Never Retreat, Never Explain, Never Apologize

Never Retreat,
Never Explain,
Never Apologize
My Life,
My Politics

DEBORAH GREY

KEY PORTER BOOKS

Library and Archives Canada Cataloguing in Publication

Grey, Deborah, 1952–
  Never retreat, never explain, never apologize : my life, my
politics / Deborah Grey.

Includes index.
ISBN 1-55263-620-8

  1. Grey, Deborah, 1952– 2. Reform Party of Canada—Biography.
3. Canada—Politics and government—1993– 4. Politicians—Canada—Biography. I. Title.

FC636.G74A4 2004   971.064'8'092   C2004-904157-6

THE CANADA COUNCIL | LE CONSEIL DES ARTS
FOR THE ARTS | DU CANADA
SINCE 1957 | DEPUIS 1957

ONTARIO ARTS COUNCIL
CONSEIL DES ARTS DE L'ONTARIO

The publisher gratefully acknowledges the support of the Canada Council for the Arts and the Ontario Arts Council for its publishing program. We acknowledge the support of the Government of Ontario through the Ontario Media Development Corporation's Ontario Book Initiative.

We acknowledge the financial support of the Government of Canada through the Book Publishing Industry Development Program (BPIDP) for our publishing activities.

Key Porter Books Limited
70 The Esplanade
Toronto, Ontario
Canada M5E 1R2

www.keyporter.com

Text design: Jack Steiner
Electronic formatting: Jean Lightfoot Peters

Printed and bound in Canada

04 05 06 07 08 09 6 5 4 3 2 1

"Never retreat, never explain, never apologize;
get the thing done and let them howl."

NELLIE McCLUNG (1878–1951),
REFORMER, LEGISLATOR, AUTHOR, AND ONE
OF THE FAMOUS FIVE.

This is how I have lived my life. I have never backed away from, nor regretted, apologizing when I have been wrong. However, when on the right path, it is possible to get sidetracked by the naysayers. Then it is essential to never retreat, never explain, never apologize....

Contents

Foreword

If you like people, politics and the interplay between the two, you're going to love Deborah Grey's rollicking tale of her fifteen years in the federal political arena.

Shortly after her election to the House of Commons, I introduced Deb to ninety-three-year-old Douglas Campbell, the former Premier of Manitoba. Mr. Campbell was first elected to the Manitoba Legislature in the 1920s as a candidate for the fledgling Progressive Party. He was also a personal friend of Agnes Campbell Macphail, a fellow Progressive and the first woman ever elected to the Canadian House of Commons.

After meeting Deborah, Doug turned to me and said, "It's remarkable. She's a lot like Agnes Campbell Macphail, she really is!" And it proved to be true—each making Canadian political history in her own way.

In 1989, Deborah went from teaching school in Dewberry, Alberta, to sitting in the House of Commons as the newly created Reform Party's first elected Member of Parliament. She went on to win three more times before retiring undefeated in 2004.

In between, she served as Chairman of the Reform Caucus; unofficial den mother to dozens of newly elected Reform MPs; star performer in the Commons' daily Question Period; Reform's most popular public speaker and campaigner; co-chair of the Canadian Alliance (predecessor to the new Conservative Party); and Leader (Interim) of the Official Opposition—the first woman to hold that office.

During her time in politics, she was either in the ring or in a front row seat at such controversial political events as the Meech Lake debate, the Charlottetown Accord referendum, the collapse of the Mulroney Conservatives, the Quebec secession referendum, the fight to balance the federal budget, the coalition-building that led to the new Conservative Party and all the major scandals of the Chrétien administration. She provides candid firsthand impressions of the prominent political personalities she has clashed or cooperated with along the way, from Jean Chrétien and Paul Martin to Lucien Bouchard, Stockwell Day and Stephen Harper.

For me, personally, the two most meaningful aspects of Deb's story are the expression of her genuine fondness for people and her personal Christian faith in her relations with others and in her practice of politics.

Deborah Grey is that rarest of creatures—a principled democrat, a genuine political reformer, a winsome Christian and a passionate Canadian all rolled up into one vibrant and committed person. Her story will inspire and instruct everyone who reads it.

Preston Manning
Calgary, Alberta
July 2004

Introduction

THE CLAW MARKS WERE DEEP and would remain in the door and the folklore of that old homestead shack. They told a story of raw terror and the protective nature of a purebred German Shepherd named Jireh.

It was a bitterly cold night in northeastern Alberta in December 1979. I lay in bed, frozen in fear. I had been teaching at Frog Lake Reserve for some months now, and was accustomed to folks from farms or the reserve stopping by for a visit or directions or gas. But never had I heard such loud honking, followed by many voices, screaming. Jireh leapt up, barking furiously. As car doors opened and closed and the voices got nearer and louder, she lunged at the door. She clamoured to get out and get at them. I could hear her claws gouging the wood. All I could do was picture a headline across tomorrow's newspaper: "Young Single Schoolteacher Murdered Overnight." Panic gripped me.

Why did I think I could do this? What made me think I could live here alone, so far from any town, and meet the challenges? Why was I, a city kid, trying to convince myself (and others) I could live in the bush and be completely content?

At that moment, the answer to all of these questions haunted me. Jireh barked and wanted nothing more than to protect me; I wanted nothing more than to die quickly, and not have to suffer.

All this noise and seeing my life flash before my eyes took mere seconds. The screaming stayed loud, but suddenly took shape. Was that singing I heard? Impossible! But wait—was that Fritz's voice? Unmistakeable! Was that a Christmas carol? Absolutely! A little off-key, words unclear, but sure enough, it was carollers. I got out of what I thought would be my deathbed, calmed Jireh down and opened the door to my dear friends Fritz, Jerry and Jeannette, Liz and Jack, who'd dreamed up this "spreading of good cheer." As you can imagine, at each place they stopped to carol, their hosts had "spread good cheer" to them. By the time they reached me, the good cheer was evident and they all tumbled inside, anxious to snuggle up to the cozy wood stove!

When my heart and my stomach traded places again and settled down, I told my pals they were lucky to be alive—I had a gun as well as a German Shepherd! Then I served coffee, crackers and cheese and we all had a great time as I hosted my first-ever shivaree!

As I reflected on the questions I had asked myself in those moments of terror, I clearly recognized the answers. I, as a city kid, had always loved the bush, and was not only capable of living on my own there, but relished it. And although brave, yet perhaps a little crazy, I knew I was not foolhardy. I was careful, yet not so cautious as to be paranoid. My dog, Jireh, was faithful and I had complete confidence in her to protect me. I also knew that God had looked after me to this point in my life and surely would continue to keep an eye on me, no matter where I ended up.

This teaching job came at the end of many long years of university. By then I was so anxious to teach that I accepted the offer immediately, after driving out to the school at Frog Lake in the middle of my final exams. The Chief and Council and the Superintendent of Schools with the Department of Indian Affairs interviewed me. When asked, "When can you start?" I replied, "My last exam is April 24th; I can begin the 25th." "Deal."

I packed my few personal belongings in my old red Dodge and drove the three hours northeast of Edmonton to my new home—a teacherage trailer, one of six, out behind the school. As I pulled into the driveway, a middle-aged woman was walking near the school. I stopped to say hello.

"Are you the new schoolteacher?" she asked anxiously.

"Yes, my name is Deb Grey."

"Oh good," she said, looking pleased and relieved. "I've been looking after that class since the last teacher left—am I ever glad to see you!" It turned out that she was the principal's girlfriend and not a teacher, but available to fill in. I wondered what lay in store for me.

Although trained as a high school English teacher, I had accepted a position teaching Grade 4. It was a bit of a surprise to discover that some of the kids in the class could not read. This presented a huge conundrum, because I did not know how to teach reading! What was I to do? To these kids, I was simply another *mooneyow* (Cree for "white woman") who, at the ripe old age of twenty-six, was coming to teach them. I was, in fact, the fourth "teacher" in their lives that year alone. You can guess what sport they thought they could have with number four during the unfolding warm, long days of May and June, as the school year drifted to an end.

Having been a student myself for what seemed like an eternity, I knew a little about teacher-student psychology. And the first lesson I'd learned (mostly from the negative side of teachers not understanding this) was that teachers must not only teach—they must also learn. So, during my first few days on the job, I searched for a way to do that. After I'd learned names, listened to stories and heard folklore about the seahorse that lived in Frog Lake, it was time to venture outdoors. Over those days, we studied each other, tested each other and started to trust each other. We put up a sign on our portable classroom door: Gone Fishing! (This is when you pray the superintendent doesn't come around to see how the rookie teacher is doing!)

The kids were excited to show me the creek that ran for a short time in the spring. Down we went, through a wonderland of wild crocuses poking through a hillside that was blackened from an early spring burning. The brilliant green of new grass and the bright clusters of crocuses on that background of black charcoal was like a beautiful painting to me that day. I knew I was about to learn more than I would probably ever teach anybody.

Down at the creek, the kids were ready to show me their stuff.

Amazed, I watched one kid take off his shoes, roll up his pant legs and stand completely still in the creek. He bent over, arms in the water, hands cupped. The entire class was silent. Suddenly, in one lightning-quick movement, he splashed, squealed with delight and tossed a fish up on the bank! The class howled their approval. Another kid went in and harvested another fish, then another kid. It didn't take long before the plot unfolded. They all looked at each other, knowingly, and then I heard what I knew was inevitable: "Your turn, Grey-eyes." (They had nicknamed me that upon my arrival.)

"But…I don't think I'm that fast…but…you guys do this lots and I never have…but…but…but…" We all knew that I was being watched, tested and initiated. Did I have what it took to earn their respect and prove to them I could learn as well as teach? Down I went into the creek, barefoot, pant legs rolled up. A couple of the kids came in with me and coached me. I did as they said. I cupped my hands and waited. I saw the fish coming downstream and when I thought it was the perfect moment, I grabbed (I thought) with lightning speed. I felt the cold, slimy thing slither through my hands, but I came up empty. The kids laughed and encouraged me to go at it again. I missed another time or two, but soon I nabbed a fish with precision and speed and heaved it up on the bank. Oh, the squeals of joy! The excitement on each face! The incredible feeling of pride and bonding we all shared! After much fun and bragging, we all went back to our classroom, the kids all agreeing that this old "Grey-eyes" might not be so bad after all. It seemed to me they tried harder with their reading and times table from then on.

During the spring, I scouted out the countryside and learned of an old homestead site that was abandoned. The Gunderson family had come from Norway and homesteaded there in the early 1900s, and the original house was no longer being used. I decided I did not want to live in a trailer lined up with all my colleagues. I could hear coughing two trailers away or a family feud four trailers over, and I needed a little more room to breathe after living cooped up for so many years in basement suites. So I set about fixing up the Gunderson place, with the blessing of family members Vernon and Fay, who owned the land and lived just up the road. My aunt and uncle, Marely and Harold, drove up from Vancouver and we went to work. We built and installed cupboards, patched walls and windows, secured doors, then tried to seal off the upstairs to keep heat in and bats out. Unfortunately, the bats could still sneak down and I became a bit of an expert at picking them off in mid-air with a short length of two-by-four. I bought an old wood stove from some friends on the reserve. We hooked that up and it was my only source of heat for cooking. There was no running water, but I did have power and a small oil heater. I had an old tin bathtub with an electric cattle-trough heater coil to heat up the well water. During the dead of winter, I either showered at the school or at the home of my friends the Hancocks. During the rest of the year, however, I had an outdoor bath in the most wonderful surroundings. If someone was coming Jireh would bark, so I could dash inside the back of the house while they were coming to the front.

Outdoor tub, outhouse, chopping wood for daily fires—just how was it again that I, the city kid, could live in the bush and be completely content...?

CHAPTER 1

Growing up Grey

JOYCE, MY MOTHER, MUST HAVE NEARLY DESPAIRED, thinking that her fourth child would never arrive. It was June 30, she was overdue by weeks, not days, and had three young girls at home to look after. Just to get out of the house for a break, she asked my father, Mansell, to take her for a drive. Stanley Park in Vancouver, British Columbia, was gorgeous that evening. Nobody knows exactly why, but the trip was enough to put her into labour, and away they went. I was born some hours later, at the Grace Hospital, on July 1, 1952. What a great day for a birthday! Obviously I knew what I wanted even back then, and this was a perfect time to arrive—I don't believe I have ever been late since.

My two maternal great aunts, Belle and Nell Russell, suggested I be named Gabrielle. Thankfully, though, Mom and Dad didn't go along with that. (A politician named Gabby Grey? That would have been too good to be true for the *Royal Canadian Air Farce* or *This Hour Has 22 Minutes!*) Instead, I was named Deborah Cleland Grey, the middle name commemorating my mother's father, Cleland Russell.

I joined the Grey household after Leslie, seven, Alexis (Skipper), four, and Alison, three. We lived in a middle-class neighbourhood in Dunbar, an area close to UBC. My father was a roofer who had his own company, Marine Roofing and Sheet Metal. Ours was a happy home, at first, with laughter, good health and enough money to live comfortably. But our lives soon changed. When I was two, my father contracted tuberculosis and spent a number of months in the sanatorium. No sooner had he recuperated from that, when he suffered a broken back in a skiing accident. It landed him in the hospital again for a number of weeks, and he spent further months resting at home in a full body cast. Needless to say, things were difficult for our family, financially and emotionally. My father came from a background of alcoholism, and I wonder if my mother always secretly worried whether it would surface in him. Both his parents, Jack and Phyllis, had suffered from this affliction. It was how they had learned to react to difficulties. Two such serious blows were evidently more than Dad could cope with and he turned to alcohol to escape. Even though he recovered from his health problems and his business prospered again, the seeds of trouble were sown. It became easier to drink for any reason—or for no reason. Soon we all learned to read the signs and walk on eggshells when things looked as if they might break loose.

I do remember some happy occasions with my dad. I was a tomboy and loved to go with him on jobs and climb up the ladders to rooftops. It was adventurous and seemed so daring. I knew he was there and would protect me if anything went wrong. We also went on family camping trips. I loved the peace of the bush, the sound of the water, the smell of a campfire and the taste of roasted marshmallows. We girls all fought like crazy, but were glad of one another's company and for having someone to play tag or hide-and-seek with.

Both sides of my extended family lived nearby and they enriched our lives. My Nana Russell (widowed when my mother was eight years old) lived up in Kerrisdale with my mom's only sister, Joan (who some years later changed her name to Marely). Nana McTier and her second husband, Hugh, lived at Broadway and Oak, near my father's only sister, Carol, who was also unmarried. We did not have one first cousin—a rarity in those days, I'm sure. Also, my great aunts, Belle and Nell, lived up in Dunbar. We loved having family gatherings. Often we kids would put on some kind of a show or a singsong. For me, the bigger the audience the better! All of these people fulfilled certain functions or roles.

Nana Russell was a great baker and snuggler. We loved to be with her, drinking hot chocolate and feeling special. Aunt Joan was our confidante; she always knew when we needed someone to talk to because there were times when Mom "just didn't understand the way things worked." Nana McTier and Uncle Hugh provided getaways and sleepovers, and we took full advantage by staying up late, which we were not allowed to do at home. My Aunt Carol loved to go camping and often took us along. How we loved going with her; we felt so grown-up, leaving Mom and Dad behind. I owe my love for the bush mainly to Carol. But she found four of us quite a handful, I'm sure. On almost every trip, she would blow up and say, "That's it! I'm not taking you kids camping ever again!" But we knew that soon she would arrive again, saying, "Well, kids, ready to go to Silver Lake camping for the weekend?" We had her figured out, but she was awfully good to us. Belle and Nell were retired schoolteachers who were unbelievable walkers. Most Saturdays, we would go to Stanley Park on the bus and walk—no, march—around it. My short legs had to do double duty to keep up! We also had sleepovers at their place and loved listening to stories of their adventures when they returned from trips overseas.

Then, one by one, my sisters all went off to school. When Alison started, I was very lonely. I'd always had company, but now I had to learn to amuse myself. During the day, I spent hours on my bicycle and visited the neighbours, adults and kids alike. I already had a fascination with numbers and letters, probably because I was with my older sisters all the time and learned them by osmosis. I cooked up the idea that I was going to practice my numbers and printing, so I grabbed an unsuspecting neighbourhood pal, Mary Alice, and we sat on the boulevard of Blenheim and 24th Avenue (close to our homes), writing down licence plate numbers when cars would drive by. Now, this does seem like a strange pastime, I'm sure. But we took it very seriously. We had red pens and we filled every page of a scribbler with columns of plate numbers— we had books full of them! Every day after school my sisters teased me unmercifully. "How many licence plate numbers did you get today?" they'd ask mockingly. I, so proud of my work, did not fall for their taunting, but would open up my latest scribbler and flip the pages as if it were some precious document. I credit this ridiculous pastime as the main reason I developed my excellent memory and ability to retain and retrieve what may seem like completely insignificant details and trivia. However, if anyone ever needs a name or a phone number, who do you think they ask?

One other striking memory I have of my preschool days was having to go to bed so early, well before my sisters. I remember thinking this was fundamentally unjust. I have always been (and still am) a night-hawk. After supper, my sisters were allowed to go over to the schoolyard and play ball. I had to go to bed. What made it so painful was that the school was only one block over and I could hear the noise of balls being hit and great cheers for the runner. I sat up in the windowsill, with the window wide open, pining for the day when I could join them. That feeling, and the constant song of the robins on those summer evenings, are indelibly imprinted on my memory.

About the time I began Grade 1, things were deteriorating at home. Dad was drinking more, Mom was frightened and, to make matters even more difficult, Dad thought another child, a son, would be a good idea. To ease tensions, Mom and Dad "got away" for a few days and Nana Russell stayed with us. She took me to my first day of school. I was quite nervous, because I am left-handed and I had heard horror stories about how they tried to change you over. My teacher was young and this was her first teaching position. My Nana said, "This is my granddaughter, Debbie, and she is left-handed. I don't want you to ever try to change her to become right-handed. Is that clear?" She was so soft-spoken and gentle, but I think she put the fear of God into that poor young woman. I remember her eyes getting big and round as she said weakly, "All right," and then her voice trailed off.

Not long into that school year, our lives changed dramatically. I was walking down the back lane one day, coming home for lunch. My mom said, "Come and see your new brother." I replied, "I can't have a new brother. You haven't had a big tummy and you haven't gone to the hospital." Being the youngest, I'd had the benefit of sitting in quietly on the "facts-of-life" sessions that my older sisters were getting. But when I came into the yard, sure enough, there was a cute little boy, ready-made.

Shaun was two-and-a-half and he could walk and talk. An automatic baby brother! This was great fun for all of us girls and we initiated him into the Grey family immediately. It took a lot of adjustment on our parts, because a sudden arrival does not allow for a "getting-used-to-the-idea" gestation period. We also soon discovered that he had experienced a great deal of upheaval already; he had been in two foster homes and now was coming to us.

So now our family was seven. Needless to say, this did not help my father's addiction to alcohol. The added financial pressure of a growing family and an inability to address the root problems simply exacerbated the symptoms. It wasn't long before Dad was spiralling downward, losing his temper and losing the respect of his family. Some nights, he would not come home at all, and we went to bed wondering if he was dead or alive. I remember going by Shaun's bedroom and listening to him crying. He sobbed, "I've had two dads already and now this one doesn't want me either." Such is the cruelty of alcohol.

My pain and grief started showing itself at school. I paid no attention to the teacher as I gazed off into space, wondering what we might face tonight or tomorrow. I remember my teacher saying to me, "Debbie, you are not paying attention to your reading." I answered, "You're right, and you know why? Because my father didn't come home last night. I'm scared and I don't know where he is." She stared at me in stunned silence. There should be a course for teachers that equips them to look beyond some silly reader or multiplication tables when a kid seems preoccupied with real, painful life.

On a family camping trip, when I was seven, I learned another frightening lesson. We were at a lake and all of us girls were in the water with Dad. Mom and Shaun were on the shore. I was riding on my dad's back, a wonderful, safe place to be. He swam out to the raft and dropped me off. We girls had a great time jumping in the water and climbing back up the ladder, only to go again. Some time later Dad swam back out to us. I did not know he had been drinking more while on shore. He came up on the raft and after a short time said, "Well, you might as well learn to swim." Then he threw me into the water, too far from the ladder to grab it. I screamed and thrashed around, somehow knowing that

I had to make it on my own and that he would not come in after me. My sisters watched helplessly; they could all swim, but seemed paralyzed with shock. My little life flashed before my eyes. Somehow, I made it to the raft and clung on for dear life. When I came to my senses, I made a major life decision: "I will never totally trust that man again."

Because of that terrifying experience, I knew I needed to conquer my fear of water. I realized that if I did not deal with it immediately, it would haunt me forever. After I regained my composure, and with my sisters to help me, I began to venture a little farther from the ladder. Slowly but surely, I learned to relax and make it back. The panic subsided and the distances lengthened. Over the next few months, I managed to learn some strokes and become a fairly good swimmer. In fact, I became a lifeguard at fourteen and ever since that fateful, frightening day I've been a "water baby." I have always had an innate ability to tackle challenges head on, and this was certainly one that I forced myself to conquer.

About that time, I made another major life decision: "I will never, ever drink." After seeing the destruction and unravelling of such a good person as my father, I decided it would not be worth the pain and risk of even trying it.

While I was still in primary school, Dad started staying out several nights at a time. I had no idea where he was or if he was okay. When he did come home, Mom had instructed us not to grill him, for fear that it would set him off again. I found this very difficult, because if I usually wanted to know anything, I just asked. Dad hated himself for drinking and disappearing, but seemed powerless over it when the next urge hit. The patterns and powers of addiction were all too familiar and all too frightening. Away he would go again, sooner or later, and we were left to fend for ourselves and pretend that all was well in the Grey household.

In the late 1950s and early 1960s, talking about alcoholism was just simply "not done." I wonder how many families out there were going through the same agony, but put on a façade of everything being just fine. The prevalent attitude was that nobody should know about those "hidden secrets." Even though some families lived with alcoholism and others had to face violence or sexual abuse, back then parents were expected to stay together "for the sake of the children." I've often questioned my own parents' decision. But perhaps it was only a recognition that superhuman efforts are needed in *any* family to raise normal, well-adjusted children and this was certainly their desire. Even if it seemed impossible to deliver, the objective was sound.

After several of Dad's home-again, gone-again ventures, it was impossible to hide our situation from the extended family, or from our friends, neighbours and school. Several times Mom and Dad would get away together, thinking that a quiet holiday would give them time to communicate and resolve the conflict.

We kids would be left at home with live-in nannies. One of them, Mrs. Cameron (not her real name), taught us how to do the cancan and eat peas off our knives. We enjoyed all the fun she provided and at least it took our minds off our family's pain. Her time with us was cut short, however, as Dad had begun drinking on their getaway and Mom came home early, by herself, on a bus.

Another time, we had another nanny, Mrs. Shepling (also a fictitious name). She was a quiet old soul, and should never have been assigned to a family of five energetic, mischievous kids. She had extremely long hair and would retire to her bedroom every evening at about seven to brush it, and would be gone for two hours. Then she'd poke her head out to see what was going on in the rest of the house. You can guess! We had the run of the place with nobody to ride herd on us. We played games, chased each other around and, best of all, were overdue on "bedtime" every single night. It was marvellous. One time when she did her peek-a-boo check on us, my sister, Skip, was heading past her room and upstairs with arms outstretched, carrying four pieces of toast stacked up on each arm.

"What is that?" the woman demanded.

"Toast," Skip replied, as she proceeded on up the steps. I remember thinking this would cause an ugly showdown. Normally, we were not allowed to be cheeky or talk back. This landed us with an automatic pass to our rooms, at any time of the day or night. As I waited for Mrs. Shepling's fury to fly, I watched her stare up the stairs after Skip, who disappeared down the hall to her room. Then our caregiver turned, went back into the bedroom and carried on brushing her hair. Our free rein with her was cut short, also, by Mom returning prematurely from another disastrous getaway.

When I was nine, we kids went with Mom to Stanley Park for an outing. Leslie had a part-time job, so she wasn't with us. As we headed home, a woman drove through a red light and hit us broadside. Our car flipped over several times, just missing a light pole, and came to rest in a gas station. I remained conscious and crawled out immediately. The others were pinned in and it took what seemed like forever for the paramedics to get everyone out. We were in various states of confusion and had some injuries, none of them life-threatening. We were taken in ambulances to St. Paul's Hospital in downtown Vancouver. Mom was not seriously hurt but was traumatized by what had happened to her children. She was assured that we were all going to be okay, although Alison had had a concussion and was a bit woozy. They put us all in fuzzy housecoats that had been warmed up.

After sitting still for quite a while, Alison and I decided we should go on a tour of our ward. I pushed her in a wheelchair and away we went. We wandered up and down the hallways, turning this unfortunate experience into an adventure. After a while, we heard a loud, familiar voice challenging the medical staff. It was our father, and we instantly recognized his "had too much to drink" voice. "Quick," said Alison. "He's coming—hide!" We ducked into a small alcove, and although we got out of the hallway, it did not hide us.

As we heard Dad coming down the hall, we heard him say, "What do you mean I can't see my wife and children? Where are they?" We huddled together, but he spotted us. He looked us over and, realizing we were obviously alive and well, told us to lead him to our mother's room. As soon as he walked in, the tirade began. "What do you think you were doing? Don't you know that you could have killed those kids?" I am sure she was devastated to be treated like this, especially when everyone knew, including the police, that she was not at fault. He made such a fuss that the doctor told him he had to leave. Somehow they got him out of there and Alison and I resumed our walk, feeling heavy-hearted and frightened to go home.

Some hours later, my Aunt Carol came and took us home. Although Dad's car was there, we hoped he would be asleep. But as I knocked on the back door, I could see through to the living room, and he was awake, sitting on the couch. He just sat there, looking at me with a smirk on his face. We all knocked and said, "Please let us in." Nobody felt in great shape; we were all sore and wanted to get in and go to bed. He ignored us. Finally, I crawled up a tree, got across onto the roof and into my bedroom window. Then I came downstairs and unlocked the back door for my family. That was one more painful incident that confirmed my theory about not being able to trust my own father.

It was not long after the accident that we had another scary experience in a car. Dad had a convertible and we loved to go for drives. He was turning left and cut off an oncoming vehicle way too close for comfort. Mom screamed, "Mansell, look out!"

The car missed us, but Mom's words obviously irritated him. He said, "What's the matter—too close for you? I'll show you close," and around the block we went to do it again. The second time, I just closed my eyes, sure we would get hit and be thrown from the car. The oncoming car missed us, but barely.

The last straw came one weekend when Dad sold his business to his long-time secretary. Our livelihood was gone and so was our father.

CHAPTER 2

Homewood: A Heart Healed

REMEMBER THE DEVASTATION I FELT when I realized my father was actually gone. Although it was peaceful around the house, his absence was still very tangible. Like many alcoholics, he was loving and responsive when he was sober. When drinking, however, he instilled panic and fear in the whole family, because he was unpredictable and, often, volatile. At least after he was gone, we settled into a state of normalcy. The rules were clear and Mom was a quiet, steady enforcer of them. Although strict, Mom was always a great encourager of all of us kids. If we had a project or a dream she would say, "Do you want to do it? Do you think you can do it? Then go for it, and I am behind you all the way."

Each member of the family was feeling his or her own grief at the loss of our father and we tried to comfort each other, but it was difficult. Mom felt raw terror at the prospect of housing, clothing and feeding five kids alone. She had not worked for many years and finding a job seemed a daunting task, especially given the circumstances. Divorce was not a common thing in the early sixties and there was a stigma attached to it that was difficult to shake. If you could not hold a marriage together, the implication was, you might not have been trying hard enough to be a good wife and mother. We knew a little bit about the life of a divorcee through my Aunt Ardath, Mom's very special, long-time friend. They had grown up together and Ardath's two girls, Susan and Joanne, were like cousins to us. Ardath had raised her two girls alone, with the assistance of her parents, Mr. and Mrs. Wallace. Their family business, Regal Lamps and Shades, was prosperous. Mr. Wallace knew of our family situation and offered Mom a job. She began immediately and worked there for many years, until we were all grown and gone. She was their secretary, bookkeeper and worked on the sales floor as well.

Overnight, then, we became the forerunners of the "latch-key kids" generation. In fact, for a short while, we did have a woman who came over after school so somebody would be there. We got used to having Mrs. Netter around, but of course she was not our mother. We were not the best-behaved kids, as we were going through all the stages of grieving the loss of our father and adjusting to the new reality of being part of a single-parent family.

We went to a family counsellor, but it didn't go well. He did not give us concrete tools to deal with our grief and anger and adjust to our new life. Particularly painful was the fact that the kids at school knew we were going to a counsellor, because of our absence from classes. Although we had some wonderful neighbours who hired "the Grey girls" to baby-sit and were very supportive of my mother, some neighbourhood parents were judgmental and referred to us as "that divorcee Joyce Grey and her five hellion children." This was not an easy label to live down. It seemed easier to live up to it. And I did. School became harder; other kids were increasingly critical and taunting. I turned tough so I could pretend it didn't hurt. I started fighting back and picking on other kids first, thinking that might be a defensive move to fend them off and keep them from any offensive attacks. I knew I did not like this part of me, but at least it deflected the pain I was feeling. It was certainly not a solution.

I have always been quick-witted and able to think on my feet. This only made things worse at school. I got the strap in Grade 2 for talking to other kids too much, as well as being sassy to my teacher, Mrs. Hall. Not only was I afraid of getting the actual strap, but also facing my mother when she found out what had happened. When Mrs. Hall lifted the strap and swung it down, I pulled my hands away. The strap kept going and whacked her on the legs. Even though I thought that was a brilliant move on my part, my little victory was short-lived. I got it twice as hard the second time. It burned into my hands and my heart. I remember confessing that to Mom as soon as I could after school, before the teacher had a chance to get to her. Direct communication became one of my hallmarks.

Although the strap taught me a few things about talking too much, it did not cure my inner need to pay back the pain that had been inflicted on me. I began to steal and get into more and more trouble at school. I found it impossible to focus on my schoolwork. Although I managed to carry on and get decent grades, I became keenly aware of how teachers and students alike reacted to difficult personal situations. Soon, I started noticing other kids who were being picked on, or teachers who were the butt of kids' scorn and ridicule. Although I certainly did my fair share of taunting teachers and baiting kids, I did find myself, occasionally, becoming an advocate if I saw what I considered to be injustices being committed against others. For instance, if I saw a kid being picked on unfairly by another kid, or a teacher, I would march down to the office and give an account of the incident and declare whom I thought to be the guilty party. Also, if I saw a teacher being unfairly leapt upon by kids, acting with malice, I would face up to them and address the issue. This made me a hero to some, a villain to others. I didn't really care a whole lot—I simply wanted to see justice done.

My need for adventure and activity was met by taking long bicycle rides all over Vancouver. I knew the city well and felt completely safe. Riding down to the Fraser River to pick blackberries was always exciting. It was a challenge to lean my bike up against the bushes, and use scraps of lumber or branches as scaffolding. No matter how stable it felt, the result was always the same: over-reaching, falling off my perch and being pierced by a thousand thorns. But I kept going back for more. (Could this be a foreshadowing of my political career?)

Another favourite ride was all around Point Grey, UBC and the Spanish Banks beaches. I loved the water and felt at peace with myself when I was near it. The constant sound of the waves seemed to wash over my pain and keep it at low tide. I enjoyed my solo time on these rides. One year, I spent the summer almost entirely alone, in the old Golf

Course at Arbutus and 33rd, teaching myself how to whistle. I loved the idea of being able to call people with my very own, identifiable whistle. Consequently, I rode around practicing, and also spent untold hours sitting up in a tree, trying and trying until I actually heard a faint noise resembling a whistle. I had driven Mom crazy trying it on her, making only a blowing sound. By the end of the summer, working on it every day, I finally mastered whistling. I knew Mom was proud of me even though she did get tired of hearing it. To this day, she will stop in her tracks if she hears my whistle or come immediately to her front window in Victoria, even if I surprise her and she doesn't know I am in town.

I am a social person and although I do not mind being alone, I prefer being with people. My favourite bike rides were with my cousin Susan. She would ride from her home in West Vancouver, I from Kerrisdale, and we would meet in Stanley Park. We would ride around the park, walk on the seawall, collect shells on the beaches and tell each other our girl-secrets. She lived with her grandparents, the Wallaces, in a grand old house on a large piece of property. I spent a lot of time there and we had wonderful times exploring and being mischievous in their neighbourhood. Our family went to their place every Boxing Day for an enormous meal and presents. Mom was grateful for the opportunity to work for Mr. Wallace and earned our livelihood there for many years.

When I was thirteen, Susan suggested I come to summer camp with her. I loved camping and being in the bush. She said Camp Homewood, on Vancouver Island, was "a little religious," but not too bad. The water activities and beautiful surroundings would make up for that. I was not really interested in anything religious. Our family had attended St. Mary's Anglican Church some years before, but not regularly or for any length of time. Nonetheless, I could certainly trade a little religion for a week away from the city. We needed to take a Bible to camp. I did not have one so I rode my bike to the church and stole one.

Camp was wonderful. I loved it. I did find chapel, quiet time (can this be possible for me, even yet?!) and fireside a bit much. But I listened anyway, enjoyed the songs, and did well with memorization of verses. The most fun for us was sneaking out of the tent at night, not to do anything bad, but just to enjoy the adventure of "the chase." I have one piece of advice for camp counsellors. Do not use flashlights to look for your young charges! We were sitting up on the rock bluff in the trees and knew exactly where they were! We only needed to keep ahead of the lights. When they got back to the tent, we were already there, snuggled up in bed!

One counsellor actually found my mischief amusing and seemed genuinely interested in me as a person. She was Elaine Strom, niece of Harry Strom, a member of the Ernest Manning government in Alberta. I appreciated her because she cared enough to listen to my story. I learned from her about what it meant to "be a Christian"—not everything in life is perfect, but God can help you walk through it. I knew I had a soul and a spirit, but it seemed so far away. Because I had been so deeply hurt, I buried my feelings of needing any higher power in my life. I knew, though, that there was another dimension and, sooner or later, I would need to address it. Some of the Bible verses I memorized told me that God loved me, no matter what. I found this hard to believe because my father loved me, too, but he had left. I knew it wasn't my fault, but at the same time, I had that nagging feeling that if I had only cleaned my room faster, or done the dishes when told, I might not have sparked him off and he might not have left. Now I was being told that no matter what I did or said, God was there and loved me. I felt comforted by that, but He was still distant from my life.

I went back home after camp thinking about what my purpose on earth was, and what might become of my life. I continued to get into trouble with teachers and students alike. My worst time was in home economics class. It was such a colossal bore and the teacher, Mrs. Pillsbury, took her sewing classes quite seriously. I hated sewing and was compared regularly to Leslie, my oldest sister, who was a gifted seamstress. This, obviously, did not help. When making a blouse, I had the darts halfway between my bust and my waist. She remarked, "You look like a saggy, baggy elephant." I sassed her back and earned a trip to the office (one of many).

During that school year, I had my first experience of a lifelong love affair with motorcycles. Alison had a friend who came around to see her on a large, loud Harley-Davidson. Mom was less than impressed, I'm sure, but had learned that if she were to protest too loudly, it would only drive Alison toward him even more. This fellow thought a good way to win Alison over would be to have an ally—and what could be better than a kid sister singing his praises? So away we went. It was love at first ride. I knew I would be a biker forever. I loved the smells and the feel of the wind. I was not caged inside, but open and free. The only thing I didn't really enjoy was the loud and rough ride of the Harley. But, oh, was I hooked! The romance between Alison and "Mr. Harley-Davidson" did not last, but mine surely did. I have now spent thirty-seven years riding and have enjoyed every mile.

At school, I was still struggling with who I was and wanted to be. I was overburdened with the guilt I felt for contributing to my family's breakup. Mom explained to us that alcoholism was a sickness, but I still felt somewhat responsible. I needed to be set free, but I didn't know how. At the end of Grade 8, after an explosive exchange with the art teacher, I found myself in the vice-principal's office again. He explained that I could not carry on challenging everybody all the time. I truly felt the teacher had been unreasonable with a student, but, apparently, it was not my responsibility to address it and solve it. He told me that he was going to put me on probation for three weeks at the beginning of Grade 9. If I didn't shape up, I would be suspended. Realizing I was in deep trouble, I gave him my word that I would do better next year. He needed to believe me and trust me. We shook hands and I left school for my summer holidays. I had no idea how I was ever going to live up to my promise. I only knew that I had no options left. Something had to be done, because I did not want to be kicked out of school.

Elaine Strom wrote me a letter and said if I could get the money together to go back to camp, she would also come and arrange it so I could be in her tent. (Later I learned that all the other counsellors said, "Good. You can have her. We can't control her.") I saved the needed amount and away I went, alone this time, because at the last minute my cousin Susan couldn't go. Because she wasn't there, I was less rambunctious and caused less stress and friction than the year before.

I knew that Elaine had a deep faith and that she really believed the stuff she was telling me. Jesus died to forgive the sins of every single person, even me. He rose again and conquered death. I was actually quite worried about death, because I always wondered if I would see my dad again. The chances of him dying from drinking and driving or freezing to death were above average. Also, my sister Skip had had an operation on her shoulder for tuberculosis. It was unnerving to be in the children's ward of a hospital. One of the girls that Skip befriended died and it brought us face-to-face with mortality. My aunts, Belle and Nell, had neighbours who lost their daughter, Linda, to leukemia. We had played with her all of our lives and we watched her die at age eleven.

So when Elaine told me that all I needed to do was accept this forgiveness, I was tempted. "But," I remember thinking, "everyone will think I'm a religious fanatic. Maybe when I'm older—twenty or so." But as she explained the freedom I would experience, I knew this was what I wanted. But I still fought off the urge to yield and be set free of my guilt and shame. I remember that when I left on the last day of camp, Elaine was standing on top of the railing at the ferry landing, crying. I was so touched that I meant that much to her. I'd suspected she would be glad to see me go.

I thought deeply about my life on the way home on the Greyhound bus. If I died that night, where would I go? The question concerned me, but more than that, I longed for the freedom of forgiveness. That night, August 5, 1966, I knelt beside my bed and prayed, "Lord, I don't know who you are or what you are. But I am prepared to let you take over the management of my life. I accept your forgiveness." No lights flashed, no bells rang. I simply knew that my sins were forgiven and I was a new person.

CHAPTER 3

High School Salvaged

I KNEW THAT I NEEDED TO DEAL with the issue of my probation as soon as school began. So, on the first day of classes, I went to the office and knocked on the vice-principal's door. Mr. Macpherson opened it, looked at me and said, "Already?" He was obviously thinking I was in trouble on day one.

I laughed and told him the story of how I had been to Bible camp and become a Christian, and assured him that there would be no more trouble from me. He looked at me, made a face and said, "I haven't heard *that* one before." I also rode my bike to St. Mary's Church, told them the story and returned the Bible.

My life changed a great deal, and many of the kids I hung out with did not care for the regenerated me. I was shunned and called a fanatic. I did not have any truly close friends at school throughout my teenage years. I threw myself into athletics and excelled at that. I became a long-distance runner, threw the discus, played basketball, volleyball and field hockey. I have always been very competitive, and that spurred me on, whether in team or individual sports. Mom did not allow us to go out and socialize on weeknights, but I was permitted to run. I enjoyed that, because I could burn off some of my abundant energy. It also gave me quiet time to think and pray. My dog, Frisky, often accompanied me and we both enjoyed it. The odd time I took advantage of it and met a pal at the park for a short visit, but I was fearful that Mom would catch me. She had an uncanny way of finding out what was going on. One day, my Mom's Al-Anon pal, Joan, said, "Oh, Joyce, I saw Skipper today." Mom seemed pleased and asked her where, just as a matter of interest. She had seen her down at the corner of Georgia and Denman, close to Stanley Park. Mom still didn't think anything of it until she asked what time. It was smack in the middle of the school day. Joan said, "Oh-oh. I think I just got her into trouble." Skip was grounded, and I learned from her mistake.

Even though my life had become much more settled and focused, I was still mischievous and sassy. With Mrs. Kliman, the cooking teacher, I didn't fare any better than I had in the sewing department with Mrs. Pillsbury. The day she announced that we were "making Golden Grog for Fifty," I laughed hysterically. What an unappetizing name for a hot drink. And how often do you have fifty over? Down I went to the office to see Mr. Macpherson. When I told him why I was there, he laughed out loud, too. Then he walked me back to the classroom and told me no matter how hard it was, I had to keep from giggling and apologize. I appreciated his understanding.

During that year, when I was fourteen, I took my bronze medallion and became a lifeguard. This enabled me to participate on the staff at Camp Homewood. I spent every summer of my high school years there and it was always like going home. I had close friends there and I would fill up on that during the summer and it would carry me for the school year until camp time came around again. I loved the bush, the water, campfires and offering kids a very special opportunity to bond with others the way only the experience of summer camp can.

During the school year, I worked part-time as a waitress at the White Spot restaurant. I loved visiting with, and entertaining, my customers. It was a difficult day when my boss told me I would have to serve liquor. I politely refused and explained to him that I was an abstainer and this would go against my deeply held beliefs. He was astounded. He countered; I re-countered; he fired me. I was shocked, but willing to pay the price because I wanted no part of serving liquor to anyone. The staff circulated a petition for my reinstatement and I was re-hired in the kitchen as a short-order cook. It was a wonderful compromise and I spent several years there, earning money for school.

One special friend I made during my White Spot days was a woman named Ev. She had waitressed there and it turned out that I had known her husband, Don, for years. He was a pal of Larry, my sister Alison's husband. Ev and I shared a love of the water and spent a lot of time together canoeing at several local lakes. She was in a crumbling marriage, and when I shared my faith with her she responded to the same celebration of freedom and forgiveness that I had experienced. With a new lease on life, she decided to go back to school for retraining. It was exciting to watch her study and discover that she had a keen desire and ability to learn.

Between Grades 11 and 12, I spent the summer at Homewood again, but also worked at a resort on Quadra Island called April Point. I worked as a cook and paddled a kayak back and forth every day from camp. I stayed at the home of Alf and Marg Bayne, the directors of Homewood. They were a wonderful couple who loved kids and had dedicated their entire lives to the ministry of summer camps for kids, many of whom were underprivileged. I loved them dearly and appreciated the profound impact they had on my life.

They truly loved the outdoors. They worked, ate and even slept outside all the time. One morning I tiptoed out of the house at 5:30 A.M. to head down to the waterfront to paddle over to April Point. I came around the side of the house and saw the couple sleeping on the front veranda. At times, my *joie de vivre* and complete spontaneity is a great asset. At other times, it is a curse. Without thinking, I lifted a corner of the blanket, stuck my face up close and whispered, "Good morning." A woman opened her eyes and stared at me in complete shock. I, too, was wide-eyed. I had never seen her before!! I said, "Who are you?" They were Joy and Ben Warkentin, cousins and company of Marg and Alf. Naturally, she said, "And who are you?" "I'm Deb and I'm sorry. See you later," and I ran down the hill to the wharf as fast as I could. That morning, I'm sure my kayaking time over to April Point could have set an Olympic record.

It was at the resort that I met my first serious boyfriend, Paul. He ran the custom cannery where we canned fish for the guests at the lodge. One day he went to light the smokehouse and the pilot light was out. Without thinking, he lit a match and the whole thing blew up, burning his face and hands badly. He did mend, but it took a long time. As I had helped down there a little, and knew the operation, I was seconded from chef duty to run the cannery for the rest of the summer. When he was well enough, he came to give instructions and oversee the operation. We got to know each other and became good friends.

He was a student at UBC, so he spent the school year in Vancouver. Mom really liked him and he came to the house regularly and helped me with my math. I was great with humanities and terrible with math and sciences. I knew I wanted to be a teacher and needed math to graduate on the matriculation stream. It was hard for me to conceptualize, but Paul helped me a lot with formulae and problem-solving.

While in Grade 12, I needed to make plans for post-secondary education. I wanted to go to university, but I also thought some Bible school training would be good for me, to provide me with a good foundation. My dear friend Elaine, with whom I corresponded regularly, gave me good advice. She said, "I'm not going to tell you what to do, but I'll tell you my experience. I have so many friends who wanted to do the same as you. They thought they would get their degree first and then take some Bible school training. But as soon as they got their degree (and after so many years of living on nothing), a job offer came along. They grabbed it and never made it to Bible school." Ohhhhh. I knew that would be me to a T. I decided to apply and was accepted at Burrard Inlet Bible Institute, just outside Vancouver in Port Moody.

As I was finishing high school, I thought back on the trouble I had gotten into years ago. Things were going better now, and my life was taking shape. I was living alone with Mom, as Shaun had gone to private school on Vancouver Island. I have fond memories of sitting on Mom's bedroom floor, the two of us playing jacks together like kids, and chatting about the day's events. Even though we laughed a lot, she still ran a tight ship and demanded full respect. Just before I finished high school, an event occurred that drove this point home. I had supper made when Mom arrived home from work one day. While getting the meal on the table, I asked her what I could make for my school lunch the next day, as we were out of peanut butter. She replied that I could make egg sandwiches. I wrinkled up my nose, ever so little, thinking about the smell of my locker after the sandwiches sat there for several hours. Mom saw my face and asked, "Are you complaining about the food around here, Deborah?" (I knew this was serious, because she called me by my formal name.) "No, Mom, I'm not. It's just that egg sandwiches smell after a while. That's all." (I had lived with her for seventeen years, after all. I knew not to push back.) She responded, "You sound like you are being ungrateful. I think you should go to bed and think about your attitude." And to bed I went, at 5:30 in the afternoon, with no supper. I was furious, I was hungry, but I was obedient. I laugh as I think back on it now and wonder how many kids these days would go straight to bed before supper just because they were told to. Mom had earned my respect and had made it through many difficult years as a single parent. I admired her tenacity and appreciated the way she could discipline severely, yet maintain her warmth and pride in me. Shortly after the egg-sandwich episode, you can imagine the smile on her face, and mine, when on graduation night in May 1970, I received the girls' athletic award, the gold pin for drama, and the female award of merit, the all-round citizenship award. As Mr. Macpherson (now the principal) gave me the award and shook my hand, he smiled and said, "Who would have thought this?"

My enjoyment of the honour was short-lived, however. While I was on the stage I heard a noise and a ruckus in the hallway off to the side. I recognized the voice; it was my father—drunk. I had not seen him for a long time and wondered how he had known about my graduation, let alone talked his way into the school and found his way to the gym. As I walked down the steps from the stage, he appeared at the doorway. Our eyes met. I felt utter humiliation. But I'd be hanged if I'd let him ruin such a special night. I visited briefly with him and he came to the dance for a short while. He disappeared and I did not see him again for some time.

Before I left for the summer with a Homewood friend, Lynn McNaughton, I spent a lot of time with Paul. We had become very close, but I was completely shocked when he asked me to marry him. I felt I was definitely too young. Besides, I was going across Canada for the summer and then to Bible school. He was finishing university and moving back to the Island. These were all factors, but the primary problem was that we did not share a common faith. I had loved and appreciated him a great deal, but I was convinced that when children come along or you face a serious crisis, you must be "equally yoked" in your faith. Paul told me that he had made offers to come along to church with me simply to win my heart. How I appreciated his honesty, but what a lesson I learned about going along with something when you know deep down it will probably not work out in the end. Better to end something at the beginning than to have your heart tied up and then broken down the road. After that encounter, although very painful, I was now free to move forward. Lynn and I bought an old Valiant station wagon from her dad, which he had fixed up and made ready for a long journey.

We were gone for the summer, travelling thousands of miles across Canada, down through Chicago (to visit my dear friend Elaine, who was now living there) and back up around the Great Lakes. I had always loved maps, and this was such a terrific chance to see so many places that I had dreamed about as a child. We camped, swam, drove, visited with old friends and made new ones. What an idyllic way to spend your first summer as an adult. It not only gave me a tremendous sense of freedom and adventure, but a deep appreciation of my country and its regions. I remember standing on Parliament Hill, awed by its immensity. This was the hub from which decisions would emanate to us in the regions.

After two months on the road, with a total car-repair bill of six dollars (we had bought two used tires for three dollars each—one in Chicago, one in Ontario), we arrived home healthy, happy and broke.

Mom's theory was that once we were adults, we were to fend for ourselves. For eighteen years she had provided for us, but one rite of passage to adulthood was to provide for ourselves, starting the day after high school graduation. I had seen my sisters move out, one by one, and accept their roles as independent adults. They did not whine, they did not beg, they simply knew the rules and lived by them. Now, as a full-time college student and a part-time cook, I, too, had joined the adult world.

CHAPTER 4

Bible College: A Firm Foundation

THE FIRST TIME I DROVE OUT to Burrard Inlet Bible Institute, I was amazed at the size of the old log building. It was massive, and sat perched on the hill above the ocean, peaceful and picturesque. What a wonderful setting for me to begin my post-secondary studies.

Classes began the day after Labour Day with about thirty-five students enrolled. There were kids from all across Western Canada, some of whom I knew from Homewood. Lynn and I lived off-campus and rented a small suite together. It worked well because I still worked part-time at the White Spot and was coming and going at all hours. We settled into the routine of classes, homework and social time, getting to know the students and staff. I found the classes very helpful, as my knowledge of the Bible was limited. The discussions were particularly interesting and even though there were differences of opinion or interpretation, we all agreed on basic principles and doctrine.

The principal, Dr. Wesley Affleck, was a kind, scholarly man who took a real interest in each student. We all loved him and wanted to do our best for him. In the dining hall, over meals, we listened to his many stories about teaching, missionaries whom he knew, church life and family life. His wife was our cook and you certainly did not want to get on her bad side.

Along with classes, it was mandatory to sing in the choir. I loved to sing and looked forward to those days. I was put in the alto section, because my voice is deep. In fact, it is deeper than alto, as I tried to explain to the choir director. Unfortunately, she didn't accept that, so I stayed with the altos. I simply sang an octave lower than the rest of them. After a while, the director told me to just mouth the words, as she didn't like the sound I made. She embarrassed me in front of all the students. I was humiliated and angry. I took off for a few days and hitchhiked up to Edmonton to see a friend from my Homewood days, Molly Fraser. It was good to be away from the school and the frustration of wrangling over the choir. When I got back, I finished the year doing what the choir director told me to do, because I needed the credits.

Imagine my excitement when she announced, at the end of the school year, that God had called her and her husband to the mission field in South America! I figured that God was looking after me just fine, thank you very much. A new choir director came in for my second year. Her name was Verneal Kallevig, and I wasn't thrilled about having a private audition with her after the previous go-around. Nonetheless, I had to meet with her and she asked if I could sing. I told her that I could, but explained about my experience the year before. She asked me to sing for her and I agreed, provided she turn her back and not look at me. I sang a little chorus and she turned around on the piano bench, amazed. "You have a beautiful voice," she said. "But it is too low for alto. You should be singing tenor." I had no idea what that was, but when she moved me over to stand with the guys, I could immediately "hear" it, and away I went. What a thrill to know what I was doing and fully join in, instead of simply mouthing the words. I am still grateful to Verneal because she met me where I was and turned my musical world upside down. I have been happily singing harmony now for well over thirty years.

I spent quite a bit of time visiting with Ben and Joy Warkentin, whom I had met on the veranda of Marg and Alf Bayne's house at Homewood. They lived in Burnaby and had two teenaged sons, Glen and Grant. I often drove my motorcycle into their basement and the boys and I would work on whatever the problem was. We had a lot of fun together. I remember thinking that if I were ever to wed, I wanted my marriage to be like Ben and Joy's. They both enjoyed each other and had a lot of fun. If they woke up in the middle of the night, they would get up and go for coffee. They were always willing to do things that kept them from getting into a rut. They celebrated Christmas in July, had "tacky queen" nights and dress-up days for family and friends.

In my second year of Bible school, I was involved in a terrible car accident on grad night. The second-year students always organized the grad, and I was bringing a load of students and supplies back to the school from the church. I went to turn out of the church parking lot and looked to the left up the gently sloping hill. It was clear, so I pulled out. Then suddenly a car came flying over the crest of the hill and crashed right into my door. We were thrown around and into the ditch. We got out of the car and checked each other over before the ambulance arrived. The kid who hit us was drunk, and staggered over and sprawled across the trunk of my car. I was not feeling very gracious about that, but was too sore to protest. We were all taken to the hospital. I sustained the worst injuries, since my door took the full impact. My back was damaged, my uterus and pelvis tipped and I had several lacerations. I was told that I might not be able to have children and because of the back damage, could possibly be in a wheelchair by the time I was thirty-five. This was very difficult to swallow, but I knew that my life was in God's hands, no matter what. I convalesced slowly over the spring and summer and felt better by the fall.

I lived in the dorm for my third year of college. It was a great time to really get to know my fellow students. For instance, I figured out quickly who I could say "Good Morning" to right away, and who would growl at me before her first cup of coffee. I found this strange because I had always woken up cheerful and started yakking immediately. We all played tricks on each other and had a lot of fun, but mostly we shared the deep things in our hearts and tried to live out our Christianity in a practical, meaningful way.

Chapel was an important and welcome part of Bible school. We had speakers who served with various missions all around the world. I was interested in Spain because my sister Skip had been living there for a few years. After my graduation from Burrard in April of 1973, I spent a summer doing mission work in the western part of Spain with Operation Mobilization. It was forty-four degrees Celsius every day and my hair got bleached white in the sun. Some village folks thought that I was Phyllis Diller, the comedian, because she was the only woman they had ever seen with fair hair. I served on a team of six women and we worked with people, distributed literature, sang and shared our faith. I loved my time there but I found the heat almost overwhelming. We had no shelter but the shade of a eucalyptus tree, camped in fields and swam and bathed in rivers. One night we got arrested for speeding and taken to jail. The Guardia Civil, the local police force, were not about to let us go lightly. Fortunately we had some Spanish girls on our team and they and the police were all hollering at each other in Spanish. Finally the police made us empty our pockets. When they counted all of our money, they announced that this is exactly what our fine would be, and let us go. We did not have one dollar left but had enough gas to get us across the border into France and to another O.M. team who gave us enough money to get back to Belgium, where we were to catch our charter home.

While serving with O.M. I got to be friends with a couple of girls from Irma, Alberta. They were Sandra Lawson and her cousin Lil Younker (whom I had met some years before at Homewood). At the end of the summer, I stopped over in Alberta to visit them and their families. I loved the farm and enjoyed my time there. We rode horses, did chores and "coffeed" with the neighbours, a staple activity of farm life. Sandra and Lil were studying at the University of Alberta to become teachers. I headed home to Vancouver at the end of August.

During that school year, I served on the Bible school staff as the cook. I was kept busy cooking for approximately fifty, including students, faculty and staff. I had cooked for large groups at Homewood, so this was not a frightening task. But it was still somewhat unnerving, wondering what everyone would think (and say) if I completely messed up a meal. I do remember thinking about my Grade 9 home economics teacher and the "Golden Grog for Fifty" episode. I could have used her recipe now!

One of my favourite characters at Burrard was Maurice. He was a handyman there and we got to be good friends. He was eccentric in many ways, brilliant but unusual. For instance, when one of the students needed some repair work done on her car, she was concerned because she didn't have much money. Maurice had the solution; he would fix it. He had no pit to work in, so he threw a couple of old mattresses on the ground and he and a few of the guys flipped the car on its side to work on it. Her eyes nearly popped out as she wondered what the finished product would look like. Surprisingly, the car survived, but I don't believe she used his services again.

Maurice also had an old dune buggy that the students would tear all over the property in. He had trails through the woods and an enormous swing that went out over a very steep embankment. He also made films and rigged up gadgets all over the campus, from a fountain to a talking tree to an electrified chair in the dining hall. The night before I was leaving for Spain, we drove up to the top of Mount Seymour, near Vancouver. He told me that he wanted to do something with me that he had not done before. I was a bit nervous, hoping that I had never led him on in a romantic way. When he leaned toward me, my heart skipped a beat. He reached behind me into the back seat of his Jeep and pulled out two guns and a couple of tin cans. "I have always wanted to come up here with you and do some target shooting," he said. When I got my breath back from the anticipation of what this occasion might be, we had a hilarious time together. Everyone needs to have such a unique individual as Maurice in his or her life.

I decided that one year on staff had been a great experience, but if I were going to go to university, I had to get started. My dorm roommate, Connie, had moved to Fort Langley after graduation and was working at Trinity Western College, a Christian liberal arts school. If I didn't sign up now, perhaps I never would....

CHAPTER 5

University: A Matter of Degrees

L IFE AT TRINITY WAS MUCH DIFFERENT than it had been at Burrard. There were rules, but not nearly as many as I was used to. I did not live on campus but roomed with Connie, a few miles from the school. I carried a full load of classes, played sports and had a part-time job working three or four nights per week on the graveyard shift at an old folks' home. Like many university students who do anything they can to make ends meet, I don't remember when I slept. However, I enjoyed my time working with the seniors, who told fascinating stories about their pasts. I was spellbound, and tried to picture them as young and strong, occupied with busy lives and families. Now, sadly, not many family members came to visit them. Much of their time was now taken up with wishing and hoping…for what, probably even they weren't quite sure.

One of my favourites was an old gent named Mr. Lumsey. Many nights he would have a tantrum and run away. This was before the days of high security and automatic lockdown doors. We tried to secure the doors but he always found a way to sneak out. He'd be gone in an instant, clothed only in his pajama tops. This was a regular occurrence, and the drill was the same each time; I would chase him down Main Street and get him stopped. He was so agitated that it took a few minutes to calm him down. "I won't stay there any longer," he yelled. I asked him why not. "Because they won't give me tea, that's why!" I responded, "Listen, I know where they keep the tea and I promise I will give you some when we get back." He didn't believe me and protested that this was simply a ploy to lure him back. As we walked slowly back, I tried to reassure him that I would be willing to take the risk of getting into trouble with the other staff to make good on my promise of getting him some tea. He was pretty calm by the time we got back and we settled into a tea party for two. By then we were pals and he told me wonderful stories of his younger days.

There were equally colourful characters at Trinity, even though I never saw any of them in just their pajama tops! Robert Thompson, a professor, had been the leader of the federal Social Credit Party in the House of Commons. He had also spent many years in Ethiopia setting up school systems, and became a trusted advisor of Haile Selassie, the emperor. He spoke about his experiences in the House and overseas. They were fascinating adventures and I was thrilled listening to them all.

Dr. Neil Snider was the president of Trinity and had dreams of enlarging the campus, enabling it to become a degree-granting university. The music department was excellent and I was hoping to be involved as part of a choir or small travelling group. I was told by the music director, "Women don't sing tenor." I looked at him, shook my head, walked out his door and never sang a song while I was a student at Trinity. I learned another valuable lesson that day about how not to deal with students.

My first school year was extremely busy with classes, work and developing relationships with the students and faculty. The next summer I secured a job working as a lifeguard down at Aldergrove Park, which had a small lake in it. I had a two-way radio that I could use to communicate with Jay, the park manager. A lot of the time it didn't work, so I was completely alone. The lake was a favourite hangout for kids and drinking parties were the norm. I would try to chase them out and pretended that my CB was working, even when it wasn't. But they were not afraid of me, and things often escalated to the point where I needed to call the police to have them removed. I was fairly nervous because all these hooligans needed to do was block off the road so that

I couldn't drive up the hill to safety. I prayed that somehow I would be able to feel safe for the rest of the summer.

A few days after I made this request to God, I saw a bunch of young kids down at the lakeshore. They were playing in and out of the water with a big German Shepherd, all having a great time. I walked around the shore and told them to get their dog out of the water, as the lake was man-made and treated regularly, so animals were not allowed in it. They said, "It's not our dog." When I looked at them doubtfully, they insisted, "Honest, it's not. We've never seen this dog. He just came up to us when we were playing." I still didn't totally believe them and said, "Whoever the dog belongs to really doesn't matter. He's not allowed in the water anyway." The kids wandered off into the bush, with the dog happily trailing along behind them.

When I finished my shift, I went to deliver my CB to Jay at the park office. He said to me, "Look, Deb, we found a stray dog." I looked in the direction he pointed and recognized the dog immediately. "That dog was down at the lake with some kids." He had spoken to the kids, too, and ended up keeping the dog when they left. She was tied up on a chain, and I went closer. Jay said to be careful because she had growled at him and he wondered if she might be vicious. I did not realize the chain had some slack in it and she lunged up at me. I was terrified, thinking she would attack my face. Instantly she was on me, licking my face furiously and wagging her tail. Jay said, "Look, she likes you." We played together for a few minutes and she was as affectionate as a pup. I was leaving for my two days off and Jay suggested I take her with me. If anyone came to claim her, I would return her when I came back.

We bonded right away and had a great couple of days. I was staying with Ev and she and the kids loved the dog, too. During my days off, I was reading in my Bible from Genesis 22. It was the story about Abraham sacrificing his son, Isaac. Just before he was ready to plunge the knife down, his hand was stopped supernaturally. He looked up and noticed a ram with its horns caught in the branches of a bush. He took the ram and sacrificed it instead. He named the place, "Jehovah-jireh, meaning 'the Lord provides.'"

Suddenly, I realized that this dog was an answer to my prayer! She could keep me safe when I was dealing with the rowdies down at the lake. I named her Jireh and she made the rest of my summer easier. When carloads of troublemakers arrived, I would pull her collar tight and she would snarl and growl. Word quickly got around and my problems were solved!

During this time, my dad was spending time at a recovery centre for alcoholics in Maple Ridge, across the Fraser River from Fort Langley, close to Trinity. He had tried desperately to sober up over the years and this was one more attempt. I rode my bike to the Albion ferry, went across the river and visited with him when I could. He had struggled many times, sober for a time and then falling off the wagon when the pressure got too much. I don't know how many times he got very near celebrating one year of sobriety then didn't quite make it to his one-year cake at AA. I prayed for him regularly and wished that he would overcome his addiction. While he was at this place, we had long talks about it and I tried to encourage him the best I could. As I had always been an abstainer, I could not understand the power and pull of alcohol. I let him know that I loved him, no matter what, and wanted him to get well. I was a student at Trinity when Dad had his fiftieth birthday on January 8, 1975. I wrote him a long letter telling him about my life and how much I missed him when he had left when I was a kid. I told him about going to camp and how that changed the entire focus of my life. It was because of that experience I could forgive him for what had happened to our family. It was because of that experience I could love him unconditionally, even though I had been bitter for so long. Also because of that I had decided to be very cautious about who I would marry, if ever. I would not marry someone with whom I could not share my faith. I told him he might not have many chances left to sober up. Fifty is a positive turning point for so many people and I wanted that for him. I committed to praying for him every day and assured him that I loved him a great deal. I know that the letter had an impact, as did a visit from an old friend of his who laid it on the line with him in much the same way I had. He remained sober, got his one-year cake, and now is ready to receive his thirty-year cake. Hurray!

In October 1975, my second year at Trinity, I was asked to drive the college van to Kelowna to pick up a load of donated apples. I set out early in the morning with Connie, Ev and Jireh. Not far down the road, in Abbotsford, we hydroplaned on the freeway, skidded and rolled off the highway down an embankment. I crawled out and so did Connie, but Ev and Jireh were trapped inside. The ambulance came quickly and we were all transported to the hospital. Ev was critically hurt, with head injuries and a badly damaged shoulder. Jireh was taken to the vet with broken legs and a cracked pelvis. I was traumatized, not knowing if my dear friend Ev would live or die. After surgery she did recover, but needed months of physiotherapy and fulltime care. I continued on with classes, but went down to part-time for the spring semester. It was a very difficult year, and though Ev made progress, it was doubtful whether she would ever be able to use her left arm again.

Over the next year she did make great gains, but still had difficulty maneuvering. She had been upgrading her education and working as a flag girl on the road, but couldn't do that anymore. Eventually she was able to finish her real estate course and worked as a real estate agent for several years. I completed my course work at Trinity in the spring of 1977 and got ready to transfer to UBC...or so I thought.

My aunts Belle and Nell had moved out of their house, which was close to the UBC campus. My Uncle Harold and I renovated it and I was expecting to rent it while I was going to university. However, my mom and Aunt Marely decided to sell it instead. This left me wondering where I would stay and if I actually would be attending UBC. I decided to take a short break and flew up to Fort Chipewyan, in northern Alberta, to see my friends Sandra and Lil, who were teaching there. Conveniently, Alberta Transportation was in town hiring crews to work on a summer project: paving the runway at the airport. I was hired and made a quick trip back to the Coast to get my gear and Jireh. I spent the entire summer on the work crew, earning and saving money for university. It was a truly spectacular part of the country, at the tip of the Great Canadian Shield, on the shore of beautiful Lake Athabasca and with no roads out to civilization. Whenever the heavy equipment broke down at work, we would go camping to the bush. When we heard the plane bringing parts, we knew they would have it repaired by the next day, and headed back to work. I also did a little substitute teaching when the equipment was broken down. It was great experience to be in the classroom, and especially to get paid for it.

Sandra had taught in Chip for two years and earned her permanent teaching certificate. Now she intended to go back to school and take RN training. She'd made plans to move to Edmonton and attend Grant MacEwen College. I then thought about rooming with her and attending University of Alberta. I applied, was accepted and we came out of the north in time for me to go back to Vancouver, ride my motorcycle up to Edmonton and get registered for classes.

I was shocked to discover how cold Alberta winters were. I had never experienced such extremes before and wondered how I would last. I had always ridden year-round in Vancouver. It was especially tough walking to university because I didn't have a lot of money and couldn't afford to pay to park the old car that we'd bought from a family member of Sandra's. What money we did have was used for gas to drive down to Sandra's parents' farm in Irma, about two hours southeast of Edmonton. We spent many weekends there and enjoyed getting out of the city, as well as the care packages her mother gave us.

I graduated in the spring of 1978 with my Bachelor of Arts degree, with a double major in English and Sociology. I started working toward my Bachelor of Education/ After Degree that summer by taking two full credit courses. That fall, I did my junior high English student teaching placement at Winfield, an hour and a half southwest of Edmonton. Sandra's sister, Marj, taught there and I stayed with her. She had a motorcycle, also, and we would ride after school. There were gorgeous fall days and the leaves were spectacular. The harvest was in full swing and the smell of grain being swathed and combined was heavenly.

I enjoyed the junior high students a lot. They had so much raw energy. "If a person could find a way to harness that, the rest of the job would be easy," I thought to myself. I did find several ways to harness them: by engaging them in conversation, role-playing, story-telling and choral reading. It was a good six-week session and I loved working with the kids.

My senior-high teaching placement was at Tofield, forty-five minutes east of Edmonton. Anne Taylor, an excellent educator and mentor, was my sponsoring teacher. I had to teach Shakespeare and I did not feel at all capable of doing that. But Anne was a great encourager—somehow I managed to get through Hamlet and so did the kids!

During the spring semester, while finishing my course work, I made several applications for teaching positions. I heard back from the Department of Indian Affairs, and was asked to come for an interview at Frog Lake Indian Reserve. I had no idea where that was, but I set up a meeting with the Superintendent at St. Paul and we planned to drive together from there. After it was all over, I had accepted a position teaching Grade 4.

Sandra had finished her RN and was heading back up to Fort Chip to be a nurse. As there were no roads up there, I kept the car. We said good-bye at the airport and then Jireh and I headed northeast to our new home at Frog Lake.

CHAPTER 6

Frog Lake Reserve: A Minority View

AS I PULLED INTO THE DRIVEWAY, a middle-aged woman was walking near the school. I stopped to say hello. "Are you the new schoolteacher?" she asked anxiously.

"Yes. My name is Deb Grey."

"Oh good," she said, seeming pleased and relieved. "I have been looking after that class since the last teacher left—am I ever glad to see you!" It turned out that she was the principal's girlfriend and was not a teacher, but available to fill in. I wondered what lay in store for me. I drove on to discover my accommodation, one of six trailers lined up behind the school.

It was a bit of a surprise to discover that some of the kids in my Grade 4 class could not read. This presented a huge conundrum, because I did not know how to teach reading! What was I to do? To these kids, I was simply another *mooneyow* (Cree for "white woman"), who was coming to teach at the ripe old age of twenty-six. I was, in fact, the fourth teacher who'd come into their lives that year alone. You can guess what sport they thought they could have with number four, as the school year drifted to an end during the warm, long days of May and June.

Having been a student myself for what seemed like an eternity, I understood a little about teacher-student psychology. And the first lesson I'd learned (mainly from the negative side of teachers not under-standing this) was that teachers must not only teach, they must also learn. So, on my first few days on the job, I searched for a way to do that. After I had learned names, listened to stories, and heard folklore about the seahorse that lived in Frog Lake, it was time to venture outdoors. Over those days, we studied each other, tested each other and started to trust each other. We put up a sign on our portable classroom door: Gone Fishing. (This is when you pray the superintendent doesn't come around to see how the rookie teacher is doing!)

The kids were excited to show me the creek that ran for a short time in the spring. Down we went, through a wonderland of wild crocuses, poking through a hillside that was blackened from an early spring burn-ing. The brilliant green of new grass and the bright clusters of crocuses set on that black charcoal backdrop was like a beautiful painting to me that day. I knew I was about to learn more than I would probably ever teach anybody.

Down at the creek, the kids were ready to show me their stuff. I stood, amazed, as I watched one kid take off his shoes, roll up his pant legs, and stand completely still in the creek. He bent over, arms in the water; hands cupped. The entire class was silent. Suddenly, in one light-ning-quick movement, he splashed, squealed with delight and tossed a fish up on the bank! The class howled their approval. Another kid went in and harvested another fish, then another kid. It didn't take long before the plot unfolded. They all looked at each other, knowingly, then I heard what I knew was inevitable, "Your turn, Grey-eyes." (They had nicknamed me that upon my arrival.)

"But…I don't think I'm that fast….but….you guys do this lots and I never have….but…but…but…" We all knew that I was being watched, tested, and initiated. Did I have what it took to earn their respect and prove to them I could learn as well as teach? Down I went, into the creek, barefoot, pant legs rolled up. A couple of the kids came in with me and coached me. I did as they said. I cupped my hands and waited. I saw the fish coming downstream and when I thought it was the perfect moment, I grabbed (I thought) lightning-fast. I felt the cold, slimy thing slither through my hands, but I came up empty. The kids laughed and encouraged me to go at it again. I missed another time or two, but soon I nabbed a fish with precision and speed and heaved it up on the bank. Oh, the squeals of joy! The excitement on each face! The incredible feeling of pride and bonding we all shared! After much fun and bragging, we went back to our classroom, the kids all agreeing that this old "Grey-eyes" might not be so bad after all. It seemed to me they tried harder with their reading and times table after that.

During the spring, I scouted out the countryside and learned of an old homestead site that was abandoned. The Gunderson family had come there from Norway and homesteaded in the early 1900s, and the original house was no longer being used. I decided I did not want to live in a trailer lined up with all of my colleagues, where I could hear neighbours coughing two trailers over, or a family feud four trailers away. After living cooped up for so many years in basement suites I needed a little more room to breathe. So I set about fixing the Gunderson place, with the blessing of family members Vernon and Fay, who owned the land and lived just up the road. My aunt and uncle, Marely and Harold, drove up from Vancouver and we went to work. We built and installed cupboards, patched walls and windows, secured doors, then tried to seal off the upstairs to keep heat in and bats out. Unfortunately, the bats still found ways to sneak down and I became a bit of an expert at picking them off in mid-air with a short length of two-by-four. I bought an old wood stove from some friends on the reserve. We hooked that up and it was my only source of cooking. There was no running water, but I did have power and a small oil heater. I had an old tin bathtub with an electric cattle-trough heater coil to warm up the well water. I bathed in the most wonderful surroundings of the great outdoors, with faithful Jireh to bark and let me know if someone was coming; I could dash inside the back of the house while company was coming to the front.

That same spring I got a note from Susan McCaslin, my English prof from Trinity Western. She was doing a poetry workshop in Calgary that July, and wondered if I could attend. It did not work out for me to go, but on the pamphlet I noticed the name of Maxine Hancock, distinguished author and speaker, who would also be making a presentation at the conference. I did not know Maxine, but when I saw that she was from

Marwayne, Alberta, I did a double take. On the way to Lloydminster, I had passed by the town of Marwayne. "Wow!" I thought. "Maybe I could find a Christian friend way out here in the middle of nowhere." I went to the phone book and flipped to Hancock. I called the first one, "C. Hancock". A young boy answered and said, "This is the Hancock residence. Mitchell speaking." I asked if this was where Maxine lived, and he replied, "Yes, it is. Who's speaking, please?" I felt like a fool because she was an international celebrity and would not have a clue who I was. "Deb Grey," I responded. "From Frog Lake." (as if that would help!) A moment later, Maxine came to the phone. I introduced myself and told her I was new in the area and was teaching at Frog Lake. She and Cam taught at Marwayne School, but were in the middle of a strike and were probably finished for the summer. I had just finished also, as we got out a little ahead of the public schools. She invited me down for dinner the next day and I accepted. I still had enough city kid left in me to think that dinner was the evening meal, and showed up then. They'd been expecting me at noon, for that was the time for "dinner" on the farm. Fortunately they were gracious and took me in anyway. I loved all their kids immediately: Geoff, fourteen; Camille, twelve; Heather, ten; and Mitchell, eight. They were bright, vibrant, mischievous yet respectful. What a huge part of my life they all became.

In the fall, I was transferred up to junior-high language arts, math and remedial reading. It was a steep learning curve as I had no training in these areas, so class prep and staying one step ahead of the kids kept me busy. We all settled into the school year smoothly and developed a comfortable routine. Life was filled with school activities, community events and involvement for me with the Dewberry United Church, where the Hancocks attended.

When there was a professional development day, or any break from school in Marwayne, the Hancock kids loved coming to school with me on the reserve. It was an experience for them to be in a minority and it was good for my Native kids to interact with them. There was a lot of cross-cultural exchange and goodwill, which benefited us all. There were also occasions when the Hancocks could come and experience the pioneer lifestyle at my old homestead shack. They got a kick out of using the woodstove and outhouse, and sitting around the campfire for hours at a time. I also enjoyed going to their place; it had a warm and welcoming atmosphere and there was always stimulating conversation (as well as running water!)

At school, we were always trying to find ways to involve the parents in their kids' education. We came up with a bright idea to have a feast and combine it with parent-teacher interviews. Somebody shot a caribou and donated the hindquarters to this event. We were going to have a terrific feed and talk to the parents at the same time. The morning went well. We were all getting our classrooms ready to display the kids' work. I went to the kitchen, just before the expected mealtime, to discover a big caribou leg lying on the counter, bloody, raw and hairy. We skinned the leg, cut it up and got it in the oven. Needless to say, there were not many people still around to share the feast by the time it was ready in the late afternoon.

Another time, I was driving home from school and a muskrat ran right in front of me. I could not avoid him and he was killed instantly. I thought this would be an opportunity to practice my skinning abilities, so I threw him in the trunk and took him home.

I did not too bad a job, I thought, and stretched it out on a board to dry. A few days later I had a knock at my door. There stood a tall, burly wildlife officer. He showed me his badge and told me he had heard that I had been hunting muskrat without a permit. I grabbed my pelt, still on the stretching board and started babbling that I had not hunted him, but killed him on the road with my car. I wondered what the charge and my penalty would be if he didn't believe me. He sat there a long time looking at it and said, "Not a bad job of skinning." I thanked him, but was anxious to hear my fate. He smiled and said, "You know Fritz, right? You told him about your muskrat adventure and he told me to come here and scare you." "And you did!" I replied. We had a good laugh and I sure gave it to Fritz when I saw him next. He farmed west of the Frog Lake store and had come to my place with Vernon Gunderson to clean out the chimney a while before.

I loved the rustic atmosphere of my home and the daily chores that I became accustomed to: chopping wood, building a fire, wandering to the outhouse and bathing outdoors. Many of these activities were time-consuming, but there was a great sense of satisfaction when they were completed. I felt relaxed as I settled into the easy rhythm of life in the bush. I enjoyed visiting at neighbours' homes, but also appreciated the quietness of my place, where I could do my reading and marking while I sat tucked in by the fire. Winter evenings were long and dark and it was easier to go to bed earlier than usual. It was a bitterly cold night in December 1979 when Jireh and I went to bed, thinking this would be no different than any other night.

After a while, we were awakened by the sound of a car, then people screaming. Jireh leapt up, barking furiously. As the voices got louder and the people got closer, she lunged at the door. Her claws gouged the wood as she tried to get out to attack the intruders. I lay in bed frozen in fear. All I could do was picture a headline in the next day's papers announcing my murder. Raw terror gripped me. Jireh barked and wanted nothing more than to protect me; I wanted nothing more than to die quickly, and not have to suffer. All this noise, and the vision of my life that flashed before my eyes, took mere seconds. The screaming stayed loud, but suddenly took shape. Was that singing I heard? Impossible! But wait—was that Fritz's voice? Unmistakable! Was that a Christmas carol? Absolutely! The tune was a little off-key, the words unclear, but sure enough, they were carolers. I got out of what I thought would be my deathbed, calmed Jireh down and opened the door to my dear friends Fritz, Jerry and Jeannette, Liz and Jack, who'd dreamed up this "spreading of good cheer." As you can imagine, at each place they stopped to carol, their hosts had "spread good cheer" to them. They all tumbled inside, anxious to snuggle up to the cozy woodstove!

When my heart and my stomach traded places again and settled down, I told my pals it was lucky they hadn't died—I had a gun as well as a German Shepherd! I served coffee and crackers with cheese and we all had a great time as I hosted my first-ever shivaree! Jireh enjoyed the company once they were on the right side of the door. I was always grateful for her protective nature and felt safe knowing that she stood between me and anybody who might want to harm me.

One day in the spring, we had a track meet at the school. It was pouring rain, the field was a pool of mud and we were all completely soaked. As I was having coffee in the staff room at noon, the principal came in. "Deb, you have company." I had no idea who it might be, because the school was miles from anywhere. I walked out to the main office and saw a tall, blond older man. He said, "You probably don't remember me, but…" I recognized him immediately and said, "I sure do. You are Art Yerex." He could hardly believe that I remembered him. He and his wife, Reta, lived at the Coast. She was a sister to Grayden, the man my Aunt Marely married when I was a teenager. I had seen them a couple of times over the years, but not since Grayden had died in 1974. It was now 1980 and there Art was, standing in the office at Frog Lake School! He and Reta had been on a trip in their motor home to Saskatchewan and were driving back along Highway 16, the Yellowhead. Just outside of Lloydminster, they saw the turnoff for Frog Lake. Art said, "Didn't Marely say that her niece was teaching at Frog Lake? Let's go find out." And so began a series of yearly journeys by Art and Reta to northern Alberta to see me. They stayed for several weeks each year and I loved their arrival as much as that of the geese and the loons.

I had gotten to know Fritz better during the school year and spent time at his farm playing cribbage as well as celebrating calving season. He owned a house down at the lakeshore that a family of missionaries had lived in for some years. They were gone now, so I worked out a rental agreement with him and moved into it during the following summer. The Hancocks had heard that the junior and senior high-school English position had come open in Dewberry, and I applied for it. They gave me a good recommendation and I was hired. I was sad to be leaving the reserve kids, but also glad that I would be teaching in my area of expertise.

I moved my stuff out of the Gunderson place and down into my new home—a two-bedroom bungalow about forty feet from the northeastern shore of Laurier Lake. I spent an idyllic summer swimming, kayaking and listening to the loons. Surely it couldn't get much better than this.

At the end of the summer, my mom came up for a visit before I started back to school. I picked her up in Edmonton; we had supper, then drove home to the lake. It was late, but the evening was gorgeous. Just north of Vermilion, an oncoming vehicle flashed his lights at me. I stopped and got out. "There has been a hell of a wreck up ahead," he said. "How far to the nearest farmhouse?" I told him there was one about a half-mile back and we went on ahead to see if we could help. A couple of miles up the road, my headlights picked up a car in the ditch. All was quiet and dark when we walked toward the car and I shone my flashlight on it. One young man was hanging out through the windshield, dead. We looked for anyone else in the vehicle. It was empty. We assumed that he had been alone.

Sadly, we were wrong. We heard a gurgling sound off in the ditch and went to investigate. Several metres away lay another young man, badly broken up, but still breathing. We talked to him and tried to comfort him. While we were with him, we heard more noise coming from even farther away. Mom stayed with the second young man and I followed the noise and discovered a third, barely breathing. Soon the police arrived. The young officer was just as traumatized as we were and asked if I would walk with him to the victims. He recognized the driver and told me that he had just talked to him last week about alcohol and speed. Mom was still comforting the second one, talking to him and telling him we were right there with him. He died while we were standing beside him. Mom then moved to the third one, speaking quietly to him as well. He made it to the hospital, but died very soon as well.

We were in a terrible state of shock as we drove home, silently, to the lake. I felt physically sick when I arrived. I was so glad to have my mom there with me. Not only was she a comfort to me but I was also so impressed that she stayed with each young man, speaking gently to them both before they died. I can't imagine anything worse than dying alone in a ditch. I wondered if these kids were from Dewberry and were supposed to be in one of my high school classes on Tuesday morning.

CHAPTER 7

Dewberry: A Sense of Community

I T WAS WITH A HEAVY HEART that I began my first day of school at Dewberry. As I watched my strong young high-school students, I could not help but think of the three families that had lost their sons. I talked at length about the accident with my classes, as some of them had known the driver. He was from Vermilion, but the other two were exchange students from the Maritimes. They had spent the summer in Alberta and were due to fly home the very next day. How devastating that must have been for their families. It gave me a good chance to talk to my students about the consequences of drinking and driving.

I commuted twenty miles each way from the lake daily, so I spent a lot of time on the road myself. However, the glorious fall days helped to heal my shock and fear of what I might witness next on the country highways. The crispness of the autumn sun and the brilliant golden leaves made me realize how much I loved the bush in northeast Alberta. Each day after school, I was happy to round the southeast shore of the lake and enjoy the splash of gold and blue reflected in the water. Jireh was always on hand to meet me and she delighted in wandering down to the shore as I prepared for a late afternoon kayak ride. There is a magic about paddling in the fall; the silence broken by the drone of swathers and combines, the smell of harvest in full swing, thousands of geese overhead on their way to a warmer winter, the days getting shorter and the smell of dying and decaying cattails in the sloughs. I loved it all and was so grateful to be able to live not just in the country, but also right beside the lake. Each night as I did dishes, I would look out the kitchen window and watch the beavers swim past the house, only to return some time later, hauling back an enormous branch that was going to provide winter protection for their lodge. Often I would go down to the beach and sit, watching these industrious creatures, amazed by their tenacity and perseverance. I will always remember the sound of them slapping their tails to warn others of my presence. The sound could be heard across the lake. Also, about this time of year, the loons headed south, leaving me yearning for next spring and their magical, mournful call.

Soon after the school year began, Sandra moved down from Fort Chipewyan. Her father was not well and she wanted to be closer to home. Also, a job came open at our school as Jean Vivian, the Grade 3/4 teacher, became quite ill. Sandra and I became roommates again and she slipped quickly and comfortably into our school and community.

And so, school got into full swing after a difficult start. My students were very welcoming, although it was always a challenge to see how far you could push the new teacher. As the classes were small, I had a chance to learn names and family connections quickly. When I asked my Grade 11 students their names, it seemed fairly simple; Darren, Morley, *Cindy*, Myrna, Barb, *Cindy* (there were only eleven students in the class and I thought it pretty strange that there would be two girls by the name of Cindy), Kelly, Mike, *Cindy*. "All right!" I exploded. "You may think this is pretty funny, but I don't know how stupid you think I am. I want to know what your real names are, and I want to know now." They looked at me and said, one at a time, "Miss Grey, I am Cindy Maddex"; "I am Cindy Timanson"; "I am Cindy Nelson." Oh, did I feel foolish!! I told them how sorry I was. We all had a good laugh and, although they surely had some fun at my expense, they realized that here was a teacher who could actually say "Sorry." It was a good day for all of us.

I enjoyed being part of a community. Every day after school, I would go to the post office, the Co-op, the bank. The people who worked in all of these places were my students' parents, relatives or friends. Everybody knew everybody and I quickly got used to the idea of being known by anyone I met on the street. The locals enjoyed studying the new teachers—what we wore, what we drove, how much homework we gave their kids. But they were all extremely friendly and I had more invitations for coffee than I could accept in any given week.

To help familiarize myself with the community, I had my Grade 11 English class do an autobiographical assignment, one chapter of which was their family history. This enabled me to see who was related to whom, and to study family trees and backgrounds, so that I would know more about the history and culture around me. This proved invaluable because I got to know many people before I had even met them. I'm sure they were impressed when I told them that I knew they were so-and-so's great aunt. This exercise was helpful for me as well as interesting for my students.

One of the first places I went for coffee was to Dora Fitzpatrick's. She was the mother of one of my Grade 11 students, Myrna, who had written a chapter in her autobiography about the death of her father, Gordon, exactly one year before. He had been hunting just north of their farmhouse and had a fatal heart attack in the field. It had been a terrible shock for the whole community, not just for Dora and her family. I was so glad to have known that before I went to their place for coffee. She welcomed me into her home and into her heart, and we have been very special friends ever since. Over that next decade, she would often phone the school and say to Alice, our secretary, "Tell Deb and Sandra there are fresh cinnamon buns and coffee ready right after school."

One of my Grade 9 students was a Mennonite girl named Laura Thiessen. Her family had moved to the Dewberry area from B.C. and they were the first of many Mennonites to settle in the area over the next few years. One Friday, I let my students play Scrabble at the end of the day. Laura groaned and said to me, "You need to meet my mother. She loves playing Scrabble." I met Hilda at the Christmas concert that first year, and we made a date to get together for coffee and a Scrabble game. When I got there, I received such a warm welcome from the whole Thiessen family, I knew right away that this friendship would be a long one. And it has been. Hilda and I have played thousands of games over the last twenty-some years, and although as a Mennonite she is a pacifist, at Scrabble she is anything but! We are both very competitive; but more than that, we just love to play each other, win, lose or draw.

At church, several of us decided to form a Gospel singing group that would travel to neighbouring communities. We called ourselves "HIS" and our initial group was comprised of ten people. Eventually it was whittled down to five and remained at that number for many years. We sang in virtually every community within fifty miles of Dewberry and did some weekend touring to more distant destinations. We had a ball, and not only enjoyed singing, but also the times we had together of storytelling and riding in the van that I'd bought so we could all travel together. We shared more laughs than any other group of people I have ever been part of. Meredith, Lorraine, Bonnie, Shelley and I shared a bond that very few get to enjoy.

The school year was filled with classes, marking, fall turkey suppers, volleyball games and tournaments, Christmas concerts, curling at Heinsburg (where it was generally colder inside the curling rink than outdoors), occasional trips to Edmonton, singing with HIS, ice fishing and celebrating spring by betting on when the ice would disappear from the North Saskatchewan River and our lake. It was always wonderful to come to school and announce that the river was open. That event, and baseball games starting, signified that spring had officially arrived. As I drove through the river hills in early May, I wondered if I could spot a hint of green on the trees. I tried to convince myself that I could, but it seemed to be a hopeful wish and nothing more. But then the very next morning there was a definite tinge of green, hardly noticeable, though you could see it if you really tried. And the very next day, the green was unmistakeable. What a miracle is spring!

At the end of a long school year, summer holidays were a gift to students and teachers alike. How I loved lazing around at the lake, recharging my batteries, swimming, kayaking and enjoying campfires at the lakeshore. The summer evenings were magical as I watched the late sunsets, the northern lights and the myriad shooting stars. Many nights we went up the trail to Wilf and Rose's to play cards and have night lunch. They loved to get up to the lake for the summer. I always said that Wilf and Rose came back in April and the loons arrived in May.

After teaching in Dewberry for a few years, I noticed an ad in the newspaper for foster children who needed a home. I wondered how, or if, they would find placements. Sandra and I talked about it and thought we should at least offer to help. We had a home, jobs and a stable lifestyle. We did not know if Social Services would take single foster parents, but we called and offered our services anyway. We went through the battery of tests and interviews and were accepted. The only stipulation was that the kids needed to be of school age so they could go with us every day. A whole semester went by and we actually forgot, since we hadn't heard anything and had busy lives at school, church and in our community.

Sandra and I had pooled our resources and bought Meredith and Lorraine's farmhouse from them, as they had just built a new place. Fritz's son Darrell and his wife, Doreen, were going to move into our house. We purchased a lot just around the bay on the point. We named it Shoreline, after Mom's bookstore in Vancouver. During the spring of 1984, we had built a basement and moved the house thirty miles up to the lake. Most of our spare time was taken up with preparations for renovations and getting moved in.

During this time, in April 1984, I was called to the phone in the staff room at school. The voice said, "This is Alberta Social Services. I understand that you have offered to be a foster parent. We have two children, an eleven-year-old girl and her nine-year-old brother. Would you be willing to take them both?" I was completely dumbfounded at hearing anything from them at all, let alone asking if we would take two children. "When would they come?" I asked. "After school." "TODAY?" "Yes, we really need a placement soon." I told her to wait a moment and I raced down the hall to Sandra's classroom. I told her about the call and she said that we could not refuse if they needed a place that badly. I went back to the phone and told the social worker we could take them, but could we at least have one day to get things ready at home? She agreed, so we had to get two bedrooms ready overnight and adjust to having kids in the house, a gestation period far shorter than most parents experience.

And so Andrea and Teddy became part of our home and our lives. They came from a difficult family situation and were frightened and wary. We talked to them gently and told them that they would always be safe, warm and have enough to eat. Living at the lake was much different from being in town. It was quiet and peaceful, but when you are not used to that, it takes some getting used to. The same is true for basic house rules. When it came to chores, the kids were given a choice: "You can do dishes or go to bed. It's your choice." Teddy stood at the sink for a long, long time when it was his turn for dishes. He did not like the choices offered to him. He decided that he didn't want either and took off up the lane and out of sight around the bend. I was about to give chase, thinking I would have a tough time explaining to the social worker how I let this kid run away in the first few days he was with us. Then I thought that this could turn into a regular merry-go-round if I continued the game. I went to the shore in front of the house and saw him getting smaller and smaller as he walked along the shore across the lake. I was getting worried, but I held my ground. Soon he stopped, stood at the water's edge for quite a while, and then started homeward, ever so slowly. He walked hesitantly down the driveway, went into the house to the sink and finished the dishes. He never did that again, and I was grateful that I lived so far from any place that a kid would want to run away to.

The children also had to get accustomed to our philosophy of work and spending. Shortly after they arrived, we had a discussion about bicycles. Teddy was anxious to have a bike, as there were so many country roads to ride on. We explained that each of them would be getting an allowance of ten dollars every week. Five of it would go into the bank for savings for special purchases, and five could be spent on anything they wanted for treats. If he chose to save more he would be able to get a second-hand bike sooner. His response to me was, "Phone the welfare." I told him that we worked for what we wanted and that he would earn his own bike, not just call the welfare people to supply him with one automatically. He grudgingly saved his money and bought a bright red used bicycle for thirty dollars. He was so proud of that bike and it meant more to him than any "free" bicycle ever would have. Andrea also bought herself a bike from her savings and loved the freedom it gave her. Life offers many lessons if we are willing to learn them. The kids settled in well and were happy, responsible members of our home.

A couple of weeks after the kids arrived, we all went on a camping trip to Elk Island Park, near Edmonton. I do not think they had ever camped in a recreational vehicle before. Andrea jumped up into the bunk above the cab of our camperized van. Teddy claimed the table that folded down into a bunk-bed. I loved watching them as they experienced this new adventure.

We headed home on Sunday afternoon. As we rounded the south side of the lake, Fritz was parked on the road waiting for us. He came over to our van and told us that the police were at our place, as our home had been broken into. We appreciated him telling us the news, but we also realized that it must be quite serious to warrant him sitting on the road waiting for us. There was no way we could have braced ourselves for what we witnessed when we walked in the door. Food was strewn all over the kitchen, furniture was tossed about, my bed was filled with food, now thawed and rotting, that had been taken from the freezer. Drawers were emptied out, cash taken and clothes, radios and tape decks were all gone. Worst of all, our car had been stolen, driven up the road a mile or two, rolled into the ditch, and then set on fire. We wondered how the thieves could have managed to get past Jireh, our faithful guard dog. However, Wilf and Rose had just arrived for the summer and Jireh, excited to see them, had spent the night up at their place. When she heard the car engine start, she probably didn't blink an eye, as that sound was so familiar to her. She, obviously, felt no need to investigate.

We all felt completely violated. Everyone whose house has been robbed makes this statement, but it is only comprehensible when you have experienced it yourself. It feels so much like a rape; your privacy and intimate belongings have become public to a complete stranger. At least we prayed it was a complete stranger. The police grilled us about the children, who were from nearby Frog Lake Reserve. The RCMP wondered if family members were angry about the kids being placed in foster care and were retaliating. This was even more frightening, because it meant they might pay us another visit. We spent many nervous nights after that, but I made sure Jireh stayed at home by tying her up close to the door.

Finally the police found the culprits, a group of young people from another reserve. There was no connection to Andrea and Teddy, which made us very grateful. They had found their way to the lake somehow, and gone from cabin to cabin, looking for food and drink. None of the other owners had opened up their cabins yet for the summer, and we were the only ones who lived there year-round. Naturally, finding the place warm and full of food, they made themselves at home and did their hateful deeds. The offenders got forty hours of community work in St. Paul for their sentence. I told the police I would give them forty hours of work at my place. It seems to me that this would have been a better use of their time. They could have seen the faces of their victims and maybe, just maybe, there might have been real remorse and retribution. Eventually, we got everything cleaned up and our personal belongings replaced, but we were glad to be moving to the new house and leaving these memories behind.

Teddy and Andrea became completely involved with the project of the new house. The old walls were lath and plaster and had shaken loose with the move. We ripped them apart with a crowbar and the kids hauled load after load outside. What a tremendous help they were. It became a "family" project and we spent all summer insulating, dry-walling and painting. The days were hot, so we would all work for a while, then jump in the lake and have a swim. Then we'd return and work with our wet clothes on, repeating the cycle each time we dried off.

I learned a tremendous amount about renovating during that summer. I had booked a drywaller to come out and refinish the main floor of the house. He did not show up, and my neighbour Wilf said, "Oh, it's nothing to drywall. It's easy. You can do it with no problem. But don't get eight-foot sheets. There is too much crack-filling. Get ten-foot sheets." I appreciated the advice, measured the square footage, purchased the required amount and had it delivered to the lake. Little did I know that, firstly, we could hardly lift the sheets and, secondly, there was not a wall in the whole place that could use a whole ten-foot sheet. One of the things that I loved about the house was that it had so many windows. Consequently, I had to cut up every sheet and fit it around windows and doors. I learned a great lesson not just about renovating, but also about taking neighbours' advice blindly!

Eventually we finished the project and moved in before school started in September. The kids claimed the two bedrooms upstairs. They chose their paint and wallpaper, probably the first time in their lives that they had such an opportunity to claim ownership. They'd helped with the job and were proud of their accomplishment.

Although the project was so exciting for all of us, the summer season was not without loss. Jireh was getting older and suffering from hip dysplasia, which is common in purebred German Shepherds. She was not able to run and come to a comfortable stop. Her back end twisted around and she fell over sideways. It broke our hearts when we had to take her to the vet in Lloydminster to have her put down. The kids had fallen in love with her and were very sad to have to say goodbye. Picking up a brand-new Shepherd pup on the way home made that horrible day much less painful for us all. She was a six-week-old roly-poly ball of fur with big criss-crossed ears and feet the size of hamburger patties, and we named her Juno.

We still grieved the loss of Jireh deeply, but this crazy, mischievous pup stole our hearts the moment she got out of the truck. She learned the trails down to, and around, the lake with the kids. She pulled stuff all over the yard and chewed everything that she could get her puppy teeth into. Training her gave the kids a great project and we marvelled at the job they did. Her nature was kind, her temperament gentle. It wasn't long before the entire lake population fell in love with her and she became the Laurier Lake community dog. During the summer she visited everyone along the east and northern beaches, and all winter she was a visitor and friend to every ice fisherman on the whole lake. When we came home from school and rounded the lake's edge, she recognized the sound of our car, and started running full tilt toward home. It was always a race, but generally she arrived first and was so excited to greet us.

Our lives were rich with school, time at the lake, visiting neighbours, friends and family. Sandra often took the children to Irma for weekends. They enjoyed life at the farm; helping with chores, feeding pigs, riding on the tractor and playing with Sandra's nephews. We also got out to the Coast two or three times to visit my family. The first time the kids saw the Rocky Mountains, it was almost too much for them to comprehend. When we got close to Hinton, I said, "There are the mountains, kids." Teddy was sitting behind my driver's seat and glanced up when he heard me speak. He leapt up on his knees behind me, grabbed the back of my seat and started rocking it with excitement. He squealed with delight and was astounded how high the mountains were, then asked how we were ever going to get over them. We all laughed as he provided a running commentary while we wound our way through the valleys and peaks.

He was equally exuberant when we reached the Pacific Ocean at Vancouver and rode across on the ferry to Vancouver Island. The kids had seen pictures of the ocean, but nothing really prepares you for the immensity of the real thing. Andrea, thoroughly delighted, but enjoying it more quietly, also drank in the beauty. They were able to see all those sights from ground level, but we also flew out to the Coast and their first flight was similarly exciting. Seeing the Rockies from 35,000 feet was magical for them. All these rich experiences filled the kids' minds with good images to play in their memory-bank movies for the rest of their lives.

It was a huge shock when the call came that announced what "the rest of their lives" would be. In 1986, a new *Child Welfare Act* was passed and it affected us directly. The gist of it was that almost regardless of circumstance, children are better off with their nuclear family. We found this difficult to accept, as things were no better with the kids' mother. Her first comment was, " I would like to have my two babies back. And how much difference will it make on my cheque?" We were heartbroken.

As a foster parent, you know from the outset that the placement is temporary and eventually you must say goodbye. But you never know when or under what circumstances. You always have the hope, but never the assurance, that things have improved in the family home. It was with heavy hearts that we watched Andrea and Teddy drive out of our lives with the social worker in the fall of 1986. I will never forget their expressions as they looked back down our driveway, tears streaming down their faces. Within days, their bicycles and cross-country skis had been pawned. They had saved their money for them, they bought them, they owned them and then they lost them, just like that. Even now, some eighteen years later, I weep while I write these lines.

We grieved their loss, but when the next call came some weeks later asking if we could take in a twelve-year-old boy, we immediately agreed. Knowing the raw pain of bonding, then having that bond broken is difficult, but always worth the effort. We were told that Willy's mother was addicted to booze and bingo and needed three months to deal with it. I was surprised that they suggested it would only take that long to overcome two major addictions. We prepared to have him longer. And we did. He was with us for six months and then returned to St. Paul to his mother. They moved to Montana shortly after that and I have not heard what became of him.

When he arrived at the lake and we asked him what he liked to do, he replied, "I like TV and video games." I told him that he would be 0 for 2 at our place for those, but that we did have a kayak and other outdoor equipment that he might grow to enjoy. He got angry and said that he didn't want to stay because he was a town kid and didn't like the bush. I tried to impress on him that this was not an option open to him, so he would need to work on adjusting his attitude. He was a bright kid and realized that he might not win this battle of wills. Within days he was spending time cross-country skiing with Juno alongside, getting between his legs. The two of them ended up tangled upside down in the snow, laughing and wrestling with each other.

That spring, we were doing some outdoor work, clearing a path down to the lake and making a little bridge across a low, wet spot in the meadow. Willy was anxious to help and I explained to him about using an axe to clear brush. He became quite adept at it and many times I smiled as I watched him go down through the bush, hearing his cheerful voice saying, "I just love to work." We all worked hard at the project and Uncle Art's spring visit was well timed. Timbers were laid down, boards were cut and we soon had a wonderful bridge across the slough.

At school, Willy kept his grades up and fit in well with the other kids. Often, while we stayed late with marking, meetings or coaching, he would read or play in the schoolyard. One day he wanted to go to the store and rent a video to watch in Sandra's classroom while he waited. He had not whined about not having TV, so we were happy to let him watch a movie. He went downtown and rented a video with his allowance money. While getting ready to load it in the VCR, he looked at the cover and said to Sandra, "Oh...occasional nudity." Sandra shrieked and said, "Willy, what movie did you rent?" He smirked and said, "Just joking. I got *Big Red.*" We really did love his spontaneity and terrific sense of humour.

That spring we made a trip to the Coast and Willy was just as excited about the Rockies and the Pacific as the other two kids had been. We camped at Fernie, in the Kootenays, visiting with Ben and Joy Warkentin, who had moved there some years before. To Willy, everything was an adventure and he drank up each new experience with enthusiasm. How we enjoyed watching him fish, skip rocks and light a campfire. For a "town kid," he adjusted amazingly well and loved the challenge of rural life. We were grateful for the six months he was with us and were sad when he left. But our lives were richer for his being with us.

During the summer of 1987 I was out in Vancouver visiting my family alone. It was suggested to me that I take a fifteen-year-old girl whose family I was close to. She and her father were very similar in personality and they constantly clashed. Her mother felt caught in the middle and perhaps a year away for their daughter would be a good thing for all concerned. Sandra and I agreed, so young Sonya flew up to Edmonton with me at the end of the summer. On the flight, I discussed her temper with her. I had known her since she was born, and had witnessed several of her tantrums over the years. I said to her on the plane, "Sonya, I want you to give serious thought to, and work on, your temper this year. I do not think it is acceptable for you to go to your bedroom when you are angry and slam the door so hard it echoes throughout the whole house. If you do that at our home, do you believe me when I tell you that I will remove the hinges and take your bedroom door off completely?" "Yes, Deb, I believe you." That was the only time that topic was addressed and not once did we have an outburst of anger the entire school year.

Just as classes began, we received a call from Social Services, asking us to take a fourteen-year-old girl who was in lock-up at the Youth Assessment Centre in Lac La Biche. This would be a special challenge, so we had a family conference to discuss the pros and cons. In the end, we decided to take her and she arrived soon after school started. Jessica had difficulty going to school with us each day and did not fit well into a small, closely knit school. Every day we had to debrief and suggest techniques to help her cope. Soon, we saw growth and were encouraged by her willingness to try to communicate with students, staff and us at home. We noticed her laughing and teasing, sure signs that she was getting more comfortable with her surroundings and the people who were part of her life. We had long discussions, and she asked a lot of questions about life, love and friendship. She had been severed from primary relationships and found it difficult to relate to people that were in close proximity. It wasn't long before we heard the two girls giggling and having late-night discussions. We were thrilled, and made little attempt to shut them down.

At Thanksgiving, Jessica went back to Lac La Biche for the weekend. We don't know exactly what happened, but she ran away from there and was not apprehended for some months. Our guess is that she had begun to feel at home, bonded to some degree, and perhaps found the possibility of losing that trust too much to handle. Better to cut it off now than be disappointed down the road, which was the only pattern she had ever known. Nonetheless, she did not return to us, but we thought of her often and wished her well.

Soon after she left, we were asked to take another teenager, Shauna. She was thirteen and was a cheerful, friendly girl. She fit right in and was a great sport, willing to participate in any adventure from kayaking to pitching a tent in the front yard. The girls spent many nights out there, even on school nights, provided they didn't talk too late. When Art and Reta arrived for their spring visit, their motor home was close to the girls' tent and they could report if they heard late-night noise! Shauna had many positive experiences at our place. When she left we missed her cheerful demeanour. We were sad to hear, some years later, that she had been in a car full of teenagers and was killed in a tragic accident. Alcohol had been a factor.

Sonya was going to be turning sixteen in August, and was anxious to learn how to drive before she returned to Vancouver. As you could get your learner's permit and drive in Alberta at fourteen, we spent the spring practicing driving on the quiet country roads. My car had a standard transmission, so we lurched along, stalling regularly. However, she got a little better each time out.

After this interesting, but somewhat stressful, year, Sandra and I told Social Services that we were going to take a hiatus from fostering. They begged us not to, but we felt it necessary. That summer we went to the British Isles for a well-deserved and total break. She had relatives there and we were gone for a month. We traveled throughout England, Scotland and Wales. I particularly loved Scotland, the homeland of my mother's ancestors. Riding across the ferry to the Isle of Skye in the Hebrides, I could hear my aunts, Belle and Nell, singing the song I had heard so often as a child, "Over the Sea to Skye." The weather was less than perfect; in fact we had rain every day but one. It was the rainiest summer since they had started keeping records in 1869. We didn't care much. We just kept our rain slickers handy. Everything was so different from life at home, we simply wanted to make the best of every experience, wet or dry!

We arrived home to the news that Wayne Gretzky had just been traded to the Los Angeles Kings. This was a huge event and the radio waves were full of commentary. We were inundated the moment we arrived and the heather-covered Scottish moors suddenly seemed far away.

Even more disturbing was the news we received when we returned to the lake. There was a phone message saying that my aunt Reta had just been diagnosed with pancreatic cancer and was in the hospital in Vancouver. It looked very serious and could we come right out? We unpacked our suitcases, did laundry, repacked and were on the road within hours. We spent a couple of days with her and wondered if this might be the last time we'd talk to her. We began school on the Thursday before Labour Day, then took off again and drove through the night back to Vancouver to spend the weekend with Reta. She was bright yellow and feeling very weak. After a special couple of days, reminiscing about all the visits to our lake, we said our goodbyes, feeling that this time we would not see her again. It was a sober drive home to Alberta and tough to settle into school.

Soon classes got into full swing, and I thought that this would be a normal school year, as all the others had been throughout my teaching career. Boy, was I wrong!

CHAPTER 8

Politics? Are You Kidding?

O N SEPTEMBER 15, WE WERE INVITED UP to Liz and Jack White's farm to celebrate Sandra's birthday with cake and coffee. Mulroney was about to call a fall election, and as we sat around the table, we griped about the current political situation. We had all voted for the Progressive Conservatives, thinking they would get the country's finances back on track, but that had not happened. In fact, to us they had not appeared "conservative" in any sense of the word. Deficits were ballooning and our large contingent of Alberta MPs did not seem to carry much weight in the Mulroney cabinet. As a Westerner, I felt betrayed in many ways. Firstly, the time zones relegated us to playing catch-up on voting day. Majority governments were announced before any of us had even gone to the ballot box. Secondly, the National Energy Policy had devastated Western Canada's oil industry. Billions of dollars were bled out of our economy to Eastern Canada, and the results were catastrophic. Thirdly, Winnipeg had initially won the contract for maintenance work on the fleet of Canadian Forces CF-18 fighter jets. Then, suddenly, and with no explanation, the contract was awarded to Montreal. That was another blow levelled at the West.

As a voter and taxpayer, I found this very frustrating. As a teacher, I used the opportunity to talk about Western alienation and the anger it created, even though I was completely non-political. On the streets, in coffee shops and around family tables the feelings of betrayal and exasperation were palpable.

So, on that fateful evening of September 15, there we were, voicing our concerns over cake and coffee. Since 1972, every single seat in every single election in Alberta, had gone Conservative. We'd all had high hopes that when they formed the government on September 4, 1984, things would turn around. Alas, things only seemed to get worse. I asked Liz, "What do you know about this new Reform Party? Are they a bunch of Western separatist wackos?" I am a proud and passionate Canadian and had no time for the separatists, whether in Quebec (Parti Québécois) or Western Canada (Western Canada Concept). She answered "No," and to prove Reform wasn't separatist, she told me Preston Manning was the leader and that the party's slogan was "The West Wants In."

The Manning name in Alberta always evoked the highest respect. Preston's father, Ernest, had been our premier from 1943 to 1968 and had been loved and well-respected. His Social Credit government had been scandal-free, likely the only one in Canada that could be so described, then or since.

Liz told me that the party was brand-new and that she was a member. She was convinced this was the way to go. I was surprised by my good friend and neighbour—a nurse, farmer and avid fisherman—because she hardly seemed like a political activist! Even though the party was less than a year old, it was preparing to field candidates across Western Canada in the upcoming election. I asked who would be going up against Don Mazankowski, our popular, well-known incumbent MP. She replied that, under redistribution, we were in a newly carved-out constituency called "Beaver River." I announced that I was going to get politically involved, take my responsibilities seriously and attend an all-candidates' forum during the campaign. What commitment! What action! What a stand I was taking against the great evils of Ottawa! After all, I had always voted but never cared enough to actually go to a forum and listen to the candidates' platforms. I was rising up to defend my rights as a voter.

"Who is running for Reform here in Beaver River?" I asked. "We don't have a candidate yet, Deb…why don't you run?" Liz replied.

"Don't be ridiculous," I responded. "First of all, it's September, and I'm up to here with school preparation. Secondly, I already get enough hassle as a schoolteacher—'too much money, too many holidays.' Why would I want to sign on for more abuse? Thirdly, I don't want to be labelled a politician. Those pot-lickers disappear to Ottawa and then you won't see them again until it's election time. You tell them what to say to Ottawa and they come back spouting what Ottawa says to you. Thanks, Liz, but I don't think so." After a few minutes, she tried again. "But, Deb, we don't have a candidate and you would do really well. You can get up and talk and you aren't afraid to take anyone on. I dare you!" Uh-oh! Those fateful words. I pondered them for only seconds. I had never backed down from a good dare—ever.

Soon, she was on the phone to Pat Chern, a Reform riding association director, from Smoky Lake. Liz chatted with her for a few minutes, then called me to the phone. I got on the line and nervously said, "Hello?" Pat's friendly voice said, "Hi there. So, you're thinking of becoming the candidate, are you?" I nearly laughed out loud, but managed to contain myself enough to say, "Hardly, but I'd love to read some information about your party and platform." She mailed it right away and I picked it up at the Dewberry post office the next Friday, September 23.

I grabbed it, threw it in my vehicle and drove off after school for the two-and-a-half hour trip to Edmonton. I was flying to Vancouver for my brother Shaun's wedding. I got to the airport and was sitting in the waiting lounge, reading away. I was fascinated and thrilled. Finally, somebody had put down on paper all the things I had felt for so many years. Fiscal responsibility—yes! Social program sustainability—yes! Democratic accountability—yes! Individual and provincial equality—yes! That was it—I had always been a Reformer, but only now did I realize that someone had put together a platform to enunciate and articulate my feelings!

While I was reading, taking it all in, I noticed an older man walk up very close to me. I looked up and said, "Hello." He said, "Hello, I just couldn't help but notice what you're reading." He had noticed the party logo and come over to chat. *Oh, no,* I thought, *he's going to ask me questions and I don't know anything.* I smiled at him and said, "This is very interesting, but I just got it and can't answer many of your questions." He laughed and said, "That's okay—my name is Gordon Shaw. I'm the vice-president of the party. I've just been up in Edmonton for meetings with Preston Manning." I managed to respond with something inane like, "Oh, that's interesting." My heart pounded, wondering at the timing of these "chance" happenings. As a Christian, I believe God organizes these things. But, no matter what you call it—providence, fate, chance, luck—the common denominator is always the same: the hair on the back of your neck stands up and the goose bumps arrive immediately!

We sat together on the plane and he asked what I did and where I lived. When I told him, he said, "Oh, that's up in Beaver River. We're looking for a candidate there. Any ideas?" I responded somewhat confidently, "Well, I teach up there and sing in a gospel group, so I get around to a lot of those towns. I'll keep my eyes open and let you know if I come across anyone that looks like a good possibility." "Great, thanks," he said. After what seemed like a long, painful silence, he said, "What about you? You look like you'd make a great candidate."

The die was cast. I reiterated what I had told Liz and he responded in much the same way she did. Was this planned? Had they cooked this up together? We arrived in Vancouver and I figured my political career had ended as quickly as it had begun. We would part ways and I would never see or hear from him again. His wife, Mary Jane, was there to meet him and he said to her, "Hi, dear. I'd like to introduce you to Deb Grey and explain about her." Mary Jane retorted with a wonderful laugh and a handshake, "I certainly hope so." We chatted for a few minutes and Gordon explained that Preston and all the candidates nominated thus far would be speaking at a big rally at the Jubilee Auditorium in Edmonton on the upcoming Monday night. He said I would find it interesting and have the chance to learn more about what would be involved in being a candidate. He gave me the phone number of Neil Weir, the campaign manager, and I told Gordon I would call Neil on Monday morning.

My head was reeling all weekend. I enjoyed being with my family and celebrating with Shaun and Cheryl. The whole time, though, I was brainstorming with friends, Uncle Art and Aunt Reta (who was in the hospital) and my immediate family. My sisters and Mom thought this would be a great field trip and a wonderful exercise in democracy. My mom encouraged me, as usual, by saying, "Do you want to do it? Do you think you can do it? Then go for it. I'm behind you 100 per cent. Think of all the things you will learn and the experiences you will have. The worst that can happen is that you could lose." I took those words as an endorsement from the whole crew, a sign that they thought this foray into the political field would be great fun and an adventure. It would also be a tremendous learning experience for us all—for me, as a candidate, but also for them, because they would pay far more attention to this election than any other to date.

I flew back to Edmonton on Sunday and drove the three hours home to the lake, arriving well after midnight. I was up early for school, and during my prep period, around ten o'clock, I thought of Neil Weir. I was still hesitating. "Why would I even bother to call him? He's busy and has no clue who I am. I shouldn't waste his time." But the nagging feeling kept eating at me. "I am a woman of my word and I told Gordon Shaw I would call Neil. No problem, nothing to lose." I dialled his number and, when he answered, I said, "My name is Deborah Grey. I was chatting the other day with…" He cut me off and said, "Hi, Deborah. Gordon Shaw told me you would be calling. Can you come to the rally tonight?"

So, after school, away I went to Edmonton again, to the Jubilee Auditorium. The candidates were introduced and they spoke briefly. I was moved by their passion and desire to serve. Preston spoke after them and I was so impressed, I drove home knowing that something incredibly powerful had taken place in my life. Here was a "politician" who made sense, had solutions for the country and was not in the least bit self-serving. What in the world was in store?

Neil Weir phoned me the next day and set up a meeting for me with Tom and Erna Holliday, members of the Beaver River board who lived in Elk Point, twenty minutes from my home. They took me to an association meeting and I met all the directors. They seemed down to earth and pleased to meet someone they might hornswoggle into becoming their candidate. The association was new and the election was drawing closer every day. They suggested I go to Lloydminster to a rally and told me they thought it was on Tuesday night. I drove into Lloydminster after school and discovered the Elks' Hall was in total darkness. In fact, the meeting was to be on Wednesday night. I thought it ridiculous to drive all that way again for a meeting that, who knew, might not be that night either.

Still, I felt drawn back there on Wednesday night and met a lot of regular folks like myself who seemed fired up at the mess our country was in, but had a genuine desire to fix it. Along with a young fellow from Saskatchewan, I bought a membership that night—my first ever in any political party. His name was Elwin Hermanson from Beechy. (Little did I know that, down the road, we would become colleagues and close personal friends.) I sought advice, prayed and wondered what in the world to do. What would my school board and principal think if I asked for time off to campaign in a federal election? How would I manage Christmas expenses if I took six to eight weeks off with no pay? How could I ever find a substitute teacher during harvest and do all the necessary lesson plans?

Because of the political landscape and climate of Alberta, I soon realized that most, if not all, of the school board members were Progressive Conservatives. Obviously, they were not amused at this young pup becoming a candidate for this ragtag band of Reformers who thought they could storm the capital and change the country.

But somehow, unbelievably, everything fell into place perfectly. I was grudgingly granted six weeks of unpaid leave, and found my own substitute teacher. The writ was dropped on October 5 for a November 21, 1988 election. I was nominated by acclamation on October 12 in St. Paul, and I was off and running on the campaign trail.

What a ball! We had no clue how to run a campaign. We got brochures and highway signs made up with the help of the national campaign. I learned the issues and how to communicate them in chewable, understandable pieces. I went door-knocking in dozens of towns, sometimes with a little team of two or three volunteers, but many times alone. I attended coffee parties and social events, mostly harvest suppers. But the events that I really enjoyed and did well at were the all-candidates' forums.

The PC candidate, John Dahmer, had been nominated for a long time, but had been diagnosed with cancer before the writ was dropped. He became quite ill, but nobody (even his own campaign team) really knew how sick he was. He was seldom seen in public throughout the campaign.

In any race, political opponents generally pick on the frontrunner, and this one was typical. At the debates, one chair was always left empty, and one night it would have a bale of hay on it ("all you had to do was run a hay bale for the PCs and you'd win"), another night a post, another night a chicken. We other candidates were present for the nine forums all over our large rural riding, which covered 28,000 square kilometres.

My team rented a storefront space in St. Paul for our campaign office. It was small, but we didn't need much room—we had precious few volunteers and had no phone banks or voter ID methods anyway. We were provided a complete voters' list by Elections Canada, but we had no idea what to do with it, so I had it in a box in the back of my vehicle for weight on the winter roads. I also carried around an axe, and pounded signs into the freezing ground and, as the campaign wore on, snowbanks.

I was moving at a dead run for the entire writ period. I simply did not slow down. This made it difficult to keep up with real life, let alone with the issues. I hardly had time to read the newspapers or follow in-depth news. My roommate, Sandra, was aware of this and did her part to help. She spent hours reading articles from papers and weekly magazines such as *Alberta Report* and *Maclean's* into a cassette recorder and then I would listen to them while I was on the road for hours traversing the riding. So I was getting the news quickly, efficiently, and inexpensively!

The financing of this electoral process was quite a hoot, also. When I was nominated, our riding account had sixty-eight dollars in it. As a teacher, I equated that with roughly one successful hot-dog sale. A good start, but...Donations came in during the writ and we managed to raise $11,000. Much of it came from fifty- and one-hundred-dollar donations from supporters. But a chunk of it came from a continuous garage sale right in our campaign office. We sold all kinds of stuff that people would bring in and our war chest got a little bigger with each meagre sale. We spent the money that we had, and no more.

Although the Meech Lake Accord was an issue in the campaign, and also the National Energy Program, the CF-18 contracts and Triple-E Senate, the 1988 election campaign boiled down to only one issue: the Free Trade Agreement. It was the defining issue. The Liberals were dead against it. In fact, they ran a fantastic advertising scheme against free trade. There was a picture of a map of North America. While a voice was decrying free trade, a big pencil came out and the eraser end of it completely rubbed out the 49th parallel. Surely we would not want to become the 51st state and be one with "the enemy," the Liberals intimated.

The debate raged for the entire forty-seven-day writ period. This issue made things difficult for us, because Reform was in favour of free trade and voters were told a vote for us would split the free trade vote and the Liberals would capitalize on that. Free trade was very important to Albertans, and they did not want to put a Liberal into any federal seat in our province.

On election night, November 21, 1988, the Mulroney Tories ended up with a huge majority and a clear mandate for free trade. They won 169 seats, the Liberals got 83 seats and the NDP, 43. Canada had spoken—the voters wanted free trade. In Alberta, the votes coincided pretty closely with past federal elections. This time, however, the constituency of Edmonton East elected a New Democrat MP, Ross Harvey, the first non-PC MP since 1972.

In Beaver River, the result echoed the rest of Alberta. The results were:

John Dahmer, PC	13,768
Ernie Sehn, Liberal	6,528
Brian Luther, NDP	6,492
Deborah Grey, Reform	4,158
Les Johnston, Confederation of Regions	131

For a brand-new political party, and with me, a brand-new candidate, we did extremely well. Sandra told me, "Any more than two votes—yours and mine—will be a bonus." We laughed and figured we did pretty well, considering all the factors: a lack of money; a new party; Alberta's traditional voting patterns; free trade, etc. The sad part was that we garnered 13.5 per cent of the vote, just shy of the 15 per cent needed to get our rebate of 50 per cent of campaign expenses from Elections Canada. But what a run! We had made new friends, done extremely well, put a little fear into the competition and had a lot of fun at the same time.

On election night, John Dahmer's wife, Donna, announced that although John was very ill, he was pleased to have been elected and looked forward to serving as Beaver River's MP. Still, nobody knew how ill he really was.

I took Tuesday and Wednesday off school to clean out the campaign office and write thank-you notes. On Wednesday's news, we heard that Dahmer's health had taken a turn for the worse and that a team from Ottawa was flying out to swear John in at the hospital in Edmonton. I returned to school on Thursday to get back into the swing and carry on with my life as it had been before the campaign. Dahmer went into a coma on Thursday and was never sworn in.

On Saturday morning, my first chance to collapse and sleep in, I was awakened by the phone at 9:00 AM. One of my campaign workers said, "John Dahmer just died. Are you ready for a by-election?"

CHAPTER 9

Beaver River By-Election

THE DEATH OF JOHN DAHMER came as a shock to us, but even more so to the PCs. Many of his campaign workers had been led to believe that he was not that sick. They were hurt, many were angry and I think all felt somewhat betrayed. Nonetheless, a by-election was now upon us and we needed to get organized.

As I was already back at school, I had no plans to put my name forward as a candidate. I called Preston Manning that same Saturday. I had never met him and had no idea if he knew who I was. "Yes, Deborah from Beaver River, how are you?" he responded when I told him who was calling. He was surprised to hear that John Dahmer had died so soon. I told Preston that I was back at school and that I assumed he would be running in the by-election. I remember saying to him, "You can consider me your warm-up act in Beaver River. I will be happy to help you campaign in any way that I can." He thanked me and said we would need to get together as a board to have some discussions. A meeting was scheduled for the following Thursday, December 1, 1988, at the home of Pat and Alex Chern in Smoky Lake. There was a good turnout and, although we were keen to do what we could for the upcoming by-election, we were all still exhausted from the forty-seven-day general election campaign.

Our strategic discussions revolved around Preston getting a seat in the House to establish a beachhead for Reform in Parliament. We chatted away about platform, funding, campaign literature and signage. It would be somewhat cheaper because he could use his same signs—that would be helpful. After a long discussion, Preston dropped a bombshell. He had, unbeknownst to all of us, just spent days driving the length and breadth of Beaver River, gauging support from various areas. He told us that people in coffee shops, small business owners and oil-rig workers had said they voted PC to ensure that free trade went through. Now that it had, they would consider voting for me as the candidate because I had become well known and done well in the general election, especially at the all-candidates' forums. Preston then went on to say that it would look like political opportunism if he were to parachute in to Beaver River. He explained that getting a toehold in Parliament was essential, but that the candidate did not necessarily have to be him. He could still be free to travel the country and promote Reform. He built a great case for not running in the by-election and asked if I would be willing to run again. We were all dumbfounded by this strategic thinking. I was probably more shocked than anybody else. I really did believe my political foray was over and was not sad about returning to my classroom. I countered with, "Well, you're not really a parachute candidate. You are only four miles outside the boundary." Others said, "We love Deb, but she does not have the profile you would have in Ottawa." A heated discussion ensued, with some seriously questioning his strategy. He addressed each person's concerns, including mine. On a very personal note, I did not have the nerve to face my school board again, asking for another leave. Besides, I could not afford more time off financially. I also worried about my students, because they'd already had a sub for some weeks and she had now moved on to another school for a long-term contract.

When all the discussion died down, the consensus was that I should be the candidate again. I said I would think it over and let them know soon. As I drove home, I rehashed all the ins and outs of the meeting. What struck me most was the realization that I had just been introduced to, and very impressed by, the most unpolitical politician I had ever met. He had no lust for power or to see his name in lights; he did not want to elevate himself to the detriment of others; he seemed completely devoid of ego. Even before I pulled into my driveway at the lake, I decided to run.

My school board, as expected, was not keen to grant me another leave of absence. Prime Minister Mulroney had six months in which to call the by-election, but we didn't know when it would happen. Parliament sat briefly in mid-December to pass the *Free Trade Act*, then recessed on Christmas Eve. Politically, things got very quiet until the New Year. Even then, we had no idea when the writ would be dropped.

Even though I was still teaching all day, I campaigned in the evenings, soliciting support for the nomination, which was contested by Richard Johnson, a medical doctor from Cold Lake. The nomination meeting was held in Smoky Lake on January 9, 1989. It was forty-two below, but we still drew a decent crowd. Richard had a boys' band playing and a virtual "tickle trunk" full of props for his speech. He brought out his stethoscope to talk about health care, a military cap to talk about defence, a hard hat to talk about the trades. His delivery was actually hilarious. In spite of his spirited presentation, I won 120 to 6 and our campaign was off and running again.

We set up our office in St. Paul in an unused flower shop. Neil Weir came out from Edmonton to be our campaign manager. His desk was in the "cooler." He had to open the doors and step into it, which was a little awkward. However, it was a quiet place for him to work. We continued to have a running garage sale, but more funds came in from all over to support our campaign. Tom Holliday was my official agent, again, and his wife, Erna, was our office manager and volunteer co-ordinator.

The writ was dropped on January 21, before the PCs had even held their nomination meeting. For them, the real campaign was securing the nomination. In Alberta, that was the only actual contest. The election itself was just a formality. I went to the PC nomination meeting in Glendon on Saturday, January 28, 1989. There were forty-five hundred people there to choose one of nine candidates in the running. It was bitterly cold, but the turnout was enormous and generated a lot of heat inside the hockey arena. I knew that only one candidate would win and that there would be a lot of disgruntled party members. So we printed up hundreds of brochures saying, "If you are not happy with the candidate chosen, perhaps you would like to consider Deborah Grey and Reform." I convinced a whole army of kids to join me in the parking lot. We plastered every windshield with a brochure. The kids thought this was great sport and I was grateful to have so much help. Still, we were all glad to get back inside the warm arena.

I spent from 1:00 P.M. to 10:00 P.M. at the nomination meeting. Word of my presence spread like wildfire and I got a chance to talk to a lot of people. My unmitigated gall at showing up shocked many, but more probably admired my nerve in facing the competition head-on. My day of adventure paid off when the candidate was finally chosen. Dave Broda, a realtor from Redwater, won the nod. Don Mazankowski and Jack Shields, veteran MPs, took the stage and one of them said, "There is a candidate here from one of the other parties who has come to see how a real party picks its candidates." A man in front of me groaned and said, "Oh, sh-t. Why did they announce that?" He didn't know I was standing behind him, so I tapped him on the shoulder and said, "Beats me…but I'm sure glad he did." He was embarrassed, but at least good-natured enough to say, "You won that one, Deborah." There was a media black-out at the beginning of the campaign, so we could not advertise. My presence at the meeting became a news event, however, and the media descended on me and played clips on the news for the next day or two!

The candidate chosen for the Liberals was Ernie Brousseau, a baker from Smoky Lake. The NDP nominated Barb Bonneau, the postmistress from Newbrook. Both were pleasant, both were novices, and both were replacing candidates who had run in the general election. I was the only repeat candidate and was familiar with the flow of the fall election.

The by-election turned into a debate about issues other than free trade, so that helped our campaign. It was not a referendum on the government's performance, because it was so early in their mandate. But the big issue became who best could represent the constituents of Beaver River. The typical battle-cry is: "You need someone at the government table who can get you stuff." This time around, people seemed to care more about having someone stand up for them rather than just get them "stuff." Alberta already had enough Tory MPs who did not stand up for them against Central Canada's powerful elites. The voters were frustrated by the CF-18 contract, Air Canada moving their head office from Winnipeg to Montreal, the National Energy Program, a lack of concern about Senate reform, the pending Meech Lake Accord (signed in 1987), giving Quebec distinct-society status enshrined in the Constitution, official bilingualism, high interest rates and so on.

We printed our "fair language policy" into four languages—English, Cree, Ukrainian, and French—and blanketed the riding. We were not critical of French; we were critical of a government obsessed by official bilingualism while ignoring other language groups who were "just as Canadian." We felt official bilingualism discriminated against unilingual Canadians and those whose mother tongue or second language was neither English nor French. A stark example of that came from a senior military person who told me that he was being transferred to Germany. He was completely bilingual in English and German and was very much looking forward to his posting. At the last minute (with furniture packed and ready to go) his posting was cancelled and he was accused of lying because he'd checked "yes" on the bilingual category on his application for the posting. We called for a fair language policy that recognized French in Quebec and English elsewhere as the predominant working language, with bilingual services in Parliament and the Supreme Court, and local areas where common sense and the market dictated. Ironically, Beaver River has the second-largest francophone population in Alberta and offered many services in French, which was practical. Under our fair language policy, that military officer would have been celebrated and posted, rather than denied and deflated.

Another issue of concern was high interest rates. The Bank of Canada tried to defend their rates, saying it was trying to control inflation. The problem was, the inflation was mostly in the overheated economies of southern Ontario and Quebec. In Beaver River, we were experiencing a recession and high interest rates only made it worse. We advocated that the Bank of Canada should be more sensitive to the regions when balancing fiscal and monetary policy. Also, much of the overheating of the Central Canadian economy could be traced directly to the federal government. In 1987–88, of total regional development spending, 71 per cent was in Ontario and Quebec. Per-capita federal government procurement for these two provinces was three to four times that of Alberta. So, while trying to quell inflation, the government was actually fanning the fire.

I did manage to get a leave for the last two weeks of the campaign. On one of those days, Preston and I flew to the Bank of Canada in Calgary aboard the "Reform Air Force," a small plane belonging to Phil Stuffco, that we had to jump-start at the Edmonton Municipal Airport. We delivered a lengthy letter for John Crow, who was the governor at the time. The media followed us into the bank foyer and up to the wickets, behind which were a couple of employees who were not used to such publicity. Security arrived, and we told them we simply wanted to make a deposit on behalf of the many voters in Beaver River. It was a bit nerve-racking, but I relaxed when a couple of the guards recognized me, told me they were Reformers, and wished me well in the by-election.

A charge that was levelled at us on a regular basis was that we were racist. It was unkind, it was unfair, and it was untrue. In fact, our policy was that immigration should be based on Canada's labour and economic market needs, and thus it was racially neutral. In fact, Preston Manning had refused to sign the candidate papers for Doug Collins, a potential candidate for the Reform Party at the West Coast in 1988, because he made inflammatory statements that we did not believe or accept.

Nevertheless, Ernie Brousseau's campaign team put out a brochure labelling us as "racist," using quotes from Collins. At an all-candidates' meeting in Redwater, Ernie had to face one of my campaign workers, Colleen Everitt, who is a West Coast Indian. She said, "If the Reform Party is racist, how is it that people like me are not only members of the party, but hold key positions on the local executive and campaign team? So, do you actually believe that Reformers are racist, or is that something a few smart-alec lawyers in Edmonton put into your brochure?" Poor Ernie—he got so flustered, he didn't know how to respond. He finally tried to disassociate himself from his own campaign literature, apologized and offered to print retractions in all the local papers. Colleen was the best neutralizer for attacks of racism, and I was grateful for her interventions.

During the election, there was a furor about Eastern Canada trucking potentially dangerous PCBs to a facility in Swan Hills. The media reported on what hazards lay in store if these vehicles crashed en route. As I was trying hard to convince voters in Beaver River that Alberta had enough Tory MPs, I was able to turn the news reports to my local advantage. At that same candidates' forum in Redwater I announced, "Alberta does not need any more PCBs—Progressive Conservative Backbenchers. Surely, we have enough of those." The acronym stuck and people talked about it for some time. It definitely made an impression.

My campaign team was aware that we were starting from far behind in the race. We were confident that we could close the gap. Ironically, the provincial government had called a general election for March 20. This was very confusing for the electorate in Beaver River. The provincial PCs stapled their campaign posters right onto my signs along the highway. Poll results showed that I was at 38 per cent in the provincial election. Also, a provincial returning officer phoned Elections Alberta and said that my name had been omitted on the ballot!

During the last part of our campaign, I started using the phrase, "Beware the Ides of March, Brian Mulroney. The Reform Party is on its way to Ottawa." At the candidates' forums, I said that and then looked to my Tory counterpart, smiled and asked, "*Et tu* Broda?" The crowds loved it.

Preston spent some time campaigning with me. He was careful not to make it seem that I needed babysitting, but we did some events together and he helped me out in many ways. One of my fondest memories is when we were in Lac La Biche. My friend Lil and I were delivering brochures door to door. We had run out and got some printed up quickly, but they had not been folded. There sat Preston in the back of his van, in a captain's chair, folding brochures on his knees. We teased him and said, "If the national media could only see you now." But Preston was remarkable; he simply saw a task that needed to be done and just got at it.

Another time we were campaigning in Waskatenau and went into the local bar. Preston asked a couple of farmers what they thought of

Deborah Grey. They replied that I could "talk common sense" and that they might vote for me. I had a rather less enthusiastic response on the Main Street in Radway. I asked an older farmer if he would support me. He said, "Well—I don't know. You got two things against you. You're a schoolteacher and you're a woman." One of my very few regrets in my political life is that I did not get his name and telephone number. I would have loved to give him a call on March 14!

For every negative experience, there always seems to be a positive one. At an old folks' home in Bonnyville, I had some wonderful encouragement. An old gent said to me, "We might as well let the women run the country. Men haven't done a great job in 125-odd years." And my all-time favourite came from an elderly woman who was walking me to the front door. She patted me on the arm and said, "I'm going to vote for you, dear. You have lovely teeth." Yikes! I suppose everybody has their reasons about whom they vote for and why.

On the last weekend of the campaign, we organized a cavalcade. Cars and trucks came from all corners of the riding (and beyond) and we met in St. Paul. We drove around, honking and waving banners. Dave Broda's office was on the main drag and we went past it several times. One friendly news reporter called Broda's office and said, "Can you count them? There must be a least four hundred of them." In fact, we had only about forty or fifty vehicles, and after my first time past, waving and smiling, I ducked each time we went by.

I asked my mother to come up for the by-election, as I thought it would be fun for her to see all my signs along the roads and get the feel of election fever. She enjoyed it immensely. I assured her that I had done my best in the campaign and although we had virtually no chance of winning, we were going to "hopefully come second" and "put a good scare into the Tories."

March 13, 1989, by-election day, finally arrived. Mom and I went to the Heinsburg Hall, where I cast my ballot. We drove around the riding, Mom getting a feel for the vast, rural constituency. At 6:00 P.M. we arrived in St. Paul to get things ready for our volunteers to "watch" the results. As this was a by-election, there was no television coverage, so we couldn't watch anything live. However, we did have some scrutineers this time around, so they could call results in, and we had someone at the returning officer's headquarters to relay results to us.

While I was getting coffee ready and putting out food trays, a reporter I did not recognize came in. I was sure I had met all the local media from Beaver River, the *Edmonton Sun* and the *Edmonton Journal*. She said she was from Canadian Press. Soon after, another stranger arrived, identifying himself as a reporter from *Maclean's*. And on it went—CBC, CTV, et cetera. Now I got nervous. Byron Christopher, an Edmonton reporter, predicted an upset. The general media consensus was "what would make a better story, 'Another PC Backbencher,' or 'Reform Party Makes History'?" I could hardly believe my ears. I had no idea that we could be that close, but I wasn't going to argue with them.

The polls closed and we anxiously awaited the results. Within half an hour, the phones started ringing. Jack Ramsay, from Camrose, who had helped me in the campaign, stood on a chair to announce the results. "Grey, 122; Broda, 56. Grey, 103; Broda, 43. Grey, 86; Broda, 48." And on it went. The trend was soon apparent. It was not long before someone called in to say they were watching an Edmonton Oilers hockey game and a bar rolled across the bottom of the screen, "Reform Party makes history in by-election in Beaver River." After it was all over, the totals were:

Deborah Grey, Reform	11,154
Dave Broda, PC	6,912
Ernie Brousseau, Liberal	2,756
Barb Bonneau, NDP	2,081

Everybody in our campaign office went crazy. We had all just made Canadian history! The media were pleased that they had made the right call when they came to our headquarters. An amazing story to cover, to be sure!

As I looked around the office and saw so many people, some of whom I had known and loved for many years, some of whom I had only met on the campaign trail, I was in awe. We had worked so hard with hardly any expectation of this outcome. It was a delirious feeling for us all. Preston and Sandra were so excited and so proud of the whole campaign team. Preston took me aside to the telephone inside the "cooler" where he had his father, Ernest Manning, on the line from their winter home in Arizona. What an honour to talk to Alberta's former premier and elder statesman! He sounded so pleased and wished me well. After interviews and clean-up, it was almost 3:00 A.M. before I got home to the lake and to bed.

The media were arriving at 6:30 A.M. to film me eating breakfast and then driving to my school in Dewberry. As I lay in bed, eyes wide open, not able to sleep, I spoke the familiar words, "Beware the Ides of March, Brian Mulroney. The Reform Party is on its way to Ottawa."

CHAPTER 10

My New Classroom:
Parliament Hill

I SLEPT PRECIOUS LITTLE THAT NIGHT. It seemed like only moments before the alarm went off. I jumped out of bed, remembering that CBC cameras would be at my place very soon. I took some solace in the fact that no matter how easy my directions were to follow, almost everybody got lost trying to find my house at the lake. Naturally, on this day, they followed them to a T and drove directly to Shoreline. I was still bleary-eyed when they parked in the yard and got set up. I'd just got my hair dried and a bit of make-up on as they clumped up the steps to the deck and the patio doors. I welcomed them into the kitchen, poured coffee and served muffins. The commentary was hilarious, as they hadn't gotten any more sleep than I had. As we all chatted and ate, we were amused to note what breakfast looks and tastes like "the morning after" one makes Canadian history. After wandering around my home, and filming Juno looking plaintively in the front window hinting for a muffin, they all clumped off downstairs and loaded their equipment back into the van, ready to head for Dewberry School.

Mom and I drove together with the CBC truck following, filming my car as it wound through the river hills. I'd made the trip daily for nine years, but somehow, that day it seemed so different, so final. I knew that, as of this very morning, my days would take me on a new path. Mom and I were almost giddy; I was thinking that this could not all be true, and she was wondering how this could have ever happened to one of her kids. It was truly surreal. I had to give her a little coaching, because the night before, when asked by the media about this history-making daughter of hers, she would burst into fits of laughter. And when they asked about my growing-up years, searching for clues about any early political aspirations, she said, "Well, she was a feisty little kid, always wearing her holster and guns." Thanks, Mom. By the time we got to the school, after a crash course on media relations, she was responding right on cue!

I parked in my normal spot and met the camera crew at the east door of the school, where my classroom was. They hoisted their cameras and away we went. When I opened the door, the principal, Lyle Fettis, met us and congratulated me. I asked him, "Do you think I could take a long-term leave?" He laughed and said, "I think we could arrange that." What I saw next moved me to tears. The entire school was lining the hallways, clapping and cheering. From Grade 1 to Grade 12, the kids and teachers felt like this was their personal victory as well as mine. In a small community, you learn to share. And we did. One of my Grade 12 homeroom students yelled out, "Way to go, Miss Grey. You smoked 'em!" Everybody roared their approval and agreement. It was a magical moment for us all. But it was also bitter-sweet, because I knew that even though it was exciting, it meant goodbyes were inevitable, and that I would be leaving the day-to-day activities of Dewberry School, probably forever.

From there, we parted company with the camera crew and headed off to Edmonton on our own. Mom was catching an afternoon flight back to the Coast and I had media interviews to do and a celebration visit to make to our head office. That afternoon I went and bought a colour TV and a VCR because I did not have either, and thought the time had surely come when I needed to watch every blessed bit of news from then on. I only had the old black-and-white TV that I had bought at the Frog Lake Store pawnshop, and it lived in the closet of my bedroom. My friends and family all laughed at me, to think that was my first big purchase after my election.

The next morning I was up at a frightful hour to go on "Canada A.M." Pamela Wallin was the host and we had quite a go. The gist of her questions was, "So, what are you going to be hollering and screaming about from the West?" I replied, "Nothing." Perhaps that was the only time Pamela has been speechless. I was sure Central Canada had heard all about the Reformers and was expecting an all-out assault. I assured her that we had real concerns and that I would do my best to let Parliament know about these without going hysterical, but also without being ignored. After the interview and a few more obligations, I drove back out to the lake to get some rest, and ponder the fact that my very private life in the bush had now become a very public life and there would not and could not be any turning back.

The next few days were taken up with finding space for a constituency office, hiring staff and so on. I could hardly keep up with the requests for interviews from all across the country, as well as get ready for my first trip to Ottawa. Somehow, everything came together and I said my goodbyes to Sandra, Hilda, Fritz, Dora, Megers and HIS, as well as the Hancocks and so many others who were such a part of the fabric of my life for so many years. Even though I would be back and forth every weekend from Ottawa, I would no longer be a part of the day-to-day life of my friends and the community.

On my first trip to Ottawa, I went via Calgary for an enormous victory supper, hosted by the Calgary Reformers and chaired by Stan Waters. Preston and Ernest Manning were both there. This was a tremendous honour for me, as I had never met Preston's father before. Also, Mr. Doug Campbell was in attendance, one of the original Progressives and the former Liberal premier of Manitoba. I felt small and insignificant in the presence of two such great reformers. Mr. Manning and Mr. Campbell spanned a generation of leadership and reform—Mr. Manning had been Alberta's premier from 1943 to 1968, and Mr. Campbell had been elected to Parliament in 1922 as a Farmers' candidate, then went on eventually to be Manitoba's premier in 1948. They had gotten to know each other when travelling to Ottawa on the train to first ministers' conferences. They were now aged eighty-one and ninety-three, respectively.

I sat and drank in everything they said that night. Ernest Manning spoke of the early days in Alberta, and the development of the huge tar sands in Fort McMurray. Doug Campbell told me stories of Agnes

Macphail, another Progressive and the first-ever woman MP in the House of Commons, elected in 1922. He mentioned how ironic it was that Agnes and I did not represent the mainstream parties and that we were women, starting something new. I was excited, but felt somewhat unworthy to be walking in her footprints.

Doug Campbell spoke, and then passed the torch from the original populist movements to the new generation of Reform. Surely bridges had been built from the past to the present, and he was the living embodiment of it, right before my eyes. He quoted, from memory, a poem by (Miss) Will Allen Dromgoole, *The Bridge Builder*:

>An old man, going a lone highway,
>Came at the evening, cold and gray,
>To a chasm, vast and deep and wide,
>Through which was flowing a sullen tide.
>The old man crossed in the twilight dim—
>That sullen stream had no fears for him;
>But he turned, when he reached the other side,
>And built a bridge to span the tide.
>
>"Old man," said a fellow pilgrim near,
>"You are wasting strength in building here.
>Your journey will end with the ending day;
>You never again must pass this way.
>You have crossed the chasm, deep and wide,
>Why build you the bridge at the eventide?"
>
>The builder lifted his old gray head.
>"Good friend, in the path I have come," he said,
>"There followeth after me today
>A youth whose feet must pass this way.
>This chasm that has been naught to me
>To that fair-haired youth may a pitfall be.
>He, too, must cross in the twilight dim;
>Good friend, I am building the bridge for him."

When he finished, I hugged him and sat down, feeling like an exhilarated, but terrified, "fair-haired youth." Would I be able to live up to the mantle that had just been put on me?

Two other older people who had a tremendous influence on me were Francis and Harriet Winspear, a couple in their eighties when I met them. They were true "Reformers," providing initial funding for the party, as well as philanthropy to the University of Alberta and to the arts. They were very gracious to me as well. My victory was great cause for celebration for them. (Francis died in 1997 and Harriet turned 100 in August 2004.)

I had long been a white-knuckle flyer, terrified by every new sound of the engines. How in the world would I ever adjust to a regular commute across the country? I prayed long and hard on my maiden voyage of this new chapter of my life. If God had got me into this crazy thing, surely He would help with the travel it required!

Upon my (safe) arrival, a man walked up to me at the airport and said, "Are you Deborah Grey?" I replied, "Yes," assuming he was a reporter. He told me that he was a real estate agent and would be happy to not only deliver me to my hotel, but would be pleased to show me some condos I might want to purchase. He handed me a pile of listings and would have sold me a property on the spot, sight-unseen. My gut instinct is pretty good and it crossed my mind that he could be a complete phony. Nonetheless, I was in such a state of bewilderment, I accepted a ride with him. He asked if I would like to see Parliament Hill on the way to the hotel, and I responded, "Absolutely." It was late March, very cool, very snowy and very late, almost midnight. I stood alone by the flame, staring up at the Peace Tower, trying to come to grips with the fact that this was my new classroom.

The realtor seemed to understand the magnitude of this occasion and was quiet as he drove me to the Skyline Hotel. He wished me good luck and was gone into the night. I was grateful to have made it safely, needless to say. He called once or twice after that to see if I was interested in purchasing any real estate. I declined as I had no idea how long my tenure would be in Ottawa. I didn't hear from him again, but I have always been grateful that somebody met me that very first night of my arrival, somebody who was well-intentioned and well-behaved. Thank you, sir.

Preston realized how overwhelming this first trip to Ottawa would be, so he asked Diane Ablonczy, a member of our executive council, to accompany me. I had met her during the by-election when she had come up from Calgary to campaign with my team. I appreciated her company and was so glad to have a friendly face with me in a strange, new town. Diane was good moral support for me when I had a meeting with the speaker of the House, the Honourable John Fraser. He assured me that I would be treated fairly, despite the fact that I would be considered an "independent," as twelve members are required for official party status. I then met with the sergeant-at-arms, Gus Clouthier, who issued me my MP lapel pin, office keys, etc. I found my way to 709 Confederation Building, unlocked my door and stared in disbelief. It was full of discarded furniture, cast-offs from other MPs who had set up their offices and ditched the rest in the empty office that had been assigned to John Dahmer. What a mess! I had no idea who to call for help, so I simply left.

Unbeknownst to me, Preston had called Carmel, who had worked for Ernest Manning when he was a Senator. She knew, and recommended, Linda Robar, who had worked for Walter Baker (Nepean-Carleton) and Alvin Hamilton (Qu'appelle-Moose Mountain). Hamilton had not run in the 1988 election and Linda had not been re-hired by anyone so far.

What an interview! We dragged a couple of chairs over to a desk and sat down. I had no idea what an MP's job description was, let alone her staff's. I believe the only question I asked was, "So, what do you know about setting up an MP's office?" Fortunately, she knew everything about it and I kept my ears open to learn. Diane asked a few good questions also. Regarding logistics, Linda said, "I hope you don't mind that I am really, really organized." I responded, "That is great, because I am really, really creative. If we don't drive each other crazy, and if you promise to spell my name right, we should get along fine. You're hired."

I was immensely pleased with myself, thinking that my staffing needs were now solved. But then Linda asked who else I would be hiring for administration, as well as who was going to be my legislative assistant, to cover political work. Astonished, I asked her if she knew anyone else. She told me about Jenny Kensall, who had worked for the Honourable George Hees (Northumberland). Neither Jenny nor Linda was bilingual, and neither had found work since the election. I did a brief interview with Jenny, with Preston in attendance, as he was in Ottawa. I hired her immediately. Linda began on March 28, started setting up the office, got phones hooked up, etc., and Jenny started one week later. Some people were convinced that they were Tory plants infiltrating my office. I had no way of knowing, but would have to cross that bridge if and when I discovered any hint that that might be true. There was no need. Linda and Jenny were excellent workers, 100 per cent loyal to me, and they stayed with me until they both retired, Jenny in 1998 and Linda in 2001.

I talked with Preston at length about who would fit the role of legislative assistant and political advisor. As always, Preston was thinking far ahead of anyone else. Although he knew of my abilities and adventurous spirit, he was also aware of my complete lack of knowledge of parliamentary procedure and political experience. Preston had spoken with, and lobbied, our best political advisor in the party, someone who already had parliamentary experience as a former legislative assistant. He protested because he was working on his Master's degree in economics at the University of Calgary and did not want to break off his studies and go to Ottawa. Preston persisted and managed to persuade him to spend just one year with me to give me a solid footing. He agreed, and so it was that Stephen Harper came to be my first legislative assistant.

Preston also arranged a meeting for me with the staff of the Christian Embassy. They are a part of a group called Campus Crusade for Christ that works with MPs, Senators and the diplomatic corps. I had breakfast with Barry and Wendy Bowater and Charlotte Deda. The latter was from Alberta and took me under her wing. I loved her immediately. Her cheerful demeanour and infectious laugh helped ease me into the cold, often impersonal world of Ottawa. She and Diane took me hunting for an apartment, and I was glad to rent one just a short walk from the Hill. With that secured, my staff hired and my office being set up, I headed home to get my constituency office up and running and prepare for my next trip to Ottawa. I had been informed that my swearing-in was to take place on April 3, 1989, the first day of the new spring session of Parliament.

Erna Holliday became my constituency office manager and we rented an office on the main street in St. Paul. She scavenged around and rustled up a beautiful oak desk, filing cabinet and leather chair for a great price. Little by little, shelf by shelf, equipment was set up and we were in business. Irene Krochmal worked with her for a short while, but Erna was basically a one-woman show. She was very capable at case-work, communications and counselling, which seemed to be a big part of the job. Many times, people were frustrated with the system and simply did not know where to turn. Often, after a chat and a cup of coffee, the person got up and said, "Thank you for your help; I feel so much better," when actually, we had not done a thing, other than listen and care about their issue or concern.

Constituency office work is important but not everyone comes there to visit. I bought a brand-new, bright red Toyota Forerunner 4x4 to travel around my riding. It became a well-known trademark in Beaver River. People saw my truck, with my magnetic signs on the side, in their town and even if they didn't come to my meeting, they told me that it was good to just know that I had taken the time to come.

My second flight to Ottawa was for my swearing-in and I was glad to have the company of my mom, my dad and his wife, Eleanor, my sister Alison and my roommate, Sandra. We girls were all camped in my apartment the night before the big ceremony. At about 3:30 A.M. the fire alarm rang, scaring us all out of bed. We raced down twenty-four flights of stairs faster than I ever dreamed possible. As I stood on the street in my night-shirt, I chuckled at how important it is to keep your sense of humour.

We got back into my place just in time to start getting the crew ready for the big event. The swearing-in took place at 9:30 A.M. in the Commonwealth Room, 238S. I was so nervous I could hardly think straight. This was unlike regular sessions of a new Parliament, when many MPs get sworn in at the same time, "like cattle," as it were. I was in this beautiful room, surrounded only by my family, friends, Preston and staff. The Clerk of the House, Robert Marleau, presided and told me that there was nothing to be nervous about. I repeated the words after him, "I, Deborah Grey, do swear that I will be faithful and bear true Allegiance to Her Majesty Queen Elizabeth II." He smiled and congratulated me. I replied, "Is that it?" He laughed and told me that was all there was to it. I was astounded. "Nothing about Canada? Nothing about my constituents?" Nothing. The whole thing took approximately thirty seconds. I could hardly believe it. But there it was—I was now signed, sealed and delivered. The next step was my introduction to the actual House later that day.

I knew nothing about the tradition of "being dragged reluctantly" up the aisle to my seat and being formally introduced by your leader and congratulated by the whole House. I received a call from Doug Young (Liberal—Gloucester), who was to be my seatmate. He asked if I would like him to walk me up the aisle and introduce me to the House, as I was an independent member and had no fellow party members to fulfill that role. I thanked him and accepted, having no idea what this was all about! The next thing I knew, Ross Harvey (NDP—Edmonton East) called and offered to walk up with me also. He was the other Alberta anomaly, being a non-PC member of Parliament.

That afternoon, I thought I would be sick, I was so nervous. I stood in front of the doors to the Chambers, wondering what I had gotten myself into. Suddenly, the doors opened and I heard the clapping. I couldn't retreat now! In we walked, and I saw the entire House standing to greet me. What a moment! I felt very apprehensive and inadequate, but exhilarated and privileged. Somehow, I made it to the table with them and Doug Young addressed the House, "Mr. Speaker, I have the honour to present to you Deborah Grey, who has taken the oath, signed the Roll and now claims the right to take her seat." The Speaker replied, "Let the Member now take her seat." I went up, shook his hand and walked around the back aisle to my seat, where I would spend the next four and a half years, waiting for more Reformers to join me. That afternoon the next election seemed an eternity away.

I sat there thinking about how many people had gone before me in these Chambers. This was the very place that my forerunner and mentor Agnes Macphail sat in. I could only imagine how she felt in the House; the very first woman in Parliament! My favourite story about her was the time she was asked by a simpering male MP, "Well, Agnes, have you ever been mistaken for a man?" She replied, "No. Have you?" I loved that quick wit and comeback. I was thrilled to see a bust of her in the foyer at the entrance to the Opposition Members' lobby. The first time I saw her I felt a strong connection and gave her a pat on the head to say "Hello" and "Thank you for what you have done for Parliament, for women and for me." I have done that every time I entered the lobby for my entire parliamentary career.

I was also impressed by the "Famous Five," all Alberta women who pressed the establishment to legally recognize them as "persons" in 1929. They were Emily Murphy, Irene Parlby, Nellie McClung, Henrietta Muir Edwards and Louise McKinney. Nellie McClung especially impressed me by her grasp and use of language. I have a plaque on my desk with one of her best lines, and I live by it: "Never retreat, never explain, never apologize; get the thing done and let them howl." I admire that kind of spunk, especially from someone who lived so many years ago, before the days of "liberated women."

I was told when I arrived on the Hill that I would be discriminated against because I was a woman. I have often been asked over the years, "How is it being a woman parliamentarian?" I always answer, "I don't know, because I have never been anything else." I have always felt equal, but perhaps I have been fortunate because I am a substantial size and I have a deep voice; consequently I have never been mocked for being shrill. Unfortunately, "shrillness" somehow seems to decrease credibility. However, I have had the odd encounter that made me wonder about how far we have come in terms of true equality. After I had been on the Hill for a while, I was sitting in an airplane on the tarmac in Ottawa, ready to head home. The man beside me asked if I worked in Ottawa. I said that I did, part-time, but actually lived in Alberta. He inquired what I did. I responded, "I am a Member of Parliament." That information went in, swirled around, and I could see that there was nowhere to store this in his mind. He looked puzzled and confused, but tried again. "Did you say you work for a Member of Parliament?" I was a little surprised but simply smiled. I only speak one of Canada's official languages, but I do that fairly well. Surely he could have understood my simple statement? By now I was enjoying myself and replied, "No, sir. I said I *am* a Member of Parliament." The information went in and around and around again. After a long silence, it clicked! He looked embarrassed and said sheepishly, "Oh, I am so sorry. I heard the words 'Member of Parliament' and could quite clearly see that you were a woman. I assumed you were just a secretary." I smiled and let him squirm for what I am sure he thought was an eternity. I finally responded, "That's okay. Unfortunately, stereotyping happens. But I do have a secretary…and his name is Robert." I am sure that was the longest flight that poor sucker ever had. (Stephen's brother, Robert, worked for me after Stephen went back to university to finish his Master's degree).

I do not know if anything prepares you, male or female, for Question Period. I could hardly fathom the sight I saw on my first day. My family sat up in the gallery and was equally mystified. Wasn't this the same bunch that had just appeared so collegial and friendly when I waltzed down the aisle? Now it seemed that they might easily come to blows at any moment. As the days went on, I saw the famous Rat Pack (Sheila Copps, John Nunziata, Don Boudria and Brian Tobin) in action. Wow! They really went after the Mulroney government about everything under the sun, but mostly the ills of the Free Trade Agreement. One would have thought it was the worst thing that had happened since Confederation!

I did talk with some of my colleagues in the lobby out behind the Chambers. As the only Independent, I didn't have a specific seating area, so most of the time I was in "no man's land." Some of them were fairly friendly, but sadly, most of them did not want me sitting near them when they had their discussions. Mealtime was even worse. When trays of sandwiches were put out on the tables, I would go to get something to eat. The Liberals said to me, "These are our sandwiches. Go to the NDP." I would walk over to their area and they would say, "These are our sandwiches. Go get some from the Liberals." I was so shocked; I could hardly believe that these remarks were coming from professional people. I got so disgusted that I usually just went for a walk and bought my lunch someplace off the Hill.

It would be a while before I would ask my first question, but the day came quickly for me to give my maiden speech. On April 12, 1989, I got my chance to respond to the Speech from the Throne. I discussed several topics that were of concern during the by-election. I said,

> Rightly or wrongly, many of our people believe that the processes whereby the federal government makes policy and decisions are executive processes dominated by that arm of the government and beyond the reach of the common people.... For example, our people feel utterly powerless to influence the high interest policy of the Bank of Canada, or the imposition of a national sales tax, despite the fact that our businesses, homeowners, and taxpayers simply cannot afford to pay more interest and more taxes.... Our people are not unsympathetic to constitutional amendments to make Quebec more at home in Confederation, but they want concurrent constitutional amendments, namely, meaningful Senate reform to make the West feel more at home in Confederation.... They will welcome the Government's commitment to a strong economy and deficit reduction, but they will be looking for strong signs of real cost-cutting at the top, and the thick layer of middle management that characterizes so many Government programs, before they will be willing to make sacrifices at their level. They will frown as they read the words that the new federal sales tax is to be "fair and equitable," and they will not believe such words. Our people, you see, Mr. Speaker, were told that the National Energy Program, followed by two years of the Petroleum Gas Revenue Tax, were to be "fair and equitable," programs and taxes which crippled the economy of Beaver River.... They will ask and expect answers to simple, blunt, common-sense questions concerning each of the Government's legislative and budgetary proposals.... They will ask: Is it necessary? Is it fair? Who gets help and who gets hurt? Is it practical?

> What does it cost? Can we afford it? The people of Beaver River
> are uneasy patriots, and look forward to the day when they
> become truly fair and equitable partners in Confederation.

I took a deep breath and realized that I had made it through without fainting. Then the Speaker got up and called for questions and comments for ten minutes! Somehow I staggered through the questions that were hurled at me. I was surprised and flattered that John Turner stayed in the House for my entire speech (when almost everyone else had filed out after Question Period). He rose and said, "I want to congratulate the Member for Beaver River on her excellent debut in the House of Commons and excellent speech. We can all understand how she got elected. The Honourable Member made a very forthright presentation here." I knew that he didn't need to stay and listen to my speech, so I appreciated it.

And so I had begun my career in the House of Commons. It was daunting but challenging, terrifying but exhilarating, gripping but completely irrelevant to the lives of my constituents. I had to somehow balance the need to be in the House as well as the riding. Thus began my weekly commute to Ottawa, a tradition that I have kept up for my entire parliamentary career. I would often fly to Ottawa on Monday and back on Thursday, in order to spend Friday in the riding office dealing with constituent appointments.

The government announced it would deliver its first budget on Thursday, April 27, at 5:00 P.M., but there was a leak of the document the evening before. It turned out that Doug Small, bureau chief for Global TV, received an anonymous phone call and obtained a copy of the "Budget in Brief" late in the afternoon of April 26. He went on TV live with a copy of the budget figures the same day. Michael Wilson, Finance Minister, went on national TV at 10:00 P.M. that evening and delivered the budget at a hastily called news conference. It seemed bizarre. There were calls for his immediate resignation. He blamed a thief for stealing the document and took no responsibility himself. Traditionally, a finance minister would accept the unwritten rule of "ministerial responsibility" and resign at once, regardless of how the leak had occurred. There was not a hint of that happening as Wilson read out the budget. During the eruption that followed, it looked like the markets might go wild. Traditionally, budgets are delivered after the markets close for the day. The next morning, the dollar had dropped half a cent to 83.54 cents U.S. and there were predictions it would go lower.

Stephen Wateridge, manager of corporate foreign exchange for the Bank of Montreal, said, "The contents don't really matter. It's the leak to the press. What a mockery is going to be made of us on the world stage." Regarding the contents of the budget and investor confidence, he also made the statement that the budget's anticipated deficit of $30.5 billion "is far worse than what was expected" (*Toronto Star*, Thursday April 27, 1989). The day after the leak, Michael Wilson announced he was going to present the budget in the House of Commons anyway. The other opposition parties were screaming for Wilson's resignation all day and when the 5:00 P.M. delivery time approached, every one of them left the Chambers in protest. I thought that the prudent thing to do would be to listen to it, so there I sat, the only member on the opposition benches, facing the government while the speech was read. It was a strange feeling, but one that only accentuated the fact that I was there as a caucus of one. It turned out that the markets were not unduly affected and eventually, after lengthy proceedings, Doug Small was absolved of any criminal wrongdoing.

The spring session went until the end of June, and I was grateful to head home for the summer to spend time in the riding and at my lakeside home to get some rest. Before the House rose, however, on June 27, I asked my first oral question. It was about the Meech Lake Accord and Mulroney encouraged me strongly to preach about its merits while I was home for the summer recess. I will discuss the Accord more fully in the next chapter. My supplementary question was regarding Senate reform. Mulroney answered me by saying, "Senate reform can only be achieved if Quebec is brought back into the Constitution. It cannot be done without that." That was news to me.

In Alberta, Senate reform was a real and serious issue. Because the House of Commons operates on "representation by population," the Senate is meant to represent the regions and their concerns. Because of the numbers of Senators in each province, this was impossible. The designations were: Newfoundland—6; Prince Edward Island—4; New Brunswick—10; Nova Scotia—10; Quebec—24; Ontario—24; Manitoba—6; Saskatchewan—6; Alberta—6; British Columbia—6; Yukon—1; Northwest Territories—1. How could the West ever get true regional representation when Ontario and Quebec had fully half of the seats in the Senate?

An Alberta Committee for an Elected Senate was created in 1983 to discuss and publicize the idea. Bert Brown, a farmer from Kathryn, was its chairman, and became known as "the Father of Senate Reform." The phrase "Triple-E" (Elected, Equal and Effective), coined by Ted Byfield, (*Alberta Report* magazine), became the buzz-word for the proposal. When Don Getty replaced Peter Lougheed as premier of Alberta in 1985, he used Senate reform as his hallmark. He committed the party to it, especially the Triple-E model. Unfortunately, he did not hold firm on Senate reform when it came to Meech Lake. Many of us thought he should have used it as a condition for signing Meech. He did not.

While I was fighting the by-election in February 1989, the Alberta government's Speech from the Throne promised a *Senatorial Selection Act*. We were pleased to hear that and were hoping to have a Senate election at the same time as the provincial one. Getty called the election for March 20, the Legislature prorogued and a draft of the Senate Selection bill died on the order paper. We were not 100 per cent pleased with the draft bill, because it said that only registered provincial parties could run. This meant that we would have to register as a provincial party just to run a candidate. The bill was reintroduced, passed and the Senate election was scheduled for October 16, 1989, the same day as the municipal elections across Alberta.

Our party officials registered the Reform Party of Alberta in order to run a candidate in the upcoming, historic Senate election. Our party's nomination meeting was held in Red Deer on August 28, 1989. We had four well-known, well-respected Reformers in the running. At the end of the day, Stan Waters took 74 per cent of the vote on the first ballot. In his speech, he said, "If I could carve two words into the heart of every federal politician, they would be: 'Cut spending.' Somehow, the voice of one who had served as the Commander of the Canadian Army was authoritative enough to convince every person in the hall that he meant business.

Stan served in the military for thirty-four years, including time in the Canadian Parachute Corps, the Princess Patricia Canadian Light Infantry, UN Peacekeeping, and NATO. He had also seen duty in Ottawa (which he mockingly referred to as "Fort Fumble on the Rideau"), and thus had both national and international experience.

After his military career, he was involved in business in Calgary, including construction, oil and gas, engineering, manufacturing, farming, real estate, venture capital and investment operations. Talk about a well-rounded, knowledgeable candidate. We couldn't have asked for anyone better to represent our party.

There were six candidates in the running for the actual Senate election, one of whom was Bert Brown, under the Progressive Conservative banner. There were three things that did not help Bert's campaign—the Meech Lake Accord, the growing unpopularity of Don Getty's government and frustration with the Mulroney Conservatives, who were in the process of introducing the GST.

The campaign was province-wide, so the candidates attended meetings and barbeques right across Alberta. I attended several events with Stan, and we had a great time together. He was as energetic as I, and we fired up the crowds everywhere we went. I told the people how much I needed Stan in Ottawa, and how important it would be to have him rattle things up in the Senate at the same time as I was doing that in the House of Commons. There was an enormous and sincere appetite for Senate reform, and the excitement of the campaign grew. For the first time, Albertans thought that an elected Senator (if not the entire Senate) might become a reality. The late summer and fall provided terrific campaigning weather, and piggy-backing the Senate election onto all the municipal elections provided much-needed publicity. There was a genuine feeling that something truly historical was taking place.

On October 16, 1989, election day, we realized the importance of having an excellent voter turnout. If it was poor, Mulroney and the government could say that Albertans were not really interested in the idea of an elected Senate. We had our GOTV (Get Out the Vote) machinery in full swing to make sure voter turnout was as high as possible. At the end of the day, Stan Waters received 257,523 votes, the highest single number of votes for anyone in Canadian history in a single election. It was an electric night for Alberta, because the whole province had voted so resoundingly, not just for Stan Waters, but in favour of an elected Senate. It was also a wonderful night for Reform and for me, because it meant that if we could ever convince Mulroney to appoint Stan to the Senate, I would have company in Ottawa, a thought that I was thrilled about. Stan soon came to Ottawa to join me for a press conference. He was as confident and unafraid of the establishment in Ottawa as anyone could be. I loved his spirit and daredevil attitude. He was fearless and could not have been a better friend to me if I had hand-picked someone myself.

On October 27, we had our Reform Assembly in Edmonton. It was a great celebration of two victories, my election in Beaver River and Stan's election right across Alberta. Party members were euphoric and we knew that this was only the beginning of the Reform assault on Ottawa. Principles and policies are essential, but they must be translated into real votes and electability. Here Stan and I were, living proof that people could be elected under the Reform banner. It was an amazing realization and we were all ready for the next campaign, whatever and whenever it would be.

That fall, several momentous events occurred on an international scale that made our victory look somewhat insignificant. Democratic reforms were taking effect in Eastern Europe and the Cold War was formally declared to be over. East Germany opened its border with West Germany and the Berlin Wall was demolished. People took chunks of it for souvenirs. Many things had led up to this point, but it was stunning to see how quickly things actually came unravelled, and how dictatorial rule fell apart virtually overnight. It was an amazing thing to witness, even from our distant vantage point. Events happened so quickly that one might wonder how tenuous the grip of the dictators actually was. Night after night, the news reported another country reacting to its newfound freedom. It was a most remarkable experience to watch the crumbling of the Soviet states, as they were all I had ever known for my whole life.

No sooner had this happened, than another remarkable international event occurred: Nelson Mandela was released from prison in South Africa in February 1990. All of my high school days, I had read in my textbooks about him being imprisoned. Suddenly, the African continent was undergoing major upheavals as well as the continents of Europe and Asia. A highlight of my entire parliamentary career was to sit in my seat in the House of Commons and hear Nelson Mandela address the Canadian Parliament. It was truly remarkable to listen to him and notice the lack of bitterness in his voice, just months after his release.

Perhaps our own constitutional and internal wrangling in Canada seemed small compared to what was going on around the world. However, the concern over the Meech Lake Accord continued to affect Canadians from every region. If Quebec's demands were not met, would we face another round of threats to leave and undergo a full-blown referendum? I dreaded the thought....

CHAPTER 11

Meech Lake: The Beaver River
Is Not a Tributary

THE MEECH LAKE ACCORD WAS A SERIES of constitutional proposals put forward by Brian Mulroney and Quebec premier Robert Bourassa as an alternative to the *Constitution Act* of 1982. Quebec had fiercely opposed the signing of the Constitution, which was spearheaded by Pierre Trudeau. He had moved to make this amendment to the Constitution after the Quebec referendum of May 1980, when Quebecers voted against seeking sovereignty. Queen Elizabeth II proclaimed the Act on April 17, 1982. The Charter of Rights, which was part of the *Constitution Act*, contained a "notwithstanding clause," which any province could use to override certain rights. Quebec tried to use the clause, but the Supreme Court rejected its claims in December 1982.

Brian Mulroney and all the provincial premiers agreed to the accord that was drafted and discussed at Meech Lake. The premiers of Manitoba and Ontario voiced reservations. However, the political elite hailed the deal right across the country. Premiers were encouraged to head straight home and pass a Meech resolution through their legislatures as quickly as possible. This raised many eyebrows in the West. If the deal was that good, why the hurry? Shouldn't it be able to withstand the test of time and intense scrutiny?

Meech contained five main modifications to the Canadian Constitution:

1) Recognition of the province of Quebec as a
   "distinct society";
2) Commitment to Canada's official bilingualism;
3) Increased provincial powers regarding immigration;
4) Expansion of the provincial right to veto; and
5) Provincial input in appointing Supreme Court judges.

The Reform Party had conducted more meetings and discussions regarding constitutional reform than any other group. Our party had been born and incubated with ideas that would make Canada work better and constitutional reform was at the heart of many of our policies. We had the sense that Meech would not be popular and would not fly in the West. As we listened more, we heard Westerners express their frustrations. Firstly, they didn't like the top-down, elitist approach taken by the politicians. The process called into question those who signed it as well as what was in the deal. Secondly, Westerners did not like the amending formula. If every province could veto substantive amendments at will, we knew that we would likely never see real Senate reform. Thirdly, there was precious little commitment to actual Senate reform in the Accord. This would set back our cause by light-years.

Westerners were often blamed for being anti-Quebec because of our reservations about Meech Lake. But that simply was not true. We were extremely agreeable to the idea of recognizing the historical uniqueness and sociological distinctiveness of Quebec. Nobody would deny that. But if Meech Lake meant conferring upon Quebec constitutional rights and powers not enjoyed by other provinces or Canadians, then we could not agree to that. And therein lay the rub. A battle was brewing.

Consequently, as I gave my maiden speech in the House in April 1989, it was an emotionally charged moment when I said, "Mr. Speaker, the Beaver River is not a tributary of Meech Lake. Its waters come from different sources and flow in a different direction." You could have heard a pin drop in the House. I was the only MP out of 295 in Parliament to officially oppose the deal. It was tantamount to heresy even to question anything in the Accord. But it was my job as a parliamentarian to scrutinize legislation and I felt it was especially important with Meech. It seemed that Parliament had got swept up in the excitement and wanted to move it through without any scrutiny whatsoever. I was appalled at the vindictive nature of the other political parties in the House and their reaction to my stand. I believed it was principled and defensible and I vowed to maintain my position, no matter what.

On June 27, 1989, when I asked my first question in the House, the emotion in the air was palpable. I asked, "Since it is now clear that most Canadians outside Central Canada reject the Meech Lake Accord and that public opinion will make it politically impossible for certain provinces to accept the Accord, will the Prime Minister now urge negotiation of a new accord that will address the concerns of these provinces as well as the concerns of Quebec?" Mulroney's response was to deliver a brief lecture about how all the provinces accepted Meech as well as all the political parties in the House. He also said, "Alberta is now a first-class province under the Meech Lake Accord and it was not before." I was certainly surprised by that revelation and did not feel first-class, by any stretch. My supplementary question mentioned Senate reform but also dealt with Meech Lake. I said, "The Prime Minister will be aware that a recent poll in the *Montreal Gazette* shows that even in Quebec, only 44 per cent of the people actually support the Meech Lake Accord. Since these are hardly the kinds of numbers to provoke a national unity crisis, why does the Prime Minister not urge the Government of Quebec to also show some flexibility instead of just twisting the arms of the smaller and politically weaker provinces?"

Mulroney's answer rang in my ears for some time to come: "... we must find terms on which Quebec can honourably rejoin the Canadian constitutional family. We have found them in Meech Lake and I urge my honourable friend to strongly defend Meech Lake and endorse it across Western Canada."

Pressure was put not only on me, but also on MPs, legislatures and citizens over the next few months to promote the importance of ratifying Meech. Politicians fanned out across the country, trying to convince Canadians about the necessity of the Accord going through. Ad campaigns were undertaken and pressure tactics used to allay doubts about the deal.

The spring of 1990 was a hotbed of pressure for the ratification of Meech. John Turner had stepped down, and the Liberal leadership race was in full swing. Jean Chrétien was not a supporter of Meech, but did not speak out about it. Trudeau spoke out against it loudly. Paul Martin, the other main leadership contender, was in favour of Meech and tried to pin Chrétien in the corner. However, anyone who spoke strongly in favour of Meech was sure to lose votes in the West. It was a delicate balancing act for them both.

The more the country heard about the details of the Meech Lake Accord, the more they disliked it. Consequently, when Elijah Harper, a Native representative in the Manitoba Legislature, sat in his place, held up his eagle feather and simply said, "No," he was not only speaking for himself, but a majority of Canadians who had no voice to express their vote about the deal. With Harper's refusal to grant unanimous consent, Newfoundland's premier, Clyde Wells, spoke out against the deal. He also had much ground-level support.

With time quickly running out for the deadline of June 23, and the national media camped outside the Congress Centre in Ottawa, Elijah Harper continued to simply say, "No." Reporters beamed in via satellite from the Liberal leadership convention in Calgary and the pressure mounted for Chrétien and Martin to say something to try to sway the outcome. It seemed that the country would burst with the tension.

In the heat of the final days, the prime minister's office called Stan Waters to tell him that he was about to be put into the Senate. He was away and they tracked him down in Whitehorse. His appointment was made, not as a concession to Reform or any commitment to real Senate reform, but to keep Don Getty and Alberta onside. We grabbed the chance, anyway, lest it be snatched away in some other negotiations. On June 19, 1990, I stood with Preston Manning and Barbara Waters watching Canada's first-ever elected Senator get sworn in to "the other place," as the House of Commons insisted on it being called. What a great day, not just for democracy and Senate reform, but for me, too! I now had a pal in Ottawa.

Soon after Stan's swearing in, I headed home to the riding. The Meech Lake final countdown was on. That fateful day, I was at my place at the lake. I was outside and Juno came up from the water. She had something caught in her collar that looked like a twig. I whistled and she came over to me and sat down. It turned out that she had a long piece of masking tape looped around her collar and stuck to it. I pulled it off and opened it up. The printing said, "Hurray, Deb! Meech Lake is dead!!" I had no idea who wrote it and never did find out. Somebody down the lake obviously knew that Juno would come home and they wanted to let me know how they felt about it. That was how I found out of the fate of Meech Lake, and the message arrived faster than Canada Post could have delivered it to me!

CHAPTER 12

The Charlottetown Accord: kNOw more

R IGHT AFTER THE DEATH OF MEECH LAKE, Lucien Bouchard quit the PC party and formed the separatist party, the Bloc Québécois. Several other Tories and a Liberal joined him, for a total of nine members. Emotions were running high and the House was very volatile. The government whip seated them close to me and he took great delight in putting Lucien right beside me. When Bouchard took his seat, I told him I thought it was despicable that he was decrying federalism while collecting a federal paycheque. I thought he should not just come across the aisle, but keep walking right through the curtains and out the door. After I got that off my chest and realized that he was not going to take my advice, we settled into a courteous, professional relationship. I enjoyed watching the government whip as he witnessed us having good discussions and the odd laugh. He thought we would be at each other's throats.

I admired the fact that Lucien Bouchard stood up for his convictions. There were still several Mulroney Cabinet ministers who were separatists, but kept quiet about it so they could keep their position of power and perks. The BQ were, at least, up front about what they believed and were attempting to accomplish.

With tensions high in the House, I kept balanced by spending time with Stan Waters. He was a great companion and helped me put everything into perspective. He was an expert at real war, not just the political battles that went on in Ottawa. We often went out for supper together. I was amazed by the number of people who would walk up to him on the street, salute and say, "General Waters, sir. I served under you at such-and-such a place and time." They addressed him with so much respect. I was proud to have him as my friend and colleague. He knew that I was belittled and ridiculed by colleagues in the House. He used to say, "If they get to you, Deb, just call me. I'll look after you." He made me feel so safe.

During the famous late-night GST debates, I would get my work done, and then head over to the Senate Chamber. Stan sat on the last seat in the corner, by the railing. Members of the House of Commons are not allowed into the Upper Chamber; however, I could sneak sideways along the railing without crossing it, sit cross-legged on the floor beside him and visit. We had some wonderful times talking about how great it would be to completely shake the place up by democratizing it. We laughed a lot, something I had not yet been able to do in that town.

In June of 1991, Stan called me to tell me he had a terrible headache and asked if I could fill in for him at a speech in Cambridge, Ontario. I was happy to oblige; I changed my travel plans and covered the rally for him. He very much appreciated that and said, "Thanks, Deb. I owe you one." Little did we know he would never be able to repay the favour. Soon after that, he was diagnosed with a brain tumour and died in September, just three months later. At his funeral, I was so impressed by his whole family, who, when asked what Stan, Dad and Grandpa would tell them all to do in this painful time, replied in unison, "Keep on Marching." He had lived with this motto, and also instilled it in his entire family. I missed him dreadfully and still do. I now had to face the Ottawa world alone again.

After the death of Meech, the "Quebec agenda" dominated the national stage for the next two years. The Quebec government set up the Allaire Committee and the Belanger-Campeau Committee to discuss Quebec's future, whether they stayed in Canada or left. The federal government struck the Beaudoin-Edwards Committee and the Spicer Commission to find ways to solve English Canada's concerns. Joe Clark was named Minister of Constitutional Affairs, to try and pull all of this information together and make sense of it. Late in the summer of 1992, all of the provincial governments, as well as Native groups, came to an agreement that was named the Charlottetown Accord. The Reform Party had always advocated the use of referendums to decide on large constitutional issues. I had pressed for that in Ottawa over the years, and three provinces—B.C., Alberta and Quebec—had instituted referendum legislation. Mulroney announced that the Charlottetown Accord would be put to a national referendum on October 26, 1992.

Yes and No sides were struck for the campaign. The Yes side consisted of the PCs, Liberals and NDP, as well as the First Nations, women's groups and business leaders. The No side was comprised of the BQ and the Reform Party, as well as Pierre Trudeau. At the start of the campaign, support for Charlottetown was approximately 73 per cent. As the campaign progressed, support for the Accord dwindled. We Reformers felt it was important for people to know what was actually in the text and to judge it on that basis. Key points in the Accord were:

1. Exclusive provincial jurisdiction over forestry, mining and other natural resources, and cultural policy;
2. Federal spending to be subject to stricter controls.
3. Federal power of reservation (lieutenant governor could refer a bill to federal government for assent or refusal) to be abolished and federal power of disallowance (federal government could overrule a provincial law) to be severely limited;
4. Social charter to promote health, welfare, education, environmental protection and collective bargaining;
5. Elimination of interprovincial trade barriers;
6. The "Canada Clause" to codify the values of the Canadian character, including egalitarianism, diversity and the recognition of Quebec as a distinct society;
7. Aboriginal self-government;
8. Composition and appointment process for the Supreme Court to be constitutionally entrenched (three of the nine

justices to be from Quebec—up to now this had just been a tradition);

9. Senate reform: Senators to be elected in a general election or by the provincial legislatures. Senate powers would be reduced; matters of culture and language would need a double majority (of the Senate as a whole and of francophone Senators);

10. Seats in the House of Commons: after redistribution, a province could not have fewer seats than any other province with a smaller population; however, Quebec would never have less than one quarter of all the seats in the House of Commons.

We distributed hundreds of thousands of copies of the Accord, asking people to read it for themselves, as they would be voting on it. Our campaign slogan was "Charlottetown Accord—kNOw more." I sent a copy to every household in Beaver River and had town hall meetings to go over it. I was amazed at how seriously my constituents took this exercise. They were not just advising their Member of Parliament what to do with her one vote in the House of Commons on their behalf. Every voter had their say and everyone wanted to know what was in it.

I wrote about some of my reservations about the Accord in my monthly news column for the local papers. Regarding the framework of the "Consensus Report," as it was called, I said that it was not a true agreement, but only a framework for future negotiations. To adopt it would not bring constitutional peace but only more years of wrangling and negotiations. Of the sixty sections in the report, twenty-seven explicitly called for further negotiations, such as First Ministers' conferences, federal-provincial bilateral negotiations and consultations with Aboriginal leaders. Regarding the section on economic issues, I believed the Accord would weaken rather than strengthen the economy at a time when economic renewal should be the number-one priority of government. Property rights were deleted. There was nothing about balanced budgets, fiscal responsibility or tax limitation. There was no guarantee to reduce interprovincial trade barriers other than an empty "'political accord." Also, the Senate proposals were less than 2-E. On a vast majority of bills, defeat in the Senate would mean a second vote in a joint session of the House of Commons and the Senate. Senators would be overwhelmingly outnumbered; true regional representation would not occur. The amending formula would also prove to be extremely inflexible in the Accord. Further amending of the Constitution would be very difficult because of the unanimity rule. This rule for constitutional amendments (approval by Parliament and all provincial legislatures) had been extended to all national institutions. This, in effect, locked in the unsatisfactory Senate, plus Quebec's right to 25 per cent of the seats in the Commons and 33 per cent of the Supreme Court seats in perpetuity.

Many constituents called and discussed the contents of the Accord with me. It was a fascinating exercise in democracy, as people claimed ownership of the issue. They had a chance to have real input and their vote would really count. I will never forget the day that a trapper north of Lac La Biche asked to meet with me in my riding office to discuss the Accord. I am no legal expert and I didn't know all the ins and outs of it, but I had studied it and thought I could help him interpret it. He showed me the copy he had received in the mail from me. He had been in the bush studying it and knew its text from cover to cover. The margins were filled with his handwritten comments and suggestions. I was so impressed that here was a regular citizen who was becoming involved with the political process in his country. I was proud of him and the rest of my constituents who took the time to become knowledgeable and make their own decision.

Another memorable night in the Accord saga was a town hall meeting in Grand Centre that was sponsored by the Chamber of Commerce. Jack Shields, MP for Athabasca, and I were the guests to debate the Yes and No sides. The place was absolutely packed out on a warm fall evening. We were given five minutes each to state our case and then three minutes each for rebuttal. That went smoothly. Then came the open questions from the crowd. I was impressed by the sophisticated level of their response. It was obvious that these people had read the document ahead of time. They had questions and they wanted answers. They asked things like, "Why are there so many asterisks on this document, signifying that the details will be worked out later?" "Why is Quebec being given distinct society status enshrined in the Constitution?" and "Why is the Senate reform proposal only halfway to a Triple-E?" Jack Shields tried to defend the government's position on the Accord, but it became increasingly difficult as the evening wore on. People were getting frustrated because there were no satisfactory answers to their questions. They got louder and so did he. I continued to voice my concerns and ask the government representative for answers. After a time, Jack lost his temper and yelled to the crowd, "You people just don't understand!" At that instant, I knew I had won the debate. Here was another MP coming from Ottawa to explain the merits of the latest deal and showing contempt for the citizens by telling them they "didn't get it." Well, in fact, they got it pretty well. They were tired of being told what was good for them. Their gut instinct was telling them they didn't like the looks or the smell of this deal.

The tone of the debate across the country had also become nasty. The Yes side was more heavily promoted with federal government dollars and No proponents were often criticized. Joe Clark resorted to calling me, and others, "enemies of Canada." These kinds of accusations are never helpful in a real and serious debate. During one appearance, Mulroney ripped up the Accord and threw it across the stage. This was to show how Quebec would feel if the deal were not passed. Westerners felt just as strongly about it, too, and felt that they were being intimidated into supporting the Accord.

On referendum night, October 26, 1992, the results poured in from across the country:

Newfoundland	63.2% Y
Nova Scotia	51.2% N
P.E.I	73.9% Y
New Brunswick	61.8% Y
Quebec	56.7% N
Ontario	50.1% Y
Manitoba	61.6% N
Saskatchewan	55.3% N

Alberta	60.2% N
B.C.	68.3% N
N.W.T.	61.3% Y
Yukon	56.3% N

The federal total was 54.3 per cent No, and 45.7 per cent Yes. The provincial and territorial totals were 7 No, and 5 Yes. The Charlottetown Accord was dead.

CHAPTER 13

Miss Beaver River Becomes
Mrs. Lewis Larson

DURING MY FIRST TERM, I was overwhelmed by the steep learning curve I faced. I was travelling across the country every week, but I also had to learn about parliamentary procedure, party politics and constituency work. It was fascinating and I loved it, but it seemed that I could hardly keep up. My public, political life was on display for the entire country to watch. However, my private, personal life still carried on parallel to the public events I participated in.

After the death of Meech in 1990, my roommate Sandra called me in Ottawa to let me know she could not find our dog. Juno had become the Laurier Lake community dog and visited with everyone around the lake. It was October and there was a lull between the "summer resident" and the "ice fishermen" seasons. During this time, Juno usually stayed fairly close to home, so her absence seemed out of character. Sandra had walked around our place, called and looked everywhere, but there was no sign of her. I suggested that Sandra look over at the green trailer close by, as I remembered the people who owned it had been there the weekend before. She called later to tell me that she had gone there and found Juno locked inside, thrilled to see her and quite anxious to get out. I called all over the countryside to find someone who could let Sandra in. I found someone who had a key and they came to let her out. Juno was so happy to get out and get home. She had a long drink, then almost immediately started to get sick. She fell down the steps and became delirious. When Sandra called back to tell me this, I found the owners again in Calgary and asked if there was anything in their place that she could have got into. They told me that they had winterized the place and, in doing so, filled the toilet with antifreeze. Juno had been locked in their house for four days and had drunk the liquid, probably just before she was rescued. When she got home and drank a lot of water, it spread quickly throughout her body and into her brain. I called the vet and he said there was nothing he could do to save her. Sandra took her to Dewberry and he kept her alive until I got home from Ottawa the next evening. He put her to sleep the next day, and I dug a big hole and buried her on the crest of the hill overlooking the lake that she loved so much. I missed her dreadfully and found it so painful to break the news to all her fishermen friends as they came to the lake over the next few months. Everybody said that with Juno gone it was just not the same coming to the lake anymore.

The next spring I lost my dear Aunt Marely, who had suffered from cancer for a few years. She had been burned from radiation and her quality of life was completely ruined. She went from being robust and cheerful to skeletal and incoherent. I had such fond memories from my youth, but also from her visits with Harold to the lake over many years. Their visits often coincided with Art and Reta's and we all had a great time together. We laughed a lot and enjoyed many good times over coffee. She died in May, and I also grieved thinking about Reta, who, miraculously, was relatively well that spring, but I knew that it might not be long before I would have to say goodbye to her, too.

Soon after Marely's death, Sandra decided that she was ready to move on with her life. I had been basically gone now for over two years, Juno was dead and she felt it was time to make a change. She was accepted at Regent College at UBC, and moved there for the fall semester of 1991. I drove out with her and spent an enjoyable week before I headed home to prepare for the fall session of Parliament. My place at the lake seemed pretty quiet and lonely without Juno and Sandra. I reflected on the several losses I had endured over the last year and felt like an onion having layers peeled away. Somewhere underneath the layers of pain was a resolve to learn, grow and carry on, always trying to see the positive side of change and to find joy in the middle of difficult situations.

On October 19, 1991, a few weeks after Stan Water's death, I had a Saturday night free in Edmonton, since I was speaking at the west end of the riding, just outside the city, on Sunday morning. I talked to my good friend Donna Larson, who ran our Reform Party head office in Edmonton, and asked about getting together. She could hardly believe that I had a night free and said, "Wonderful. Let's have supper together. We'll make reservations. I am going to bring Keith's brother Lew along. He is living on his own and he could use a decent meal." I said that was fine with me but asked, "Is he boring?" She replied, "Oh, no. He's kind of crazy. You'll like him." We ate at the Sawmill and had a very pleasant evening together. We all went back to Donna and Keith's and chatted until late.

We had coffee again three weeks later when I was at the west end of the riding for a Remembrance Day service. I told them that Preston and I were speaking at a big rally at the Agricom in a couple of weeks and I was also speaking and singing with the HIS group at a Christmas banquet the same weekend. We made arrangements to see each other again and Lew said he'd accompany me to one or both of the events.

The Agricom event on Friday night, November 30, was attended by 4500 enthusiastic, cheering Reformers. Preston and I raised the roof and got the crowd fired up. Our thanks came in the form of thunderous applause, cheers and a standing ovation. When we were walking out through the crowd, I noticed Lew standing near an aisle, holding my coat. He was quietly watching the crowd's reaction to me and I was quietly watching his reaction to them. He seemed perfectly comfortable with himself and I liked that. Although there was a great fuss being made over me, I loved his quiet sense of confidence and serenity. He understood that my life was very public and full of accolades, but didn't see why that should possibly bother his male ego. I felt so comfortable with him because of that.

The Saturday night church function was much smaller, but it was just as important for Lew and me to see each other in this type of setting. We met the HIS group there. When the girls saw me, they hauled me off into the ladies' washroom. "Where did you find him?" they all asked together. "Why didn't you tell us about him?" I felt like a Grade 8 girl. "You guys! I just met him a few weeks ago. I hardly know him." "Well, we think he looks great. You should marry him." Thanks, guys.

Lew and I got to know each other over the next several months. Our "courtship" consisted of having coffee while I was passing through Edmonton, either to the riding or to the airport heading for Ottawa. As I was a very public person, we were careful about where we went and what we did together. We spent a lot of time going for drives in the countryside around Edmonton, talking and sharing stories about our lives. Also, we drank lots of late-night tea at the Convention Inn South, close to the hotel where I stayed when I was in the city. We enjoyed the simplicity of just being together, away from the crowds that I spent my busy life with.

The next spring, 1992, Lew made his first trip out to the lake where I had lived for so many years. I had seen him interact with my public, political world. Now I was anxious to watch him react to my private, personal world. I was thrilled as I observed him fit right into the tempo of the bush; taking a leisurely walk to the lake, sitting silently to watch a beaver, hauling firewood to the campfire. My neighbours and friends loved him instantly. His easy manner and ability to converse about many topics were welcomed immediately. He was completely comfortable talking to Fritz about his cattle or farm machinery. Spring seeding was underway and they talked about various crops and potential yields. At church he was interested to meet my long-time friends and community folk. He had already met the HIS group and they were all glad to see him again.

I had told my dear friend Maxine Hancock all about Lew, so she and her family felt they already knew him when we went to their home for dinner. Maxine's husband, Cam, and Lew hit it off and spent time out in the shop looking at machinery and discussing zero-till, a method of farming that Cam was involved in. The whole Hancock crew seemed quite pleased with Lew and endorsed our relationship. Although I was very confident about my decision-making capabilities, I was also anxious to get others' feedback from a more objective vantage point. When you are falling in love, it's easy to overlook some aspects that might be essential to the relationship. I was glad to have input from those people who loved me and knew me the best. I asked them to be honest in their evaluations and let me know if there were caution signs that I needed to pay attention to.

Harry and Hilda Thiessen also took Lew into their hearts. Although he had been married before, they were still willing to get to know him with an open mind. Their whole family liked Lew immediately and the grandkids enjoyed teasing him and making him feel right at home. He and Harry would sit in the rocking chairs and visit for hours while Hilda and I played Scrabble.

Dora was thrilled, too, that I had a special friend. She has a completely no-nonsense approach to life and said to Lew, "We love our Deb. And we hope you do, too. She is quite the girl, but we think you can handle her just fine." She gave us her full support the day she met him.

Wilf and Rose were also glad to meet this fellow I had told them all about. He spent the weekend up the hill at their place, as we did not want to stay alone together at my home. They tried to teach him some card games, but that is one thing he had not done much of as a kid. He caught on just fine, but we all played cards at breakneck speed and I think we made him dizzy. Some time later, while talking to neighbours, Rose said, "We sure like Debbie's boyfriend, but it's too bad he doesn't play cards much." You can't please everybody all the time, I guess.

The next time Lew came out to the lake was on July 1, a few weeks later. It was my fortieth birthday and my family came up from the Coast. They were excited to meet Lew, as I had told them all about him over the last few months, and how our friendship was progressing. It was a wonderful weekend, with Lew getting to know all the "Grey girls," surely a test of any man's fortitude. They loved his easy manner and quick wit. We all laughed a lot and spent an enjoyable weekend visiting, walking by the lake and sitting by the campfire.

Parliament was now recessed for the summer. We were in the middle of the Charlottetown Accord campaign and, although I did some travelling and speaking, Lew and I were able to spend quite a lot of time together. We had not had such a long block of time together since we had met. We enjoyed being together every chance we had. I made trips into the city as often as possible, staying overnight when I had a function in the west end of the riding.

Even though I wanted to be with him all the time, I did spend quite a bit of the summer out at the lake. It was glorious being outdoors and enjoying the calm—quite a change from Ottawa. Country living is wonderful, but not perfect. Early in the summer, I had been awakened at 2:25 A.M. by what I thought was a bird hitting the window screen. Then I heard a noise at the foot of my bed, which sounded like a mouse rustling in a plastic bag. I turned on the light, peeked over the edge of the bed and discovered a bat, dazed and sprawling around on a piece of plastic. I leapt up, ran and grabbed a broom, came back and thumped him. I was shocked by the night visitor and called Lew in Edmonton. "I'm so sorry to call you in the middle of the night, but I just had a bat in my bedroom and wanted to talk to you." By the end of the sentence I was practically shrieking. He replied, "I sure wish I were closer. I'd come right over." He immediately got ten bonus points for that; all I needed was for him was to make fun of me. I did get back to sleep again and tried to convince myself that the bat had just slipped in the door while it was open at some point.

While Art and Reta were up, we had another incident. A bat flew across the living room while I was watching a football game on TV. I grabbed a newspaper, rolled it up and got him, first try. That was great, but now I knew that I had a serious problem. That evening at dusk, approximately 11:00 P.M. in northern Alberta, we went outside and watched several little creatures fly out of my chimney for their nocturnal adventure. I groaned and wondered how we would ever solve this problem. We talked at length about it and devised a plan. I called the pest control man in Lloydminster and he said he would be up to my place by dusk. He did not arrive by then and we did not know if he was going to show at all. He would not be of any use if the bats had already flown away. I went up on the roof with my flashlight and a rope with a hammer tied on to the end of it. When I saw a bat, I lowered the rope, knocked the bat off the chimney wall, it fell right through to the basement and Art bopped it with a hammer. We caught several, but I couldn't keep up with them. Next, we both went up on the roof, armed and dangerous, waiting for the expert. We sat, ready for the bat exodus. We could hear them coming up the inside of the chimney wall making a *cheep, cheep, cheep* sound. When they reached the top, they would jump, spread their wings and take off. That night, unlike all the previous ones, they jumped into my big fishing net. I flipped it around so they could not get out and bashed them with the broom. I thought I had heard that bats were a protected species, but I considered what I was doing to be self-defence and nothing more. Reta was down on the deck, howling with laughter. There we were, silhouetted by a full moon, perched on the rooftop holding a broom and a fishnet. By the time "Batman" finally arrived, we had caught about forty ourselves. He asked whether we wanted the rest dead or if he should simply release them in an environmentally friendly way. I said if he could guarantee they would never come back, I didn't care if they were dead or alive.

He announced that he would lower a sulphur "stink bomb" down the chimney and that would drive them out immediately. I would need to camp in my tent trailer for a few days. I agreed and away went the stink bomb down the chimney. We sat up above for several minutes and then he put his ear to the chimney. "Looks like we've solved your bat problems, ma'am. There won't be any more now." I wasn't convinced, so I said, "Let's just wait a few more minutes." It wasn't one minute before I heard the *cheep, cheep*. He, completely astounded, grabbed my rope and said, "Gimme that environmentally friendly hammer," and lowered it, bopping the bat on the bean and watching it fall through to the basement. So much for "Batman." We killed a few more that night the same way, for a total of forty-seven. The sulphur bomb did not stink up the house. I slept in my own bed that night, but not well.

Lew was sorry that he was not able to be in on all the bat fun, but he did put some screen up when he came to the lake later in the summer. Lew is a carpenter and excellent handyman. He knew exactly what to do. I was sorry that I had not met him before I did my renovations. I could surely have used his expertise. He replaced my deck that summer—an enormous project. It was ten feet off the ground and served as my carport. It was about one thousand square feet, larger than the whole house. I helped when I could, although I was busy doing constituency events and some travelling and speaking. When I was around, we enjoyed swimming, kayaking and long walks along the beach.

Lew also had his first chance to drive my motorcycle that summer. I had asked him earlier if he had ever ridden bikes. He had spent a year in Japan with a missionary friend many years before and had ridden a small commuter bike there. He asked what I rode and was quite surprised to find out I had a Honda 900 CB Custom. "That is a big bike," he said, eyebrows raised. We went out on the paved highway and I sat in the ditch while he went for his maiden voyage, as it is much easier to ride solo. He gunned the throttle and away he went with the front wheel coming right off the ground. I was startled and remember thinking, "Oh, I hope he is okay." It was at that moment I knew that I was completely in love; otherwise I would have been more worried about my bike than about him!

In the fall of 1992, we hardly spent any time together because I was on the road constantly, speaking at Charlottetown events and Reform nomination meetings. However, we did get some down time at Christmas and went to Victoria to see my family. We loved it at the Coast and enjoyed being together several days running. It was over all too quickly, as I had to begin travelling again on the speaking circuit. The election was expected sometime that spring, but nobody knew when.

In February, Mulroney suddenly announced that he was retiring from politics. This threw the Conservatives into a leadership campaign that lasted throughout the spring. It became quite heated at times between the two frontrunners, Kim Campbell and Jean Charest. The race culminated in Ottawa on June 12 with Kim Campbell winning. The next few days were a media frenzy and the question kept getting asked, "Will she call the election right away?" I thought it would be a good idea for her to do that because their poll numbers were dropping, with no guarantee that they would rise again before the election call. Nonetheless, she booked several summer barbeques across the country and committed to going to the G7 Summit in Tokyo.

Lew and I were watching her every move keenly. When it looked like she might put the election off until the fall, Lew made his move. A few minutes after midnight on July 1, 1993, my forty-first birthday, he asked me, "Would you like to wake up in the morning on your birthday engaged to me?" I had dreamt about this day for decades, wondering if I would ever be proposed to. My answer was immediate and convincing. "Of course!" I burst out, and snuggled into his arms. The next morning, when my mom called to wish me a Happy Birthday, Lew got on the line and said, "Joyce, I would like to ask you if I can marry your daughter." "Of course, dear. We have been waiting for you for years and years and years." We all laughed and I knew that my life would be different—richer and fuller—from this day forward.

Because Kim appeared to be putting the election off until the fall, we decided to get married before then. We had no guarantee, but we felt we'd be more comfortable being married while on the campaign trail. That afternoon, while at a July 1 function in Cold Lake, we announced our engagement and wedding date of August 7, 1993, five weeks away. There was a great cheer from the crowd. Later that afternoon, we went to Elk Point to Margaret and Lawrence Modin's fiftieth wedding anniversary and announced our engagement there. Margaret was my campaign manager and many of my campaign team were also at that function. They said, "Well, finally. At least we can get this wedding out of the way and get on with the election campaign!"

Art and Reta were at the lake during this time and were almost the first to hear of our engagement. Reta's health had gone up and down over the years and she was not well that summer. When we told them our news, Reta cried and said, "I just hope the Lord lets me live long enough to see you married." We laughed and told her that she would not have to wait long; in fact, only five weeks. She was thrilled and began to count the days.

There were a thousand things to do to prepare for a wedding in thirty-seven days. We got everything organized fairly quickly—church and hall booked, florist arranged, invitations printed, supplies purchased. The HIS group was going to sing with me, so we needed to practice together. On Tuesday, July 13, I was down in Dewberry, rehearsing at Meredith and Lorraine's. The practice had gone well and we were in the kitchen having coffee when the phone rang. Lorraine answered and recognized Lew's voice. She had a little visit and said, "Here's your sweetheart." She passed the phone to me and as soon as I heard Lew's voice, I knew something was wrong. "Are you sitting down?" he asked. I said, "Yes, sweetheart. What's up?" His voice was quiet and shaken when he replied, "Keith has just been killed in a car accident." Keith was Lew's brother, and I felt sick to my stomach as I heard him telling me the details they knew so far: he had been alone in his Porsche travelling through the Roger's Pass, near Revelstoke. He had gone off the road close to the entrance of a snow shed, crashed into its wall and was killed instantly. The police had just left Donna's place and I told Lew I would head right up to the city. The next few days were unbelievably sad. Family arrived from out of town and we spent the rest of the week consoling each other and Keith's immediate family. The funeral was on Saturday, July 17. I sang the song, "The Lighthouse," a favourite of the Larson family and mine. It was very difficult, but God gave me strength for the moment.

This was my first opportunity to meet the entire Larson family. Lew's parents, Leroy and Elizabeth, were both of Norwegian heritage and had grown up in Alberta. Leroy was a pastor and he'd served in several places in northern Alberta as well as in Weldon, a small town in Saskatchewan, where Lew graduated from high school. Lew was the eldest of six children, followed by one sister Shirley, then four more boys, Keith, David, Dennis and, finally, Jerry (born when Lew was almost twenty-one and long after he had left home). At the time of Keith's death, Shirley was living in Fort McMurray, David in Florida, Dennis in Minnesota and Jerry in Edmonton. It was good to meet them and get to know them a little bit, even under such painful circumstances. I loved them all right away and looked forward to becoming part of the Larson clan. Lew had two children from a former marriage; a daughter, Kari, who was nineteen and a son, Laine, who was almost fourteen at the time of our wedding.

Because of Keith's death and funeral, Lew and I decided to postpone our wedding until after the election. I was amazed at Mom Larson when she said, "God gives us joy and sorrow back to back. Keith is gone but we can still celebrate your wedding. Let's go ahead with it." This to me was real, practical Christianity. My campaign team stepped into the gap and continued the wedding preparations, looked after invitations, compiled the RSVPs and made cakes and food for the reception.

August 7 dawned a beautiful summer day. Our ceremony was held at my home congregation, Dewberry Community Church, approximately two and a half hours northeast of Edmonton. There were about four hundred people present. The ceremony began with a moment of silence for Keith. It was very moving. My sister Alison and Sandra stood up with me and Lew had his carpentry pal, Don, and his cousin Wayne with him. Maxine and Cam's granddaughters, Kristen (five) and Marissa (three) were our flower girls. For weeks they had counted the sleeps down to the big day, but when it finally arrived, they both got stage fright! Once they got up to the front they were just fine. The HIS group and I sang "Just You and I," which, along with my solo, "You are the Wind Beneath My Wings," went off without a hitch (or a tear, thank goodness; if I had started to cry, I don't think I could have finished the song). Maxine gave a practical message and I appreciated her insight, as always. Once we were pronounced husband and wife, there was a great cheer from the crowd and a few notes from the organ sharing our moment of celebration and confirming that I was no longer an "unclaimed treasure," as so many had teasingly called me over the years. (Lew said that the moment we walked out of the church we were already an "old married couple.")

We took photos at the lake, then went to the Heinsburg Hall for a public reception, attended by about six hundred. What a wonderful afternoon we spent, visiting with so many people who came to wish us well. After that, we had about one hundred and fifty back at the lake for supper and an evening celebration. At approximately 10:00 P.M., an RCMP car pulled into our driveway with lights and sirens on. The wedding guests were startled and wondered what could be the matter. I greeted the officer and asked if there was a problem. He asked if I was the property owner and if so, could I show him proof? People in the crowd wanted to tell him that this was my wedding reception and he was being, at the very least, inappropriate. But everybody seemed too stunned to come forward. I told the police I would get the deed to my land and went into the house. I came back outside with our garment bags and hollered, "Fooled you!" as I threw my bouquet off the deck and walked down the steps. Little Kristen and Marissa had been frightened by the arrival of the police, so I took them both in my arms and whispered to them that I had this planned. Nobody else knew about it, so they were quite pleased now to be in on the secret. The police handcuffed Lew and me, put us in the back seat of the squad car, and we waved goodbye to the crowd as we drove away, siren wailing and lights flashing, daring anyone to give chase. I had played so many tricks on people for so many years that I assumed this would be payback time on me. I outfoxed them all and we got delivered safely to the Elk Point detachment to pick up our truck, which I had left there the night before. We drove to Lac La Biche where we spent our wedding night, not discovered by one single person.

The next night we drove back to the lake and hid our truck down in the trees. We were not discovered there, either. We tucked in for a couple of days and enjoyed being there alone. We then drove to the Coast for another reception with our extended families and friends. We camped along the way and were gone for a couple of weeks. We'd been home for exactly two weeks when Kim Campbell dropped the writ on September 8 for an election on October 25, 1993. Lew and I have not lived together full-time since that day.

CHAPTER 14

October 1993: From a Caucus of One to One of a Caucus

THE CAMPAIGN WAS A LOT OF FUN. Many of our candidates had already had the chance for a dry-run campaign with the Charlottetown Accord. They'd tested their polling organizations and get-out-the-vote machinery. During the writ period I travelled quite a bit to ridings where we thought there was a good chance of winning. Kim Campbell made a couple of strategic errors that helped our cause. Firstly, early in the campaign she said that an election is not the forum to discuss serious policy issues regarding social programs. This was fodder for the opposition. We all asked, "If not during a campaign, then when?" She could not dig herself out of that hole. Secondly, the PCs ran ads showing a less-than-flattering picture of Chrétien and made fun of him talking out of both sides of his mouth. There was an uproar across the country and the ads were pulled. However, the image remained. Kim was also tarnished with the memory of the GST and the constitutional wrangling under Mulroney's leadership. She tried to distance herself but the public had made up their minds. They were ready to take a chance on the Chrétien Liberals and the Reform Party.

In Beaver River, Dave Broda won the nomination for the PCs. I went to the nomination meeting, as I had in '89. Broda said that they were going to "kick Deborah Grey's butt and turn Beaver River back to Tory blue." The press came over to me and asked what I thought of his claim.

I told them that although he certainly had a big enough target in my butt, we would let the voters decide that! At the first all-candidates' forum, Dave said in his speech, "What we need is a government led by someone who is strong, sensitive, straightforward; a government led by Kim Campbell." During the campaign, the Tories' poll numbers started sinking like a rock into Meech Lake. By the fifth all-candidates' forum, Broda was still saying, "What we need is a government led by someone who is strong, sensitive, straightforward..." I wanted to grab his notes and rewrite them so he wasn't walking straight into the bear pit with every speech.

I had a great campaign team and we managed to sign up many volunteers. The weather was terrific for door-knocking and I had several small teams across the riding to help me. Lew participated in the campaign to a degree, but he still had his life and work and we were both comfortable with that. I spent some of the nights out at the lake and some in the city with him. Margaret Modin, my campaign manager, and our team were very good about arranging my schedule so Lew and I could have at least a little time together.

Our general campaign slogan was: "Let the People Speak." We held dozens of public rallies and listened to people who were fed up with Ottawa and their "solutions" to Canada's problems. We contrasted our policies with those of the other parties. The three main issues we dealt with were jobs, crime and political accountability. We brought forward our "Zero in Three" plan to balance the budget in three years and offer real tax relief to Canadians. The other parties criticized our plan and said it would be impossible to balance the budget that quickly. They accused us of slash-and-burn policies that would destroy social programs. We countered that the surest way to destroy social programs was to carry such a high deficit and debt and pay so much money out on interest. In fact, approximately forty cents out of every dollar was going to pay interest on the debt alone. How harmful was that to our social safety net?

We advocated safer streets, homes and community with our "Restoring the Balance" plan. Our criminal-justice reforms included changing the Young Offenders Act, applying truth in sentencing and giving more rights to the victims of crime than to the criminals.

Under our political accountability reforms, we always asked people, "So you don't trust politicians? Well, neither do we!" This always got the crowds fired up. Neither the Liberals nor the PCs had a sterling record when it came to honesty and integrity in many of their dealings.

All of these issues seemed to resonate well with the voters. We felt that our message was getting out there despite the lack of national media attention. The leaders' debate was held on Monday, October 4, almost one month into the forty-seven-day writ period. Preston held his own and made some good points regarding spending and the deficit, and challenged people to think seriously, when they were alone in the ballot booth, about what they really wanted for their country and their kids.

The national campaign travelled all over the country. Our strategists were Cliff Fryers and Rick Anderson, a young man who had previously been a Liberal but who came to Reform because of his frustration with Liberal ideology and the party's stand on the Charlottetown Accord. To ease the tension of the campaign, one of them bought a small football and they would play catch with Preston and his special assistant Ian Todd, to relax the whole team. The ball came to be a symbol of our "game plan." At many events, it was passed around and everybody touched it, signifying they were part of the team.

After the debates, Reform was gaining momentum, not just in the West but in Ontario as well. Polls were putting us at about 19 per cent nationally and about 20 per cent in Ontario. This was very encouraging because it meant that our support had almost doubled since the start of the campaign. However, the wind quickly went out of our sails because of a situation with one of our candidates in Ontario. John Beck ran for us in York Centre. He had not gone through the rigorous vetting process for candidates, and that became evident in light of some remarks he made publicly about immigration, same-sex couples, youth crime and the environment. They were completely unacceptable and did not reflect our party policy. If he had been allowed to continue as a candidate, it would have cemented every negative stereotype of Reform that we had been trying to counter for years. Our party withdrew his candidacy immediately, but his remarks still did damage and possibly cost us some Ontario seats. Worst of all, the incident slowed down the momentum we'd established. We were able to gain some of it back during the rest of the campaign, but it is always so much better if you don't have to face that sort of problem.

Nonetheless, October 25, 1993, was a remarkable day in Canadian history. After the polls closed in the East, we started getting results immediately, even though polling stations were still open in the West. The Liberals won many of the seats in Atlantic Canada, but the PCs got one seat in Saint John, New Brunswick, won by Elsie Wayne, their former mayor who was well known and popular. In Quebec, the BQ took 54 of the 75 seats. The NDP took 1 seat, the PCs' leadership candidate, Jean Charest, won his seat of Sherbrooke, and the Liberals took all the rest. In Ontario, we garnered just short of a million votes, came second in fifty-seven ridings but actually won only 1 seat, Simcoe Centre, with Ed Harper. The Liberals took all the rest of the 101 seats in that province.

As we moved into the Prairies, things looked more encouraging for Reform. We took 1 seat in Manitoba and 4 in Saskatchewan. But then the polls closed in Alberta and the real excitement began. Reform took 23 of the 26 seats in the province. Equally exciting were the results in British Columbia: 24 of the 32 seats there were won by Reform. Wow! What a night! By the time the votes were all counted, Reform had 52 seats and the BQ had 54. The commentators raved on about who would form the Official Opposition. Surely not a separatist party that had MPs in only one province and wanted that province to leave Canada? When all was said and done, the BQ formed Her Majesty's Loyal Opposition, which, I believe, was one of the most bizarre events in Canadian history. The Speaker chose to go by the number of seats on election day and granted the Bloc the title.

I had predicted during the campaign that Reform would take 52 seats. This was not based on anything scientific; I just wanted to get more than 12, in order to reach official party status. The Charlottetown Accord campaign had given us extra momentum and our candidates had generally done well during the writ period. As an eternal optimist, I upped my prediction to 30 or 40 in my mind then, just for good measure added a few more, for a total of 52 (that was also the year I was born, so I was partial to that number!). Once the word got around my caucus that I had made my prediction of 52 and the Bloc got 54 seats, my colleagues said, "Deb, you meathead. Why didn't you say 55?" None of us could understand why the Speaker went with the number of seats on election day. Tradition has always been that the Official Opposition occupies the role of the party that is ready, willing and able to form the government, should the government fall. We protested loudly, but the decision remained the same. Even more frustrating was the fact that we had come so close in some seats. In Edmonton, we lost 3 seats by a combined total of only 329 votes. Anne McLellan won her Edmonton West seat by a mere 12 votes. This not only made a huge difference in terms of those actual seats, but it allowed a separatist party to form the Official Opposition. Never have I let anyone off the hook who says, "Well, my vote doesn't matter. It won't make any difference." Oh, yeah?

Nonetheless, Reform had won 52 seats in Parliament! It was very exciting for me, knowing that I would finally have company in the House. The makeup of Parliament would surely look different this time around. At dissolution, the PCs had 152, Liberals 79, NDP 43, Bloc 8, Reform 1 and Independents 2. After the dust settled over the three close Edmonton ridings, the standings were: Liberals 177, BQ 54, Reform 52, NDP 9, PC 2 and Independent 1. Parliament had literally been turned upside down overnight. In Beaver River, I had been re-elected with a larger majority than in 1989. I received 58 per cent of the vote. The results were:

Deborah Grey, Reform	17,725
Michael Zaharko, Liberal	7,542
Dave Broda, PC	3,824
Eugene Hole, NDP	1,050

Our first caucus meeting in Calgary was a time of introductions. Most of us had never met one another before and were not familiar with who had strengths or interests in any particular critic area. I was the only one who had any parliamentary experience, but another new member, Ray Speaker, had provincial legislature experience. Talk about greenhorns! We all went to Ottawa to get sworn in and attend the House orientation sessions. There was so much basic stuff that they didn't cover, so I did sessions on everything else I could think of. Preston named Elwin Hermanson as our House Leader and Diane Ablonczy as our whip (we called her our "caucus coordinator"). We all got together and worked late into the night to designate critic roles to our caucus. We tried to do things differently from the way it was usually done in Ottawa, putting our critics into "cluster groups." This was a good idea in theory, but it did not work well in practice. The media always want a "go-to" person for an interview and this seemed to confuse them, as well as us. After a time, we went to the regular system of senior and deputy critics.

Also, Preston wanted to change the layout in the House that traditionally had senior people occupying the front benches and put backbenchers in the rear. His attempt to do this by sitting in the middle himself, rather than on the front bench, met with ridicule from the other parties and the media. That idea was also good in theory, but unworkable in practice.

Before the 35th Parliament began on January 17, 1994, Lew and I got away on a honeymoon trip. Our friends Lloyd and Eowana Needham had given us a wedding gift of the use of their condo in West Palm Beach, Florida. We left on New Year's Eve and spent two weeks there before returning to Ottawa for the new session. It was wonderful. We spent time sleeping, swimming, walking by the water and sightseeing. It was so good to be together after the campaign and before the busy upcoming session.

What a contrast to go from Florida to Ottawa in January! This was Lew's first trip to Parliament and, although impressed by the buildings, he was certainly not enamored with the weather. The damp climate was biting and the temperature was −38 degrees Fahrenheit with a wind chill of −54! Lew said, "It doesn't matter which direction I walk, the wind is always blowing in my face!" Ottawa in winter made Alberta seem perfectly balmy.

I served as the deputy leader and was also elected the caucus chairman. It fell to me to find and organize our caucus room. We were assigned a room in the West Block, which also served as a committee room. I tried to get the House staff to arrange the tables in a large square so we could all see each other. I was told that this was impossible, because "it just isn't done this way." After much discussion and cajoling, the tables were arranged the way we wanted them.

We went through the same fracas over several photos that were in the room. I asked to have the pictures changed. This was "just not done" either, so away we went again. Most of the pictures were of Liberals and most of them were dead. We were not keen to have them staring down at us, dead or alive. Because this was now our caucus room, we wanted pictures of reformers, after our tradition. You would think I had asked for the moon. My assistant, Betty MacDonald, made this one of her top priorities and I am sure it took a year for her to get the photos up of several of our political mentors.

In the House, our caucus performed consistently better as the first session wore on. My legislative assistant, Mitch Gray, went to work in the leader's office and was a great help to Preston. The learning curve was steep as my colleagues got used to parliamentary procedure; bills, motions, petitions, committee work, debate and Question Period. I was proud of them all and enjoyed observing them become accustomed to their new role as Members of Parliament. They called me their "den mother" and I did my best to teach them the ropes and then watch them mature.

Very early in the mandate, the government delivered its first budget in February 1994. The Liberals' campaign promises in the Red Book offered something to everyone. Unfortunately, they neglected to tell Canadians how to pay for them all. When the Liberals took over, the annual deficit stood at $42 billion. They proposed to cut the deficit by $6 billion, a drop in the bucket compared to what was needed to stimulate the economy and create jobs. Our caucus did a terrific job of critiquing the budget from various viewpoints, ranging from Ray Speaker addressing how it would affect the provinces to Jim Silye saying how it would affect the business community, to several of our guys who were farmers speaking about how the agricultural sector would be affected. Our whole caucus worked with a focus that was unified and energetic. I enjoyed having a team with me in Ottawa. This was far better than being here alone. Not only was the workload shared, but also I really enjoyed many of my colleagues and was able to visit with them over supper. No longer did I have to eat alone in Ottawa, a city that can be unspeakably lonely. I had become tired of sitting by myself and having MPs from other parties come in and whisper to each other, "Look, there she is. There's Deborah Grey the Reformer." At times I wanted to jump up, poke them on the arm and say, "There, now *you've* got it," as though I were spreading some dreaded, infectious disease.

At the beginning of the term, our optimistic yet naïve caucus got involved in the "pay, perks and pension" fiasco. We had consistently called for the elimination of wasteful government spending. I had given 10 per cent of my salary to charity since 1990, attempting to lead by example. In a great flourish and with much media on hand, Preston gave up the chauffeur-driven car to which he was entitled as leader of the third party. Early in the parliamentary session, two of our MPs asked in the House if the Prime Minister would allow us to opt out of the generous MP pension plan. He smiled and said, "I think we can work that out." I knew we were in trouble right then. Our policy was to have a pension plan that started at regular retirement age and was more in line with the private sector. We also advocated no extra money for Cabinet ministers and committee chairmen. Also, we thought that donations to political parties should not be given special credits under the *Income Tax Act*. Until we had the power to make it consistent for all parties, we could not put ourselves at a disadvantage. We said that we would bring in these reforms upon forming a government.

The trouble we got into was being inconsistent with that message about the pension. Some thought that we should opt out of the pension plan before forming a government. This clearly went against our party policy and philosophy about the other reforms we wanted to institute. Many caucus meetings were devoted to whether to opt out or just try to make changes to the plan, and then implement more substantive changes after becoming government. I argued that if we opted out it was inconsistent with our policy. Debate got heated and personal. The worst part of it all was that virtually none of our caucus discussed this fully with our spouses and families. Preston really thought that we would form the next government and be able to make the plan fairer and more palatable to the public.

We were able to make substantial changes to the pension plan over the next year. When the Class of '93 arrived, the government was paying $6.00 for every $1.00 that we put in. Also, an MP could start collecting immediately after six years of service, regardless of age. That meant that I could have started collecting my pension at age forty-two. We instituted changes that saw the government contributing $3.61 for every $1.00 we put in. Also, you could not collect until age fifty-five and there could be no double-dipping (meaning you could not collect the MP pension if you were collecting a federal cheque from any other department). These were hard-fought changes and we should have declared victory and let it go, saying we would make more changes when we formed the government. Unfortunately, we continued to argue amongst ourselves and often the debate turned bitter and accusatory. I am very sorry I did not step in as the chairman and say that we would not entertain any more discussion on it. Instead, I went along with the mood of the majority and became the poster girl for opting out, because I was the only one that was already fully vested, with my six years' service completed, when it came time to opt out in September 1995. We made a big show of opting out, letting balloons go on Parliament Hill. One of the serious problems that we did not address was the fact that our opting-out clause was only operative during a window of sixty days. That meant that whoever followed us into Parliament would automatically be part of the MP pension plan. This put our group at a huge disadvantage as well. But, sadly, we did not think ahead; we were more concerned about the political gains we thought we would make.

Although very busy in Ottawa, I kept travelling back and forth to the riding on a weekly basis. It was important to me to spend time in the constituency at public events getting to meet people and hear their views. I also continued to have regular office appointment days. It was interesting to see the number of people who had virtually given up on receiving help from government departments or politicians. Sometimes people would come and tell me their story (or at least their side of the story). It sounded like they had been harassed beyond measure. Then I would call the corresponding department and find out that they had not paid income tax for several years, or been in default of UI regulations, or were trying to get someone into the country who had a criminal record. Many times, how-

ever, we were able to cut through the red tape of bureaucracy and facili-
tated a helpful and practical resolution. My staff were great at tracking
down information; Judi Babcock, Sue Malcolmson and Linda Hansen
worked well with bureaucrats and constituents. Sometimes there were
oversights or withholding of information that we were able to obtain for
my constituents. And then there were people who came in with problems
in some aspect of their life that had absolutely nothing to do with government, but thought I could help anyway. The wildest case my office
worked on was for a woman who came in saying she had difficulty with
a prosthetic leg she had received. She could not walk straight and wanted
me to help her. I responded that the initials after my name were MP, not
MD. She was not deterred and begged for us to help her. I asked to see her
leg and she lifted up her pant legs. I could hardly believe my eyes. I could
tell by the way her calves did not meet properly that something was not
right. I looked at her legs for a few moments then blurted out, "You have
two left legs!" She looked down, studied them and said, "That's the problem! I knew something was wrong, but I didn't know what." We all
howled with laughter, not knowing what else to do. She asked me to
please phone her doctor. I didn't think he would be pleased to hear from
a politician, and he wasn't. He would not believe me when I explained my
"diagnosis" of her problem. Nonetheless he agreed to see her, probably
just to get me off his back. In time she was back in my office, delirious
with joy. In fact, she had somehow received a left leg prosthesis instead of
a right. Bizarre? Absolutely! But did she care? Not after the problem was
rectified. Her response? "I can dance again!"

In the House, the Bloc was agitating more loudly about a referendum on separation. Lucien Bouchard, their leader, was very eloquent
and passionate. With the Bloc Québécois and the provincial Parti
Québécois (elected in September 1994 under Jacques Parizeau) both
stirring things up, it looked as though another referendum would be
inevitable. It seemed to me that our federal Parliament was being
hijacked and was not able to carry on the nation's business. It did not
matter what the issue was, the separatists turned it back on how they
were not being treated fairly in Confederation. I got sick and tired of listening to it and wanted to do something to celebrate Canada. I initiated

a motion that would see the Parliament of Canada "sing or cause to be sung" our national anthem, "Oh Canada," every Wednesday in the House, just before Question Period. The Bloc went wild! They refused to grant unanimous consent and it had to be referred to the Procedure and House Affairs Committee. It languished there for a year and finally, in April 1995, we sang our national anthem in the House, officially, for the first time. The Bloc refused to enter the Chambers while we sang that day and has steadfastly refused every single Wednesday since.

Lew and I spent quite a bit of time at the lake that summer in order to have some private time by ourselves, but also to get some chores done at our place. Our home needed a new roof and this was the time to get at it. We spent weeks tearing off the old roof, levelling it (as it was old and had sagged) and put on a bright red metal roof. I loved it! It became the landmark for miles around. We had a few bat problems as well, but nothing like before. Lew discovered another tiny hole they used for an exit. He put a screen by the hole that they could squeeze out but not climb under to get back in. That was the end of the bat visits forever! We got some time to relax and enjoy the lake before I headed back to Ottawa for what turned out to be a very difficult fall.

Most of the focus of the 35th Parliament was the Quebec referendum that was held on October 30, 1995. Reformers constantly asked the Liberals what strategy they had to renew federalism that might ward off the separatist threat. Their cupboard was bare. Chrétien seemed to think that if we kept talking positively, everything would turn out fine. Exchanges in the House between the Liberals and the Bloc were vitriolic. It was horrible to have to sit and listen to them go after each other. The government had nothing to push back against the separatists with. We had suggested several "changes to federalism" such as provincial jurisdictional powers, spending powers and constitutional referendums. This would, hopefully, deal with some of the root causes of the separatist sentiments. The second part of our response was "consequences of secession," or the tough-love realities that needed to be addressed in the light of a separatist threat. These consequences included negotiating principles, dividing the debt, defence and the Canadian dollar. We were accused of trying to break up the country but, in fact, we were putting into action our love and concern about Quebec possibly leaving Confederation.

One of Parizeau's first items of business as Quebec's premier was to introduce a *Bill Respecting the Sovereignty of Quebec*, declaring Quebec to be sovereign. The separatist movement was gaining ground. Ottawa's way of dealing with the looming crisis was to modify the government's 1995 budget by ensuring that there would be no significant drop in transfers to Quebec. This was hardly visionary.

A remarkable event occurred in November 1994 that nobody could have predicted. Lucien Bouchard was stricken with flesh-eating disease in his leg. I first heard about it when I got off the plane in Edmonton. As I got in the truck, Lew told me about it and said it was doubtful whether Lucien would last the night. His leg was amputated and he did recover, but the experience seemed to give him mythical status. He became the impassioned voice of the separatist cause. He outlined his vision at the BQ convention in the spring of 1995. He proposed to combine a vote for sovereignty with a proposal for a new "economic and political partnership" with Canada that would be negotiated nation-to-nation. Parizeau and Mario Dumont, the leader of the Action démocratique du Québec (ADQ), agreed to his initiative in June 1995.

When the National Assembly reconvened in September, Parizeau introduced Bill 1, an *Act Respecting the Future of Quebec*, which offered something to every segment of Quebec society, eliciting a Yes vote. Parizeau also announced that Quebec would be holding a referendum on October 30, 1995. The actual question was, "Do you agree that Quebec should become sovereign, after having made a formal offer to Canada for a new Economic and Political partnership, within the scope of the bill respecting the future of Quebec and of the agreement signed on June 12, 1995? Yes or No?" The polls were tied at 45 per cent for both the Yes and No sides. Chrétien was still trying to convince Canadians, and himself, that this was simply hypothetical. He was dead wrong. The race was on.

We argued that 50 per cent plus one had to be the determining threshold in the referendum. It had been in the last referendum in 1980 and it seemed strange to change it now. The government railed against us, saying that we would give the country away "by one vote to destroy

Canada." That was nonsense, but Chrétien didn't actually attempt to do anything about it by trying to raise the threshold. He simply raised the rhetoric and you would have thought he was fighting Reformers instead of separatists. Shame.

During the fall, polls showed that many Quebecers thought that they could vote Yes to separation yet still retain the Canadian dollar, the Canadian passport and economic union. Chrétien still believed that everything would work out just the way he wanted it to. However, on October 20, polls showed the Yes side to be ahead. This spurred many in the "rest of Canada" into action. Unity rallies sprang up across the country. Just before Referendum Day a huge unity rally was held in Montreal, attended by 100,000 people. Sheila Copps, the Heritage Minister, told us that we would not be welcome at the rally and that, if any of us did go, we would certainly not be allowed to speak. The government was more hostile to us Reformers than it was to the Bloc. Shame.

On October 30, I booked a room with big-screen TVs so our caucus could be together to watch the results. As the results came in, we all held our breath. The numbers were too close to call. I remember the tension on Peter Mansbridge's face, announcing a No vote. I thought it interesting that it really was a No vote—no resolutions, no solutions, no final result that would put this issue to bed, once and for all. The final tally was: No—2,362,648 (50.6 per cent); Yes—2,308,360 (49.4 per cent); with a margin of only 54,288 (1.2 per cent). Chrétien came on TV looking truly shaken. He vowed to respond to Quebec's call for change. Why hadn't he responded sooner? Would he even respond now? Nobody knew…probably not even he himself.

In January 1996, our party came up with some practical proposals and solutions for the separatist threat. They included realigning government powers, reforming our institutions and pointing out the realities of secession. We entitled the document *20/20: A Vision for the Future of Canada.* Under "realignment of powers," we advocated eliminating federal interference in the following areas: natural resources, manpower training, social services, language, culture, municipal affairs, housing, tourism, sports and recreation, spending power, cash transfers to provinces and charter challenges (none of these would require any constitutional change). Under "reforming of our institutions," we advocated measures in the House of Commons to allow freer votes, MP recall, and referendums; under "the Senate of Canada," we recommended making appointments to the Senate through an election process (we also wanted other reforms, but they would have required constitutional amendments); under "'the Supreme Court and Judiciary," we proposed that positions be appointed by provincial legislatures rather than the federal government. We also proposed that appointments to the Bank of Canada's board be made by provincial legislatures rather than the federal government; that lieutenant governors be appointed by provincial legislatures rather than by the prime minister; and that "constitutional referendums" be held to obtain the approval of a majority of Canadians.

On the other side of the coin, we recommended a reasonable Canadian negotiating position on terms and conditions if and when a majority of Quebecers voted for secession. Regarding the "realities of secession," we discussed "negotiating principles" (democratic legitimacy, the rule of law and the interests of Canada); "involving the provinces" (their interests must be taken into account); "boundaries" (Canada would support the rights of people who choose to remain part of Canada, which would likely mean changes to the boundaries of Canada and Quebec); "Aboriginal peoples" (same applies to boundaries, particularly to Aboriginals); "maritime boundaries"(all current marine resources would remain Canadian); "citizenship" (no Canadian citizenship for those choosing to remain citizens of Quebec); "passports" (same); "pensions" (if no agreement could be reached, all payments would cease); "dividing the debt" (Quebec would pay 25 per cent, proportionate to its share of the population); "ensuring creditor confidence" (Canada would call for a joint declaration to honour all debt obligations); "dividing federal assets" (all moveable assets would remain Canadian and the Canadian government would seek maximum returns from any disposal of fixed or moveable assets); "Canadian dollar" (Quebec could use the Canadian dollar but have no say in monetary policy); "international recognition" (Canada would sever diplomatic relations with countries that recognize Quebec before negotiations were ratified with Canadians); "international trade agreements"(Canada would retain its veto over Quebec); "special economic status"(trade deals would be negotiated in Canada's interest); "Atlantic corridor" (Canada would insist on unhindered rights of transportation through Quebec); "defence" (Quebec would not enter into any international agreements that compromise Canadian security); "dividing military assets" (all fixed military assets would be disposed of by Canada and moveable assets would be removed from Quebec); "ratifying the agreement"(the final agreement would require the approval of Canadians through a national referendum); and "rejoining Canada" (Quebec could not rejoin Canada except on terms and conditions wholly satisfactory to Canada) (Reform document, *20/20: A Vision for the Future of Canada,* January 1996). This was an enormous undertaking, but we felt it was essential. At least it showed that someone on the national stage was preparing to answer the question, "What if...?"

Besides putting a great deal of effort into the constitutional agenda, we were putting a lot of pressure on the Liberals for not keeping their campaign promise to "scrap, kill, abolish" the GST. They tried to defend the tax and backtracked on comments they made during the campaign. We had Sheila Copps on the ropes, as she had said she would quit if they didn't kill it. But on the very day that she was set to resign her seat, our party got caught in a huge firestorm, which took the entire focus off Sheila.

Bob Ringma, one of my colleagues from British Columbia, had done an interview some time before with a Vancouver Island newspaper reporter. In 1994, he had made comments about homosexuals in the workplace and apparently defended the right of the employer to move a homosexual worker "to the back of the shop." Peter O'Neil of the *Vancouver Sun* wrote a feature containing those comments when Bill C-33, dealing with equality issues, was brought forward in the House. The story broke while Preston was out of town and I, as deputy leader, was in charge. I had not seen the article or talked to Bob, so I told the press, "I am going to read the article and speak to Bob directly before I comment." I was slagged by the national media for this. The story dragged on because Preston and our caucus leadership waffled about whether Bob would be issuing an apology or be suspended from the caucus. Dave Chatters defended Bob's comments and then Jan Brown also got in on the act, denouncing "rednecks." Her remarks were hardly helpful. Unfortunately, this incident served to remind us that we needed a better rapid-response system in place when a crisis broke. The story should have only lasted two or three days, but spiralled out of control for weeks. (Incidentally, Sheila Copps won her seat in the by-election and carried on as if nothing had happened.)

The Liberals had been very critical of the Mulroney Tories and their ethics. They promised in their Red Book to clean things up and restore honesty and integrity to government. We questioned the Liberals on their ethics a lot during the 1993–97 Parliament. It seemed that they might not be any more open and honest when problems surfaced. For instance, two major public inquiries were commissioned to "get at the truth" of two tragic events. The first, chaired by Justice Horace Krever, was to get to the bottom of how the Canadian blood supply had become tainted with infections (specifically HIV/AIDS and Hepatitis C). Thousands of Canadians had become ill or died as a result. The second one was to look into the facts surrounding the March 1993 deaths of three unarmed Somalis (one of whom was allegedly tortured) at the hands of the members of the Canadian Airborne Regiment.

We watched with great interest to see if the Chrétien government really wanted to get to the bottom of these stories or if they wanted to only find blame to pin on the past administration. When Justice Krever uncovered evidence that there had been warnings about the blood supply as far back as 1982–84, when the Liberals were in power, it seemed that Chrétien wasn't keen to uncover the truth, the whole truth and nothing but the truth. The government tried to go to court to restrict the Krever investigation and made a decision to draw a line at 1986 for victims. This way they would still be able to blame the Tories for the mess and not take responsibility for past Liberal failures.

Regarding the Somalia Inquiry, there were many similarities. The inquiry tried to get to the root of the tragedy in 1993. However, the investigation revealed allegations of a cover-up and the shredding of documents at the Department of National Defence from 1993 to 1995 under the Liberal regime. It was obvious that "getting to the bottom" necessitated "starting at the top." However, the Liberals thwarted every opportunity to allow that to happen. Their "solution" was to disband the Canadian Airborne Regiment. This was a complete tragedy, as Canada was well served by this expertly trained rapid-response team. They should never have been assigned to those peacekeeping duties in Somalia, as that was not what they were trained for. Disbanding them would not address the problem. It seemed a band-aid solution for a government that really did not want to get to the root of any problem.

I was so frustrated at the arrogance of the Liberals. When we had been in opposition together I had talked with them a lot and told them I would not be impressed if they became as arrogant as the Mulroney Tories had at the end of their reign. They assured me they would do no such thing. Sadly, they had not kept their word. In the world of partisan politics, you have to gird yourself and try not to take things personally. However, I had a difficult time with the Liberals' cavalier attitude and sense of superiority. The worst thing that happened to me on a personal level took place in Question Period during the spring of 1997. I had asked a question about pork-barrel politics and somebody who was getting a sweet deal. While the Minister was answering, his mike was on and his seatmate, Doug Young, said so all could hear, "There's more than a slab of bacon talking there." I was incensed, but I was also deeply hurt. In politics you can go at each other, but there is an unspoken rule that personal attacks are out of bounds. Moreover, I considered Doug a friend, as he was my original seatmate and had walked me up the aisle on my first day in the House. This episode caused a great uproar in the Commons and then in the media. A quick note of apology sent across the House with a page would have ended the affair. I did not receive one. The press asked me for a long time if I had received an apology. I kept saying, "Not yet," a line I would still have to use if anybody asked me today.

It was in the light of these events that we were preparing for the next election. The Electoral Boundaries Commission had been working on redistribution since the last census. In Alberta, Calgary's population had grown enough to warrant a new federal seat but the province's population had not. Consequently, the Commission needed to eliminate a rural seat to make way for a new urban seat. Not surprisingly, they chose Beaver River. We made representations to the Commission during their hearings but to no avail. Beaver River would die before the next election. I was sad to see it go; it seemed so "Canadian" a name. I had no idea what I would do. Was my political life over? I had said publicly that I would not challenge any sitting Reform MP in a nomination battle. The party strategists told me to let them know where I would like to run. The only trouble was that I had no idea. Lew and I discussed it, and he felt strongly that we should not actively go looking for a riding, but wait to see how God would show us where, and if, to run. I found this very frustrating because my nature was to get busy and get things done. I had learned to trust his good judgment so I agreed to wait. And wait I did. The winter of 1996 melted into spring and the party guys were asking me regularly where I was going to run. I told them that I had no idea, but that I had to have peace in my gut. Until then I would not have a clue. This came to be quite the joke around party circles. While trying to build a national campaign and a local campaign around where I would run, everyone kept saying, "When Deb gets peace in her gut, then we'll know where she will run." I told them I hoped to make a decision by summer. The House rose and I headed home to, hopefully, find that peace. I got a couple of phone calls but no serious offers. More and more ridings were filling up with nominated candidates and the team was getting more and more nervous. I still had no riding.

September came and so did the House opening. By now I was feeling slightly frantic, but not as much as our party strategists and my friend, Bob Mills, MP, who was in charge of election readiness. I could not give him an answer. In October, we had a church conference and the speaker gave a message on *Selah*, a word in the Psalms that means "pause and reflect." It was excellent and he asked us when was the last time we did that. I was challenged, because in my hectic world it had actually been a while. The next day Lew had a dreadful cold and went to bed for a snooze over the supper hour, hoping to feel well enough to go to the evening service. As I did not have to worry about supper, I thought, "Hey! I can have some *Selah* time." I grabbed my Living Bible, which was sitting on the kitchen table. I flipped it open and it landed at

Chapter 2 of Habakkuk, a small book in the Old Testament. I thought, "This should be interesting. I am sure I haven't read this since I was in Bible school thirty years ago." I started reading and I could hardly believe my eyes:

> Write my answer on a billboard, large and clear, so that anyone
> can read it at a glance and rush to tell the others. But these
> things I plan won't happen right away. Slowly, steadily, surely
> the time approaches when the vision will be fulfilled. If it seems
> slow, do not despair, for these things will surely come to pass.
> Just be patient. They will not be overdue a single day!

I sat silent for a long while, realizing that I was not in control of this, but that Someone else was and knew completely what He was doing. I went to the bedroom and told Lew that all we needed to do was drive around looking at billboards to find our answer. He chuckled and said, "Sure, Deb."

The next week in Ottawa was hectic, as usual. We had a vote after Question Period and I waited in the lobby while the bells rang. Just when it was time to go into the Chambers, Bob Mills came up behind me and said, "Deb, I want to ask you a question. It's kind of crazy and I don't want you to get mad." I replied, "Sure, Bob. Ask me anything... and I promise I won't get mad." "Okay, here goes. Edmonton North phoned me and they said they want to put up a billboard inviting you to run there. I've heard of radio or newspaper ads, but never this. Crazy, eh?" I was going up the steps into the Chambers, stopped, turned around and said, "A what?" He replied, "A billboard." I told him to let them go ahead and I also said to Bob, "Can you slip up to my office after the vote? I'd like to show you something." "Sure," he responded, pleased that I had finally agreed to something after all this time. Upstairs, I read him the verses from Habakkuk and he stared at me, wide-eyed. I said, "Remember the part about peace in my gut? I got it." "Wow." And after a long silence he said, "Does that make me a prophet?" That moment, I knew I had found my new home.

CHAPTER 15

Her Majesty's Loyal Opposition

THE SPRING OF 1997 WAS A FLURRY of activity preparing for the election. I had moved into Edmonton and was now living there full-time. I was in a new area and many people knew who I was, but pictured me northeast of the city in Beaver River. It was a real exercise in communication to let people know that I was running in Edmonton North.

This was one of the three ridings in Edmonton that had gone Liberal in the 1993 election. Within ten days of my announcement, the incumbent, John Loney, called a press conference and said that he would not be seeking re-election. The Liberal Party appointed a candidate, Jonathan Murphy, who was not the choice of the local riding association, and that decision "from on high" did not sit well with them. The NDP candidate was Ray Martin, a former provincial leader of their party. The PCs ran a young man, Mitch Panciuk, who had been their candidate the last time around. At an all-candidates' forum he said, "We don't need any strangers here in Edmonton North," obviously taking a shot at me for moving there from Beaver River. I looked him up and down slowly and replied, "I don't think I look any stranger than you," to the obvious delight of the crowd.

Reform's campaign slogan and policy document was "A Fresh Start." We offered a six-point plan to build a brighter future together. These points were: reducing the size of government to create more and better jobs, offering tax relief, making families a priority, making our streets safe again, repairing the social safety net, and ending the uncertainty caused by the national unity crisis. It was a good platform and we were confident we could make gains across the country.

A few days after the writ was dropped on April 27 for a June 2 election, Preston and the national campaign team received a brown envelope that contained the Liberal Red Book. The Liberals had not released it yet, so Preston had a press conference in Quebec City and unveiled it for them. His remarks were entitled "Goodbye Red Book, Hello Cheque Book," indicating what all their promises were going to cost.

We had several citywide events in Edmonton that were well attended and increased the excitement and the momentum of our local campaign. Perhaps the most fun was a huge "hangar rally" held at the municipal airport. Preston arrived on the Reform jet, and when the door opened he greeted the crowd wearing his Oilers jersey. We were in the playoffs that spring and the whole city had hockey fever. I was on my motorcycle and met him at the plane. Because the press was filming us and we were on private property, we did not wear helmets. I drove him from the plane to the hangar, a very short distance. He was very nervous and said, "How do I hang on? Where do I hang on?" I told him to relax and pretend he was riding his horse. That didn't work. I felt his fingers dig into my back and I am sure I still have the claw marks as proof of that fateful ride. The national media replayed it, the Motorcycle Safety Council condemned it, radio talk shows were gabbing away about it. It sure gave us coverage! I have ridden with a helmet since before helmets were law and understand the importance of them. If we had worn them, however, the media would have likely squawked because they wouldn't have been able to see the faces under them.

Late in the campaign, we held a rally at the Butter Dome, the gymnasium at the University of Alberta, with more than four thousand people in attendance. Chrétien and Paul Martin were in Edmonton the same night and drew a crowd of six hundred. At our rally, Preston had a chair from the House of Commons and used it for his theme, "Who owns this chair? This seat belongs to you! Who will occupy it on your behalf after June 2? What will be said in your name on jobs, taxes, crime, unity and parliamentary reform?" It was an excellent visual and stirred up the crowd.

On election day, June 2, 1997, I rode around on my motorcycle to each of our candidates' campaign offices, cheering them on. I carried a news cameraman with me, so we also got some good visuals. Reformers all met at the exhibition grounds to watch the returns. Atlantic Canada rejected the Liberals, but the NDP and PCs picked up the protest vote. I was amused to see that Doug Young was defeated. My mother said to me, "That will teach him to mess with my daughter." (It had not been many months since his verbal attack on me in the House.) We lost our one seat in Ontario and were saddened by that. We were also frustrated by the Reform/PC vote-splitting, as in 1993. Reform came second in thirty-eight ridings and there were twenty-eight seats where our combined vote outnumbered the Liberals'.

Things improved for us as the results came in from Western Canada. We got 3 seats in Manitoba, up from 1 in '93, and 8 in Saskatchewan, up from 4. In Alberta we took 24 of the 26 seats, and in British Columbia 25 of a possible 34. We now had a total of 60 seats in Parliament. We did not have a breakthrough in the East; however, we increased our total number of seats, certainly a cause for celebration. And, unlike the last Parliament, we were now Her Majesty's Official Loyal Opposition! I was pleased that our campaign in Edmonton North had gone so well and I was re-elected with a total of 44 per cent of the vote. The results were:

Deborah Grey, Reform	16,124
Jonathan Murphy, Liberal	11,874
Ray Martin, NDP	5,354
Mitch Panciuk, PC	2,825

The new Parliament totals stood at: Liberals 155 (barely a majority), Reform 60, BQ 44, NDP 21 and PC 20. One sad note for me that night was the loss of one of our incumbents, Elwin Hermanson. He and I were in the same situation of having our rural ridings disappear because of redistribution. We both moved into the city (I to Edmonton and he to Saskatoon) to try and expand the Reform base. I won my seat, but Elwin lost his. However, because of his presence and help with the overall Saskatoon campaign, we did pick up the other three seats in that city. I really missed him in the next Parliament. (He went on to become the first leader of the Saskatchewan Party and made a tremendous impact on his province).

I set up a new constituency office in Edmonton North, staffed by Jodi Mulawka and Wendy Hamm. They did an excellent job and I had a seamless transition to my new constituency. However, Lew and I suffered a personal loss not long after the 1997 election. In October, my dear Aunt Reta finally succumbed to the pancreatic cancer that she had lived with since 1988. We were so glad to have her with us for as long as we did, but we really missed her when she died. She was such an encouragement to me, both personally and politically. She was excited to see the election results in June. You would think she had won a seat herself. She was so grateful to see us "boot the Bloc."

So now we were the Official Opposition. One of the first acts we undertook was to have a flag-planting ceremony in the office of the leader of the Opposition. The BQ had removed all flags and signs of anything federal. It was an important day for me and I was glad to see the maple leaf there after walking up and down that hallway for years and not seeing one Canadian flag.

The unity file was still an important, unresolved issue. It felt raw every time it was thought about or mentioned. The Chrétien Liberals were now paying more attention to Plan B (tough love) than to Plan A (renewing federalism). We tried to influence them by suggesting that there might be more positive results if the government tried to work on practical solutions rather than simply spouting rhetoric. The premiers had a first ministers' conference in Calgary in September 1997 and came up with an agreement, dubbed the "Calgary Declaration." It contained principles for strengthening federalism; equality of citizens and provinces in law; recognition of the value of diversity, including the uniqueness of Quebec; the principle that constitutional amendments conferring powers on one province must make those powers available to all provinces; and the principle of the federal and provincial governments working in partnership while respecting each other's jurisdictions. By November, polling data showed that there was a high degree of support for these positions in Quebec, even though many people were not aware of the actual "declaration."

We felt that it was more advantageous to work on Plan A, so we put a lot of effort and resources into our New Canada Act. This incorporated our best shot on ideas for strengthening federalism. They included division of powers, reforming federal institutions and democratizing constitutional changes, and they were composed into a new legislative format. They included specific measures for re-balancing powers, restricting federal spending power and creating a dispute-settling mechanism. But Plan B was also important. As the basis of that section of our New Canada Act, we used Stephen Harper's private member's bill, which he and our researcher, Scott Reid, had composed in the fall of 1996. It declared unilateral secession unlawful, provided a federal definition of what constituted a clear question and a majority in any lawful referendum on secession, and defined the course of action to be taken by the federal government in a case where such a referendum carried—including terms and conditions to be negotiated and then put to a national referendum. The next year the Liberals put forward their Clarity Bill. It looked amazingly like Stephen's work, yet they hailed it as their great idea and then scorned us for even mentioning that such a plan was necessary.

Which leads me to Liberal ethics. It seemed that the Liberals talked about ethics regularly, but seldom exhibited any. The previous Parliament saw a farce made of the Krever and Somalia inquiries. This Parliament saw a random internal audit in 1999 of 459 files of Human Resources Development Canada. The audit looked at files representing approximately $1 billion of "grants and contributions" and shone the light on some disturbing facts. It showed that 15 per cent of the projects did not have applications on file; 72 per cent had no cash-flow forecast; 11 per cent had no budget proposal; 11 per cent had no description of their expected results; 87 per cent had no supervision. Plus, 37 per cent of the 459 files showed such gross mismanagement that they underwent a second investigation to see if police needed to be brought in. We could hardly believe this, but if we had uncovered such a mess in HRDC, who knew what lay waiting in other government departments under the section that each of them had for "grants and contributions" (totalling approximately $13 billion)?

Over the next several months, we pressed the government to come up with answers to the "Billion-Dollar Boondoggle," as we labelled it. The Transitional Jobs Fund was a source of illegitimate use of these funds, but we also uncovered money going to companies and some being funnelled back to the Liberal Party. We found out that the prime minister was also involved, at one point asking for money for a project in his riding several weeks before they even applied. That's what I call "cash up front"!

The government's reaction was dreadful. They tried to chalk it up to a few "administrative errors." Trying to fight back, the prime minister would read out names of companies in Reformers' ridings who received grants. Don Boudria, the government House leader, would regularly grab a sheet out of his trusty binder to provide the PM with ammunition. We got so tired of this that one day in Question Period, I shot across, "Could the prime minister give us the answer without any help from Binder Boy?" They looked at each other, clearly caught off guard, started to laugh and the entire House erupted. That name has stuck with Boudria over the years, a name he justly earned.

We found out that nearly 40 per cent of Chrétien's personal campaign donations for the 1997 election came from companies that had benefited from federal grants and contributions. And we wonder why the public is so cynical about politicians? The next scandal we uncovered was the prime minister's involvement with the Auberge Grand-Mère, a hotel and golf course in his riding at Shawinigan. When he became prime minister, he signed a document required for conflict of interest purposes, stating that he held a third of the shares in the Grand-Mère Golf Club under a private company. A third party was now managing them in a blind trust arrangement. This all sounded acceptable; however, in the ensuing months, the media and our research department uncovered shady business decisions, political influence and questionable use of public money.

Chrétien had resigned from Parliament in 1986 and was re-elected in December 1990, after becoming the leader of the Liberal Party that

June. In the interim, he had practiced law in a private firm. In 1988, he and two partners bought the Grand-Mère Golf Club from Consolidated Bathurst, a pulp and paper company (of which Chrétien was a director) for $1.25 million. From 1988 to 1993, it had a string of bad luck; sewer problems, the clubhouse burned down, it was poorly managed and other golf clubs in the area gave it some stiff competition. Consequently, it racked up losses of about $2 million.

Chrétien and his partners had also bought the business of the Grand-Mère Inn, but not the building. That was purchased by Yvon Duhaime in April 1993 for $250,000. A year later he bought the actual building from Consolidated Bathurst for $225,000. Duhaime had owned another hotel down the road that had burned down.

Chrétien claimed that, three days before being sworn in as prime minister, he had sold all of his shares to Akimbo Development. Under our intense scrutiny and questioning in the House, all he could come up with for proof was a handwritten note with a signature that, later, a handwriting analyst could not verify as his. We continued to press him and, as that Parliament drew to a close, more doubt was cast on whether he still owned the shares or not. In January 1996, the prime minister personally called Howard Wilson, the ethics counsellor, and told him that the sale of the shares had fallen through. Wilson told him he could either recover the shares and declare publicly that he owned them or resell them. He did neither. He promised Wilson that he would resell them but kept them for three more years, until October 1999. Obviously, he had more than a passing interest in what happened to the worth of the Grand-Mère Inn and Golf Club over the past six years since becoming prime minister. He clearly was knowledgeable about what was happening with his shares; even though he said in the House of Commons in March 1999, "It is all dealt with by the person who manages the trust of my own affairs. I do not ask them any questions. I do not have the shares…" This was a pretty stark contradiction.

The government operates an Immigrant Investor Programme, which is a source of capital available to entrepeneurs wanting to obtain Canadian citizenship. It was federally administered, except in Quebec, where it was run by the province. They had received 46 per cent of all funds in recent years, but the funding went up to 65 per cent between 1994 and 1998 and up to 81 per cent in 1998. Clearly, somebody knew how to access these funds.

Only one month after Chrétien told the ethics counsellor that the sale of his shares had fallen through, he hosted an immigrant investor at 24 Sussex Drive to discuss an unnamed hotel. It turned out that Yvon Duhaime set up the meeting and that they had discussed the Auberge Grand-Mère.

The Immigrant Investor Programme was not the only source of government funds that was tapped into relating to the Grand-Mère affair. In 1996, HRDC selected one of the companies owned by a friend of the prime minister, Claude Gauthier, for a large CIDA contract. Two weeks later, his company, Transelec, paid $525,000 for a parcel of land right beside the Grand-Mère Golf Club so they were able to pay off a line of credit that was seven years old. (Also, during the upcoming election in 1997, Transelec donated $10,000 to Chrétien's re-election). There was, in addition, a tangled web of money received through the Transitional Jobs Fund. A lot of effort was being put into investments in the prime minister's riding of St. Maurice. Every time we questioned him, the PM would respond, "I am just doing my job to help the people in my riding."

Meanwhile, back at the Inn, Yvon Duhaime was not doing well with the business. In April 1996, Chrétien personally called the president of the Business Development Bank, Mr. Francois Beaudoin, on behalf of Duhaime, who needed money. In September 1996, the BDC turned down the request for the $3.5 million loan. In February 1997, Chrétien had personally called Beaudoin again and he felt extremely pressured to grant the loan. A loan for $615,000 was granted, despite Duhaime being in default on existing mortgages and racking up over $300,000 in unpaid debts. Duhaime also went on to receive grants under the Transitional Jobs Fund.

Through all of these Shawinigan shenanigans, who will ever know how all of this assistance could have affected the market value of the shares that the prime minister actually still owned, while claiming everything to be in a blind trust? I am reminded of the words to the Gospel song "Amazing Grace": "I once was blind, but now I see."

Me? Mischievous? Never!! 1956

My dad, Mansell, with my eldest sister, Leslie and me, 1954
"Here's looking at you."

The old Gunderson homestead, Frog Lake, 1979
"The claw marks were deep."

High school graduation, 1970
"Yikes!"

Alison's 50th birthday, June 3, 1999   "Girl power."
Back: Katie (niece), Kirsten (niece), Cheryl (sister-in-law), Leslie, Skip, me
Front: Tanya (niece), Alison, Mom

My swearing-in day, April 3, 1989
Sandra, Eleanor and Mansell, Alison, Mom, Linda, Robar, Stephen Harper, me

Clerk of the House, Robert
Marleau, swearing me in,
April 3, 1989

Doug Campbell, Progressive, passing the
Reform torch to me, March 20, 1989
"… a new generation."

Our wedding, August 7, 1993
"Wow!"

At Camp Homewood on our honeymoon,
August 1993   "… looks like we made it!"

Mom's 70th birthday,
July 8, 1995
Leslie, Skip, Alison,
mom, me
"Picnic in the park."

Scrum, 1991
"Help! What can I say?"

Class of '97
"Mr. Speaker!"

Question
Period, 2000
"Zinger!"

"Queen of the One-liners."

"Up, up and away!" CF-18, June 21, 1993

With Rick Mercer at West Edmonton Mall, March 2004
"Hey, fella!"

Hangar Rally, Edmonton, with Preston Manning, May 1997
"Don't hang on so tightly!"

Doing a skit at Camp Homewood, 1968
"Hats off to you!"

Luba Goy visiting the Leader of
the Opposition, 2000
"No Smoking Allowed."

CHAPTER 16

United? Alternative?

WHILE WE WERE HOLDING THE GOVERNMENT'S FEET to the fire in the House, our party was also undergoing a strategic review of how to stop the vote-splitting with the PCs, in order to actually have a shot at replacing the Liberal government. The media continued to point out that as long as this phenomenon carried on, the Liberals would be free to rule without challenge.

Our party had post-mortems across the country after the election. Province by province, in community after community, the verdict was the same—we had to find a way to join conservative-minded Canadians and build a bigger base to provide an alternative to the Liberals. Preston believed it was possible and had predicted it decades ago. In fact, he and his father, Ernest Manning, had urged a union of conservatism in their book, *Political Realignment*, in 1967. I wondered if conservative voices would ever unite, let alone in the foreseeable future. Decades had gone by and it looked as if that vision was farther from reality than ever. I knew in my heart this was necessary, but I found it very difficult to accept because of my history with the PCs and the pain I had endured during my first term. I had long talks with Preston and questioned whether the acrimony between the Reformers and the PCs could ever be healed. The Tories were deeply hurt that Reform had eroded their base and they saw Preston and me as the embodiment of their misfortune. On our side, we had a deep distrust of Joe Clark and other Tory MPs from the West who had seemed to sell Western interests and concerns down the river. As difficult as this scenario was, the thought of seeing a Liberal government in power forever did not seem particularly appealing, either! We had a mammoth task in front of us, not simply for our political future, but for the sake of our country. During the fall of 1997 and early 1998, many emotional caucus discussions were held about what the next step would entail. The public and the membership knew what needed to happen. But for many of us long-time, hard-line Reformers, it was a difficult pill to swallow. We could hardly fathom "doing a deal" with a party that many of us felt was no longer "conservative." Granted, we were watching the PCs rebuild after their humiliating defeat at the polls in 1993, but still…our very cultures clashed!

As we geared up for our Assembly in May 1998, in London, Ontario, the idea of building a bigger conservative tent was on our minds and the media's headlines. "Unite the Right" became the prevalent political phrase for the media. I found it misleading, as I do not consider myself a "right-winger" per se. I am hard-headed fiscally, but I can be soft-hearted socially. Where does that fit in the traditional left-right continuum? We needed to create a new entity that would break down old political barriers.

In his keynote address to the Assembly, Preston challenged Reformers to do just that. He built an excellent case for a united alternative to the Liberal government. They had had free rein with waste, scandals, lack of democracy in Parliament and cuts to important programs while funding ineffective pet projects. Surely the Chrétien Liberals did not deserve to rule in perpetuity—Canadians were demanding a choice! Preston stated very clearly that he was willing to put his leadership on the line, surely an act rarely seen in Canadian politics to date. He asked the delegates, "Do I risk the position of leadership which you have given me this past eleven years? The frank answer to the question is yes! But if I, as your leader, consider the risk worth taking—if the result to be gained by such risk-taking is the creation of a governing party based on Reform principles under the great banner of Reform—why should that risk cause us to hesitate?"

And so, the gauntlet was thrown. Immediately, the debate began. There were pros and cons, hesitant agreements and vehement denials, cautious optimism and accusations of downright heresy. Preston loved ideas and debate. He had them now in spades. The day after the speech, Preston's leadership was endorsed by 81 per cent and the United Alternative proposal carried with 91 per cent. I knew that something big was on the horizon, and it made me nervous, but we would all ride this out together, as Reformers always had. Even though we had disagreements on how to get to the goal-line, we all knew where it was—Preston always said, "If you want real reform, you have to send real Reformers to Parliament." Maybe this would be the way to get a big enough base to achieve power, not for power's sake, but to accomplish the reforms that we, and many Canadians, wanted.

The United Alternative convention was set for February 19–21, 1999, in Ottawa. This was to capitalize on students' reading week, so we would have a great turnout of young people. I was very interested in having youth involved. My part-time constituency assistant, Shannon Haggarty, was politically active and astute. I valued her input. Also, Wes McLeod, my new Ottawa assistant who replaced Jenny, was an avid pro-Alliance advocate. The amount of preparation and planning, and the logistics of organizing another large convention seemed a daunting task, but it all came together. Tony Clement, a Mike Harris MPP from Ontario, and I co-chaired the convention. This was a good blend of Tory-Reform culture. Tony and I hit it off well, addressed the cynicism of the media and the naysayers, and proved that we could get along just fine. We have been good friends ever since.

It was a very full weekend of introduction and interaction for long-time Tories, Reformers and many who had been Liberal or had no political affiliation. Debate was heated; GUARD (Grassroots United Against Reform's Demise) was loud and proud; supporters and detractors were equally passionate about their convictions. Bruce Stubbs, a long-time Reformer, was the head of GUARD. (His daughter, Shannon, later worked for me in Edmonton). Just as prominent as the discussions on the floor of the convention were the hallway incidents and unplanned altercations. I came out of the women's washroom to face an enormous scrum gathered around John Crosbie in the hallway. I wandered into the middle of it to have some sport with John. We had a go-round, much to the delight of the media and convention-goers. John and I were colleagues in the House and repartee was our specialty. He made it very clear that he would have no truck or trade with the likes of my ragtag band of Reformers and, of course, I retorted that given the size of his Tory caucus in the House, he couldn't afford to be particularly choosy!

At the convention, debate centred on several options: unite under the Reform banner, unite under the PC banner, merge the two parties into one, create a new party or have a local option—a selection of common candidates. After much discussion and debate, the convention voted to create a new political party. It was very exciting. Those of us who had been involved since the beginning knew the amount of work required, as we had done this before in the birth of Reform. Nonetheless, we also knew it was necessary.

The next year was spent traversing the country, trying to broaden the coalition and build bridges amongst conservative forces. Although I was convinced of the necessity of the UA, I was still somewhat apprehensive and uncomfortable. Much of the ridicule I had endured as the only Reformer in a PC Parliament was still very painful. Could I forgive and could I move on for the sake of the bigger picture? I grappled with that for a long while and was so grateful to talk it out with Preston and my very special friends Chuck Strahl, Monte Solberg, and also Diane Ablonczy and Jay Hill, both of whom I had known since the 1988 election. Jay and I had been candidates together and Diane was on the national council, so we had a lot invested in the Reform tradition. I realized that if we were going to move ahead and do the best thing for our country, I had to swallow some of my pride, my personal hurts, and give up some things in order to get others. Many long-time Reformers shared this sentiment. Was this a watering-down of policies? Was this a sellout? Was it a compromise simply to form a government? One of my dear friends in Beaver River asked, "Who ever said we wanted to form a government, anyway?" I was astonished. I had always thought that was Reform's mission. Evidently that was not a unanimous sentiment. Most of us realized that the bigger purpose was to allow Canadians from every region to have a say and claim ownership of the building process. This had to be more than Reform repackaged. It had to be new for all sides.

Even though I knew it was necessary, a very painful thing for me, as crazy as it sounds, was losing the name of Reform. I was a reformer before there ever was Reform. And, as they said so often on *Royal Canadian Air Farce*, "I love that word Refoooorm," mocking Preston. I loved it, too, and I grieved deeply giving it up. However, its memory lives on, as my license plate is REFORM 1, and always will be.

The second United Alternative conference (or UA II, as it became known) was in Ottawa again, mainly for the convenience of the Ottawa press. It garnered a lot of coverage, and was another exciting convention. Enthusiasm marked the mood of the group and when it wrapped up on January 29, 2000, I was now a member of the Canadian Alliance, our new name chosen by the delegates. As our Reform Assembly was scheduled for the same time, it piggybacked on the UA II, beginning Saturday afternoon, immediately after the birth of the Canadian Alliance.

Preston's keynote speech that night introduced the phrase and challenge, "Think Big." The crowd was receptive and seemed keen to begin building bridges and alliances across the country. Preston recapped our history, listed our victories and articulated the challenges that lay ahead. The next day, his leadership was endorsed by 75 per cent of delegates— lower than at other times, but still very sound, considering the enormous project that he presented to the Canadian public to rebuild conservatism.

The campaign now kicked off to win the hearts and minds of party members, to encourage new people to join in order to have a say, and to mount and sustain enough momentum, because a general election was not far away. Ballots were mailed out and the machinery set up for a national referendum in March, not many weeks hence. The pace was frenetic, and the caucus fanned out across the country to present the proposal. Not all members of the caucus supported the UA. Consequently, there were MPs debating each other, council members debating each other or MPs, and many questioning Preston's leadership.

The challenge for any leader, of course, is how to lead with vision and inspire his or her followers to come along. The reward for Preston came on March 25, 2000, when the Canadian Alliance was born, with a 92 per cent endorsement from Reform members. He had announced that he would step down as leader to run for the leadership of the Alliance. There were several candidates in the running, so our party was in campaign mode again, with the race to culminate on July 8, 2000. On March 27, after Preston's recommendation and our caucus's ratification, I became the first-ever woman leader of the Opposition!

————————

CHAPTER 17

Lipstick in the Leader's Office

THE DAY I MOVED DOWN THE HALL to the leader's office I was escorted by a host of media. This was an exciting event by all accounts. After all, never in Canadian history had a woman occupied the role of leader of the Opposition. For fun, I said to the gathered reporters and cameramen, "Okay, folks. I am going to do something that has never been done in this office before." Then I got out my lipstick and put it on in front of all the cameras. (I couldn't be 100 per cent sure that this had actually never been done by any leader of the Opposition because over the generations a few strange ducks had held the office, but I felt reasonably confident!) Everyone thought this was great fun and it got us all off to a good start. My staff all moved down with me, including Lana Fawcett, who had worked for me less than one week when I was appointed leader. She adapted incredibly well. Carolyn Stewart-Olsen, who was the leader's press secretary, also filled that role for me. We had travelled together over the years while I was deputy leader and we were good travelling companions. On our many trips, we had only one problem. I am a nighthawk and always wanted to go for a late-night walk or a swim after our evening functions. Carolyn wanted to be in bed by about 9:30 every night.

Over the years, I had done "walkabouts" through our research and communications departments, getting to know the staff. I always enjoyed this and wanted them to know that I appreciated them. Not only that, they were an essential part of our team and I wanted them to know that. While I served as leader, they fell directly under my authority and I tried to wander over more often.

Because of the fuss made over Stornoway, I chose not to live there during my tenure. I continued to room with my cousin Judy, but I did host several official functions at Stornoway. Life is so hectic that it is almost impossible to have a good turnout for lunch or supper off the Hill. I asked around to see if anyone would be willing to attend a breakfast frightfully early before everybody's busy day began. The answer was a resounding "Yes." And so I began a series of early-morning breakfasts for research staff, communications staff, the morning Question Period strategy team and various other groups. We would eat, visit and then I would turn them loose to check the place out, roaming wherever they wanted to go. The tours were fun and everyone felt completely at home.

I also hosted our MPs in groups of eight for supper meetings. (They did not opt for breakfast!) It is difficult to arrange such events with everyone so busy, but we did manage to get everyone in who wanted to come. The order of business was always the same: chat over supper, relax and then turn everyone loose to explore. We all had a good time and enjoyed a visit away from the Hill.

My mother and all my sisters had a chance to come down that spring as well. They loved their visit to Stornoway and we all howled at the idea that this was happening to someone in our family. They wandered happily around Ottawa while I put in long days on the Hill, but we always met up for late-night coffee at Starbucks. Lew spent quite a bit of the spring in Ottawa, too. He was involved in a building project out in Merrickville for our friend Rick Anderson and his wife, Michelle. It was wonderful to have Lew there and most of the time he was able to get back for the evening functions.

One of the yearly spring highlights for the Hill staff and the media is the Western barbeque at Stornoway. Big tents are put up and the place is always packed. Since I was lucky enough to serve as opposition leader during the spring, I carried on the tradition that Preston and Sandra had started. The day of the staff party, who showed up in town but my good friend Luba Goy, from *Royal Canadian Air Farce*? I told her about the barbeque and she came along. The troops were all thrilled to see her and she regaled them with stories and jokes all evening long. They all loved her—it couldn't have been planned any better.

One of my official duties was to meet foreign delegations or leaders. Twice I went to Rideau Hall, once to meet the president of Yemen and once the president of Algeria. They were fascinating individuals and I was pleased to have the chance to have a private meeting with each of them. I also hosted several delegations in the offices of the leader on the Hill.

I had regular strategy sessions with our research and communications staff to make sure we were on track, with the best ammunition we could muster. The senior caucus officers, house leader Chuck Strahl and whip Jay Hill, met with me for lunch once a week in addition to all the other meetings we attended constantly. Things went extremely well, both in the planning and in the execution.

My main focus while I served as leader was to keep the whole team together and unified while we were going through the leadership race. I knew that various caucus members would be supporting different candidates as they had every right to do so. It was essential that we work together, regardless of our choices, and we could not let the Liberals off the hook or allow media attention to focus on us. The whole caucus pulled together and I was very proud of the job we did that spring. We continued to hammer the government over the HRDC "Billion-Dollar Boondoggle" and "Shawinigate" scandals.

While we were hammering away at the government over these scandals, our House leader Chuck Strahl discovered that no less than thirteen of our caucus had gone to the government to ask to buy back into the plan. This presented a real problem for us because we knew that the government would keep making an opening for buy-backs and continue to divide our caucus. We had a strategic discussion among the senior caucus officers and then in caucus. After long discussions and a frustrated government House leader, Don Boudria, wondering when we were ever going to quit haggling over this issue, the government legislated us all back into the MP pension plan in June 2000. The legislation received royal assent in September and we were given exactly one year to buy back our past service if we chose. So now, we were all back in the plan. The class of '93 and I, who had opted out, were now equal with the class of '97, who were automatically in the plan, with no chance of an opt-out clause. Individual MPs needed to decide if they would buy back their past years of service. The premiums were being automatically deducted off our pay and we were no longer able to put money into an RRSP.

While we were dealing with that prickly issue in the House, the leadership candidates were all asked their opinions about it. Needless to say, it was difficult for all of them, but mostly for Preston. It was just one more issue for the candidates to address as the race progressed throughout the spring leading toward its culmination on July 8, 2000. There were five candidates in the race: Preston Manning, Stockwell Day, (who was the Alberta provincial treasurer, bilingual and a Conservative), Tom Long (an Ontario Conservative who gave credibility to the Alliance), Keith Martin (a Reform MP who wanted to put his ideas about health care out for public debate) and John Stachow (an individual citizen who used his candidacy to promote his ideas about monetary policy). Caucus had a long discussion about whether caucus officers should be actively supporting any candidate. Randy White challenged my leadership team about being neutral. We'd made the decision to remain officially neutral in the race, but I was quietly cheering for Preston, my good friend and mentor. He knew the risks of what he was undertaking. In leadership you make friends but also enemies. There will always be some who think their special talents are being overlooked or they are just not appreciated. In fact, if these people would chip in to whatever the task at hand is, they would be amazed how well-appreciated they are. Pouters are difficult team players.

The biggest hurdle Preston faced was a simplistic argument and theory that suggested a new party needed a new leader. I never did figure this strategy out, as I thought it was tantamount to throwing the baby out with the bath water. Preston had done an excellent job bringing us this far and was now just starting to be respected and trusted in Ontario, the biggest hunting ground for seats. I thought that what was needed was a new party with an experienced leader. Under Preston's leadership, our party had received more than two million votes in Ontario in the last two elections, more than the Conservatives and the NDP, but also more than on the Prairies, our stronghold.

Preston's team decided on a low-key campaign, trying to secure the base of existing party members while selling several thousand new memberships through teams across the country and at coffee party meetings. One reason for this strategy of Preston's campaign was that he and his team had been running flat out for several national campaigns over the last couple of years: the 1997 federal election, two Reform Assemblies, two UA conventions and two full-blown referendum campaigns to endorse the Canadian Alliance. Understandably, the people involved were totally exhausted. Preston did not appear at large rallies or many public functions. I thought that he should have done some of this because he was so good at explaining concepts to people and winning them over. It would also be difficult to make policy pronouncements, like the other candidates, because Preston had made so many policy speeches across the country for so many years. They would not seem as newsworthy as if Stockwell or Tom Long made them.

Stockwell, on the other hand, travelled across the country and attracted large crowds. He brought an excitement to the race and people flocked to hear him. He was bilingual and many thought that this was a necessity for a national leader. Although he had served in the Alberta legislature for some years, he was not known outside our province. The national stage is always much different than any provincial one. In Alberta, Stock was a big fish in a small pond. He had claimed to be the fiscal guru that had turned our financial situation around. In fact, Jim Dinning, his predecessor as treasurer, had made the necessary spending cuts. Others, such as Steve West, restructured government departments and their spending. When Stockwell was treasurer, oil prices were approximately $30 per barrel. Some experts said that he had one of the easiest jobs in Canada. At the national level, investigative journalists do not let anybody off the hook simply because they say something is true. They began to question his claims.

Something else that swirled around, though not prominently in the leadership race, was what became known as the "Goddard lawsuit." In

April 1999, Stockwell had written a letter to the *Red Deer Advocate* critical of Lorne Goddard, a local lawyer and school board trustee. He was apparently acting on behalf of a pedophile that was in possession of child pornography. Goddard filed a civil defamation suit for $600,000 and rumour had it that the costs for Stockwell's defense were skyrocketing. These costs were being covered by an insurance plan designed to protect MLAs. The whole affair was kept quiet during the leadership contest. There were two reasons that were rumoured to be behind Ralph Klein's support of Stockwell in the leadership race. One was to get him out of the provincial arena because Ralph was preparing for an election and would not want the subject of the taxpayer-funded insurance claim for Stockwell's defense to surface. Another was that he was seen as a potential successor to Ralph when he left the political scene. Ralph's chief advisor, Rod Love, was charged with getting Stock "out of Dodge" and on to the federal scene, then dropping him like a bomb (this is exactly what happened).

During the race, Stockwell's team rallied the support of several religious lobby groups and social conservatives. They also set up a group called "Families for Day." They became very active in soliciting memberships and support in churches, putting membership forms in church bulletins and setting up tables in the foyer of churches. As a Christian I object vehemently to these tactics. In my view, the mission of the church is to preach the Good News message of Christ. Although I believe that individual Christians should be involved in the political realm, I do not think it wise for the "church" to make pronouncements about any individual or party. Because, as sure as guns, when that person or party does something wrong or fails in some mission, the whole integrity of the church and its message will be called into question. If they were incorrect about a particular person or party issue, then could they also be wrong about their central message? This is dangerous ground to be on, in my view. During that race, I had Christian people call me who were absolutely wild about what they had seen in their church bulletin or foyer and wanted to know what was I going to do to stop it. Sadly, I could do nothing but suggest they talk to Stockwell's team, who were engaging in these tactics, as well as pray that the Christian community would not engage in internecine warfare. I tried to carry on in my leadership role by living by my personal standard of working Christianly in a non-Christian arena.

In the midst of these allegations and undercurrents, the first vote occurred on June 24, 2000. We used a one-member, one-vote method across the country, with an event held in Calgary to generate excitement and announce the vote. The party membership was approximately 200,000 and it was a logistical challenge to make sure everything went well with the count. When the results came in, Stockwell received 44 per cent (53,249 out of 120,557 votes cast), Preston 36 per cent, Tom 18 per cent and 2 per cent for Keith Martin and John Stachow. This number represented about 60 per cent of the total membership of the party. I think that many of those non-voters were likely Preston supporters who assumed he "had it in the bag" and there was no need for their one little vote. Many did not feel the sense of urgency that they should become involved in the race. This again demonstrates the need for "getting out the vote" in any campaign, large or small. Pressure was put on Preston to drop out of the race. He carried on for a couple of reasons: one was because the resolution called for someone to win with 50 per cent plus one and the other was he did not want to look like a quitter.

After the first ballot, I became somewhat more vocal and involved in the campaign. The most painful event that occurred for me during this period was responding to a letter that was sent to one of our MPs, Eric Lowther (Calgary Centre). Eric was a committed Christian and was our family issues critic. He had done a superb job of addressing issues such as same-sex marriage on behalf of our party. I had heard rumours during the campaign that some of Stockwell's supporters had been bullying MPs into supporting him or they would face nomination battles or have their critic roles taken away under his leadership. Several of my caucus came to me and said that they felt threatened but would not go public about the allegations. Although I found this deplorable, I could not get to the bottom of it. When Eric showed me the actual letter, which appeared to be threatening, I discussed it with him and asked his advice. He said it would be wise to make it public because he found it so distasteful and hoped the practice of making these threats would be stopped cold. I tried to call Stockwell to discuss it with him, but could only leave messages. He did not return my calls about this issue. Eventually, I had a press conference at my constituency office, released the letter at Eric's request and offered Stock a chance to renounce this type of tactic and announce a cease and desist order. It was a perfect opportunity to go on national television and set the record straight. Unfortunately, I became the target and Stock missed a chance to deny these allegations.

Another very sensitive part of the campaign was the branding of Stockwell as the "Christian" choice for leader. There were undertones that questioned the Christian commitment of Preston Manning. We had gone through all the attacks of the media for years ridiculing and denouncing Preston for his faith. He had been able to bring his Christian convictions into the political realm without looking like a zealot and was able to maintain his faith while serving the nation. Sadly, in the Alliance leadership race, many of Stock's supporters pitted him against a fellow believer, and that did more damage than good. It turned into a "who is the more 'Christian' Christian?" This is not only deplorable, it is small-minded and does nothing to build the Christian community, let alone the country. Church members found themselves in all-out battles regarding the leadership candidates, many of which did not mend after the race was over. I thought it unbelievably unfair to sow seeds of doubt about Preston's Christian commitment. Preston refused to enter this debate. He did not try to attract the support of the Chrisitian community as a political interest group or a "voting block." I used a tour of Alberta to suggest that Stockwell needed to get a federal seat, learn the ropes of being an MP and figure out how to articulate his social conservative views on the national stage. It was important for him to be on our team, but he was not yet ready to lead it. My views were apparently outnumbered.

On July 8, the second ballot was conducted and an event was held in Toronto. Even though Tom Long had joined forces with Preston and they toured the country together in early July, it was not enough to pull off a win. Stockwell won with 64 per cent of the 118,487 votes cast. Preston gave a gracious speech and declared the decision to be unanimous. I went to a get-together with Preston's team and looked around the room at the people, many of whom I had known and loved for years. I realized that this was the end of an era, but knew that we would have to carry on with the mission that we had started out with so many years before. I went to Stockwell's celebration party. He hugged me and said, "Thank you, Deb. I need you on this team. I really need you." I replied, "I am here, Stock. I'll do all I can to help you."

CHAPTER 18

Up the River Without a Paddle: Election 2000

LEFT THE NEXT DAY FOR ALBERTA and sat beside an old Reform friend on the plane. We had both supported Preston and talked at length about what Stockwell's win would mean—not just for our party, but for the whole conservative movement in Canada. We were concerned that the image our party had been branded with over the years had just been reinforced. Now we would have to start all over again trying to negate the "extremist," "religious" and "hidden agenda" labels that we had fought so hard to shake for so many years. We couldn't help but feel that this weekend had put us back light-years. However, we knew that the members had spoken loudly and we would have to make the best of it. We had overcome many hurdles over the years and surely this would be no different.

I did not receive a call to tell me about any transition meetings or that I had been replaced as the caucus chairman (this was an elected position, but often an incoming leader would make it known that he wanted one of his leadership supporters to fill it). I was fully expecting that to happen, and to be replaced as deputy leader, because several of Stockwell's supporters would likely be in line for such positions and obviously would have his trust. Jason Kenney (Calgary Southeast) was Stockwell's man in charge of the transition team. Jason and I had always gotten along well, but he had seemed to hold a grudge against Preston and his leadership team. Nonetheless, I had heard nothing about the transition meetings that were going on in the few days after the leadership race. It was especially awkward for me, since I was still the leader of the Opposition because Stockwell was not a Member of Parliament. He was leader of the party but could not fill the role of leader of the Opposition until he got a seat. We were told that there would be a caucus meeting on Wednesday, July 12 in Ottawa. I flew down the day before, talked to Jason and discovered that I would be chairing the large rally that would be Stock's introduction to the Hill and the national media. It was held in Room 200 West Block, a very impressive, stately hall on the Hill. It bears memories of bygone days, with black marks all over the floor from Members and guests butting their cigarettes on the floor. Hard to believe, nowadays! This day the room was filled with caucus members, staff, spouses, guests and a hungry press corps anxious to see our new leader.

I got the crowd fired up and when I said, "Please welcome our new leader, Stockwell Day," the place went wild. It was like a rock concert. There was an exciting energy and I turned around to shake Stock's hand as he came in the back door behind the head table. He jumped up onto the stage and I said, "Welcome…you're on." He looked around and then said to me, "Who's that at the head table?" I glanced over and saw our caucus officers and then Wes McLeod, my caucus chairman assistant at the end. I told him who Wes was and that he was there to take the minutes, as he did every caucus. Stock replied, "I don't want any minutes taken at caucus meetings." It is one thing to think and say this, but the part I found so unbelievable was that the room was full of several hundred people at the moment chanting, "Stockwell! Stockwell!" I said quickly, "Maybe we could discuss this another time, but right now you are on!" He seemed to snap back into the correct realm at that moment and delivered an upbeat speech about his victory, thanking all the volunteers who had worked on all the leadership campaigns. He made a special point of telling everyone that he was "not proposing any gigantic shifts or changes" to staffing as often happens with a change of leader. The assembled crowd was assured that their jobs were safe and they should just carry on as usual because we must be ready for the election. There was a great cheer from the floor. He introduced his new chief of staff, Rod Love. Those of us from Alberta knew Rod well. He had been chief advisor to our premier, Ralph Klein, for some time. He was a smart strategist and tactician. He knew everybody and was known far and wide for his withering attacks on the media. It was not unusual for him to dress them down publicly and swear a blue streak at the same time. We Albertans were somewhat amused by the incongruity of Stockwell and Rod as a team.

During caucus several MPs voiced their concerns that Stock should try to get a seat as quickly as possible as Joe Clark had become the leader of the PCs in 1998 and had still not sought a seat, which almost made him look afraid to take on the challenge. Cliff Breitkreuz mused about stepping aside and having Stock run against Clark in a by-election in Yellowhead. This was Joe Clark's former seat, where Preston Manning had challenged him in the 1988 election. However, after some thought, Cliff declined because, although he, like all of us, had been legislated back into the MP pension plan, the bill had not yet received royal assent. Consequently, he would not be eligible to buy back his past years of service if he were not still a sitting MP. If he quit right now in the middle of the summer he would lose it all. When asked by Art Hanger if a person stepping aside would be permanent or until the next election, Stock replied, "The optimum would be someone who was not running again. Compensation would be an important part of this decision." After some discussions with Stock and Rod Love, Jim Hart (Okanagan-Coquihalla) offered to step aside. He and his wife, Melanie, had just had a new baby and he announced he would not be running again. When the government had offered an opt-in clause to the MP pension in 1998, Jim and three of our colleagues had bought back in. Thus, he would not be affected the way Cliff Breitkreuz would. I'd heard that he was offered the payment of his contributions to his MP pension for the duration of this Parliament and also the amount of salary he would make between this date and the election. I remember feeling troubled after hearing about the deal. In the span of a day, here were two things that did not sit well—Stock's desire to keep no records of meetings and a cloudy exit by one of our long-time MPs.

Lew and I took ten days to drive REFORM 1 home, hoping things were going smoothly with the transition. We went through the U.S. and quite enjoyed not hearing any Canadian news. That seemed like a good thing, because I was somewhat apprehensive about what we might hear next. We had a good break, swimming and relaxing many of the days we were on the road. When we arrived home, I was ready to hit the campaign trail for the by-election that was soon called for the riding of Okanagan-Coquihalla, to be held on September 11, 2000. Stockwell was acclaimed as our candidate and none of the other major parties contested it, a courtesy often afforded party leaders. I went to the riding for the end of the campaign and by-election night. His victory was a foregone conclusion, but there was still an air of excitement and a feeling of anticipation about the general election, which would likely be held within the next six to twelve months. I left the morning after Stockwell's win, September 12. I had no idea when I left town that this particular day would go down in history as one of the worst communications nightmares our party had ever seen. That night the "Sea-Doo Affair" hit the news. I did not know it was coming. Logan, Stock's son (who was given to the outrageous) had arranged for the rental, ride and ruckus that ensued. Stockwell had practiced up on the Sea-Doo on Lake Okanagan and then came roaring up on shore for his first press conference as the Leader of the Official Opposition, clad only in a wetsuit. For his age, Stock was in remarkably fine shape and looked the part of the Okanagan jetskier. He certainly fit in well with the constituency that was now his home. However, for the rest of the country this looked like a stunt beyond all stunts. To top it off, he suggested that the House of Commons should consider a four-day work week so MPs could be doing worthwhile things in their constituencies. As you can guess, to a family struggling to make ends meet, this "time in the constituency" looked like a whole lot more fun than they might be having. After a few questions, he jumped on again and roared across the lake, water spraying right out the back fifteen feet in the air. This left people all over the country wondering if they had just witnessed a leader or a lark. To this day, his name has been synonymous with that Sea-Doo. Ever since, many Canadians cannot see such a machine without picturing him with that plume of water spraying out behind him, looking like an enormous rooster's tail.

Somehow we got through that week and on September 18, Stock was sworn in as a Member of Parliament and Leader of the Official Opposition. In his first Question Period the next day, he demanded the government reduce gas taxes. The Liberals were ready for that one and read back his record of not cutting gas taxes in Alberta while treasurer. We knew they would use his past record against him and were not too concerned about their response. However, one thing our strategic team did not understand was Stockwell's announcement on his second day on the job, September 20, that he was not going to participate in the daily "scrums" after Question Period. Instead, he would go downstairs to the bottom floor to the Charles Lynch press theatre for a question-and-answer session with the press. This was preposterous, as the media had their cameras set up in the foyer to interview all the leaders and other MPs when they exited the House. It appeared to be incredibly self-centred. It was unworkable and impractical to move the press downstairs to interview Stockwell alone. Chrétien laughed and dubbed it the "whine cellar."

On September 25, Stockwell challenged the prime minister in Question Period to "either resign because he has no support over there or call an election based on his record of being the highest taxing leader in the G-7 countries." I was sitting right beside him and I was so stunned I was sure people would read my face. Not only were we wanting to get our platform ready and the leader more experienced, we were the party that advocated fixed election dates every four years. We were barely over three years into this Parliament, and now our leader was defying strategic advice and daring Chrétien to call an election. Our research and communications people were horrified as they watched this spectacle unfold. Jim Armour, who had been our director of communications for years, had been fired from the leader's office on August 17. Phil von Finckenstein, another long-time stalwart in our communications shop, replaced him. He'd tried to spare us the embarrassment of the Sea-Doo episode, the private press conference fiasco and the nightmare that ensued when Stockwell grandstanded with the election dare. I believe it was an impossible task.

It now seemed that all indications were pointing to a late fall election. Chrétien had loved seeing Stock swallow the bait and hinted that he was just following the wishes of the Official Opposition leader. On October 5, we launched our campaign platform in Kitchener, Ontario.

On October 19, Stock appeared on the Christian broadcast, *100 Huntley Street*. During the discussion, Stock said that he prays for misguided reporters. Now, granted, some reporters are misguided, as are some politicians, teachers, mechanics, pastors, etc. In my Chritstian life, I pray for many people, but I do not think it wise to appear above anyone else or sound superior. I am ever so grateful for other people who pray for me, but out of love and genuine concern, not because they are more "religious" or "right." The responsibility of a person of faith is to live in and amongst others, not on a higher plane. This comment gave more fuel to the fire for critics that thought Stock had a hidden agenda and was a fanatic. So, three days later when the writ was dropped on Sunday, October 22, Stock did not comment on it, saying that he would be in church with his family and would not be campaigning on Sundays. (Imagine the reaction of the press when he appeared on the Plains of Abraham for a photo op some weeks later on Sunday, November 12!) As a Christian, I also go to church every Sunday and consider it as a family day. However, there are times in the political realm when you have to comment or make the best use of an opportunity, and I believe the dropping of an election writ is one of those times. You need to jump out of the starting blocks looking as if you are prepared for the upcoming race. The other leaders were on the run, energized. This looked like Stock had dared the PM to call the election and then when he did, Stock was either unwilling or unready. We lost the first whole day in the media cycle and the chance for a good, positive message. Instead, we were in the cycle, but having to fight back against a negative stereotype. And so the campaign was off, not on the best foot, but off nonetheless. Unfortunately, the official kickoff the next day didn't go much better. The location was a high-tech company in Ottawa where Stock attacked the Liberals for encouraging the brain drain to the U.S. Because nobody had checked all the details and fine print, it was discovered that the company's president had in fact returned to Canada from the U.S. to launch the company. I was in Edmonton launching my own campaign and was so frustrated when I watched the news. It meant that I would need to do local interviews, trying to do damage control by attempting to explain what I thought was unexplainable, just because someone didn't do the necessary research. What happened the next day was even worse. Our campaign team had organized a well-planned photo op at the Thousand Islands border crossing south of Ottawa. It had been cleared by immigration officials and would have been professional and effective. At the last minute, Stock decided to use Niagara Falls as a symbol of the north-south flow of Canadian brainpower. This was a terrific idea, except for the fact that it simply was not true. A reporter pointed out that in fact the river flowed from south to north. Because the event was so hastily thrown together, one of Stock's staff had made a mistake about the flow of the river. Stock's response sent chills down my spine: "We will check the record. If somebody has wrongly informed me about the flow of this particular water, then I'll be having a pretty interesting discussion with them." I knew the moment I heard those words that Stockwell Day was not a leader. The mark of a true leader is to give credit to those under you when things go well and to take the blame yourself when things go wrong (and then have a private chat with staff to straighten out errors and impose discipline, if necessary). The immediate, public casting of blame on some poor staffer who had worked so hard to get the details right for the initial media event, then had it changed on the fly, is inexcusable and shows a complete lack of the true characteristics of a leader. I was sad that the campaign had got off to such a poor start. Surely it would get better. Stock was a good campaigner, energetic, photogenic and at ease with people. One weakness, however, was an inability to always stay on script. If he could just follow the platform and not freelance, I was optimistic that we would do well.

The debate over health care raged during the entire campaign. Our party has always been accused of having a hidden agenda of wanting a private, two-tier health-care system in Canada. This is a lie. It infuriates me to watch successive governments prattle away about being the protectors and saviours of universal health care. In fact, when public health care was introduced in 1965, the problem of how to pay for it was a huge issue. The federal government committed to fund health care 50/50 with the provinces. Over the years that number has been eroded so much that the provinces, which have the jurisdictional responsibility to administer the health-care system, have a crisis on their hands. The federal government, meanwhile, sits idly by claiming that they are living up to their full commitment while clearly they are not. Our health care system is not just two-tiered, it is multi-tiered and offers different benefits to different provinces. For instance, Alberta and B.C. residents pay premiums, other provinces do not. Some provinces offer basic dental benefits, others do not. Natives have different health care benefits from non-Natives. Members of Parliament have very different benefits from ordinary citizens. It infuriates me that we can't even open a dialogue about the shortcomings of the system without being branded "American two-tier private health care advocates." This is bizarre. With the aging population of the baby-boom generation, we need to have a serious dialogue about our system. It is simply unsustainable. Waiting lines are longer, technology and equipment are increasingly expensive and capable of keeping people alive far longer than in previous eras. Patients must be the first priority and they do not care a whole lot about how they get the care or who pays for it. They simply want to know that when they need medical care it will be there for them. Whatever we can do as legislators to still honour the *Canada Health Act* but work more efficiently within it and make front-line health-care professionals more able to do their jobs is essential. We cannot remain with the status quo, beating our chests claiming to be the great defenders when the system is just not working. Unfortunately, emotion and fear-mongering always take over and the necessary debate gets pushed off the operating table yet again.

During the campaign, Stockwell endorsed the idea of innovation in providing health care. In fact, my province of Alberta has been very innovative in trying to meet the needs of patients and we have paid the price of having Ottawa heap scorn upon us. After all, the administration of health care falls to the provinces. They are the ones that have to wrangle with waiting lines, budgets, MRIs and rising capital costs. It was little help when, during the leaders' debate on November 9, Stockwell held up a sign on national TV saying, "No two-tier health care." Besides looking tacky, it assumed that we did not have it in this country already. When people had heard so much negative stereotyping about our party's stand, it seemed foolish to reinforce the phrase "two-tier health care" again. Even though there was a "no" in front of it, people hardly noticed that. Messaging is so important. Perhaps it would have been better to go on the offensive, blaming past governments for living the lie of pretending we have truly universal health care when we know the reality is quite the opposite.

Another poorly handled area in the campaign was the use of referendums on particular issues of conscience, such as abortion. Our party has long advocated the use of referendums, held rarely and wisely. Citizens long to be included in the national debate of particular issues and given an opportunity to have their say. Proof of that was the referendum on the Charlottetown Accord; even though it was regarding a constitutional amendment, the principle was the same. The issue of referendums surfaced in the campaign and could have easily been dealt with. People want and deserve a say in the affairs of their nation and citizen assemblies could be set up to discuss and devise rules for such referendums—about what issues to put to a vote, when and how. Stockwell got on the defensive and seemed unable to push back hard enough with a good policy that could be adequately defended. Rick Mercer, of *This Hour Has 22 Minutes* fame, decided to have some fun with this one and conducted a referendum across Canada to get enough signatures to change Stockwell's name to Doris Day. He actually received more than 400,000 e-mail ballots, not a bad number for a gag. I thought it was hilarious and it could have been great publicity for us. Instead, Stock and the national campaign got angry and again were not able to push back. I had some fun with it in my local Edmonton North campaign. I tried to get a referendum going to try to change my name to "Dapple" Grey, but couldn't swing it. It became a complete non-issue. One of the problems in the national war room was that nobody was actually in charge. Rod Love was the campaign manager, but had left Ottawa in disgust soon after the campaign had started. He cited frustration with Stockwell's refusal to follow a well-thought-out strategic plan. Rod flew home to Calgary and basically sat the campaign out. Consequently people who had come from the camps of Reform, the PCs and the various leadership camps manned the war room. It became literally that: tensions were often high and the various factions had not been able to meld as a team. Because of those difficult relationships, our rapid-response capability was not what it should have been.

My local campaign went very well in Edmonton North. I felt reasonably confident that I would get re-elected. So, at the beginning of the writ period I offered my services to go and help out any other ridings that looked like they were in a close race. I told the national team that they should discuss it and send me somewhere strategically helpful. I got no response and kept calling and offering. After a couple of weeks, and six calls, my calendar filled up with all-candidates' debates and meetings in my own riding and I called one last time to say that I probably didn't have many free days now. I got a call back and was sent to Vancouver for a day, Victoria for a day, Charlottetown for an evening and Moncton for two days. The folks in Vancouver and Victoria didn't even know I was coming until I was in the air. I hadn't actually considered Charlottetown and Moncton to be hotbeds of Reform and Alliance activity. Nonetheless I enjoyed my time there and did what I could to help the local candidates. In hindsight I should have booked my own schedule and gone to Ontario to help some of the candidates whom I knew to be in tight races. I thought that Rod Love was still the campaign manager and had no idea that he had gone home to Calgary. If I had known that, I would have surely done my own thing. Perhaps it would have made a difference on election night, when we lost a couple of seats by just a few votes. Who will ever know?

Back in Edmonton, my opponents fired at me about the MP pension. The bill had received royal assent on September 22, so we were all paying our premiums as of that day. The issue was whether we would buy back our past years of service. We were given exactly one year from royal assent to make the decision. I discussed this openly in my campaign and told people that I would have to consider what to do. I thought it unfair to buy back my service immediately and protect myself, because I was a sitting MP. If the voters were going to use this as a referendum on my performance or my stand on the pension issue, they could decide what to do with me on election day. If they put me out of office, then I would not be able to buy back, as I had to be a sitting MP to do that. If they re-elected me, then it was not such a big issue for them and I would make my decision after that time. The issue came up at the all-candidates' forums and I addressed it the same way each time.

My volunteers, who always called themselves "Deb's Team," were pleased with our campaign. We had 7:00 A.M. strategy meetings to prepare for events and media opportunities. Our phoning teams were working hard and our GOTV plans were ready well before the actual election. In my two runs in Edmonton, my campaign manager, Brian Mulawka, came up with the idea of making a postcard with Lew and me on the front and a short message on the back. These worked really well. For the election on June 2, 1997, we took a picture of us in the park beside a lake. The message on the back was, "It's about hope. It's about trust. It's about time. Vote Reform." For this November 27, 2000, election we had a picture of Lew and me sitting on a hearth in front of a cozy fire. The message on the back was, "It's time for honesty and dedication. It's time for integrity and respect. It's time for Deborah Grey and the Canadian Alliance." Our volunteers had a huge blitz on the last weekend dropping one in each mailbox, totalling thirty-five to forty thousand. In '97, we all came back to the campaign headquarters and had a big barbeque for our many volunteers. On the day before the 2000 vote, a cold day in late November, we hosted a huge Grey Cup party at our campaign headquarters. It was great fun and the whole team enjoyed visiting with each other after a long writ period, and was also able to answer phones and pass out literature or information to anyone dropping by.

On November 27, 2000, election day, we anxiously awaited the results. I had wondered about the creation of the Canadian Alliance that was intended to deal with the vote-splitting between us and the PCs. Today we would know. All of our local campaign teams met at the Agricom at the fair grounds in Edmonton. There was an air of excitement as we watched the results start trickling in from back East. We didn't get any seats in the Atlantic provinces or Quebec, which did not surprise us. Ontario would be the bellwether of our years of work to create a true united alternative to the Liberals. When the votes were tallied, we had won two seats in the surrounding areas close to Ottawa, with Scott Reid (Lanark-Carleton) and Cheryl Gallant (Renfrew-Nipissing-Pembroke). We were pleased to gain those victories, but terribly disappointed that we had not done better. The Liberals took every other seat in Ontario, 101 out of 103. Ouch. As the results came in across the West, we fared better. We won 5 seats in Manitoba, 11 in Saskatchewan, 23 in Alberta and 27 in B.C. for a total of 66 seats. This was an overall increase, but we were still saddened by a campaign that had gone off-script more than it had been on and was more a legacy of missed opportunities. One of the saddest losses for me was our own Eric Lowther (Calgary Centre) who lost out to Joe Clark. Joe actively courted the gay vote and received other NDP and Liberal votes who joined with him against Lowther. This made me very sad because if Joe had not won that seat, the PCs would not have had official party status and would not have had their leader in the House with them. Instead, we lost a very valuable member of our team and the Tories had new life breathed into them. Another hard loss in Edmonton was our candidate, Betty Unger, who had run a great race against Anne McLellan (Edmonton West). In fact, CTV had declared Betty the winner on national TV; then the last polls came in and Anne squeaked out yet another win. There were all kinds of questions swirling around about busing in voters from outside the riding, keeping the polling station open late, scrutineers not being allowed to view the ballots and so on. But these are all difficult allegations to prove and the difference was large enough that an official recount was not ordered. I was pleased with my victory in Edmonton North, winning with 50 per cent of the vote, up from 44 per cent in 1997. The results were:

Deborah Grey, Canadian Alliance	22,063
Jim Jacuta, Liberal	14,786
Laurie Lang, NDP	3,216
Dean Sanduga, PC	3,010

The voters had spoken. Lew and I hashed over the whole pension stuff again, and I decided to talk to the comptroller when we went to Ottawa for our swearing in.

So, now we were sixty-six and many of the seventeen newcomers had not met the caucus. We all met in Ottawa for a couple of days in December. Stockwell named Ian Todd, Preston Manning's former aide, as his chief of staff. Rod Love and his sidekick, Hal Danchilla (from Edmonton and deputy Chief of Staff), had both resigned right after the election. Nobody was terribly surprised, but still a bit unsure of the reasons why. A Christmas party was held in the parliamentary restaurant as a celebration on December 13, after our swearing in and orientation sessions. It was good to see all of my old colleagues as well as meet the new ones. I knew one of our new Ontario MPs, Scott Reid, as he had been one of our researchers. I met Cheryl Gallant for the first time and found out that she had four girls, ages thirteen, eleven, nine and seven. There are several women in all parties who have young children. I do not criticize them; they have every bit as much right to be in Parliament as anyone else does. But no matter how much we might like it to be different, women are still the primary caregivers of our children. I serve with many women who have been in Parliament for years and they had young children when they arrived. Many men and women MPs live their parliamentary lives away from their children, missing birthdays, graduations and other important events. It somehow seems sadder to me when it is the woman away. I can't explain it and I know I get criticized for my view, but it just sits deep in my heart. Thank you to all the men and women who are primary caregivers while your partners serve in Parliament. I know how difficult it is to just be away from Lew during the week while I am in Ottawa. I would not have chosen this field if I had children at home. It would be too hard to come and go, missing all kinds of special events. Sadly, we do not get a replay of our children's growing-up years.

After our meetings, we all headed home to be with those special families who love us regardless of the fact that we are public officials and in the limelight so much of the time. Christmas is always a wonderful break because both parliamentary and riding offices shut down and the phones do not ring. We thought we could settle into a relaxing Christmas season. Instead, on December 21, word came down that Stockwell's lawsuit regarding Lorne Goddard was too complex to be heard by a jury. A judge alone would hear it. Within twenty-four hours, the province ordered an immediate settlement. Merry Christmas and Happy New Year, everyone!

CHAPTER 19

2001: Our Darkest Days

AFTER THREE FULL-BLOWN CAMPAIGNS IN ONE YEAR—the party referendum, the leadership race and the general election—everyone was literally exhausted. Lew and I booked time off to go to Cozumel, Mexico, early in January. We enjoyed two weeks swimming, snorkeling, scuba-diving and sleeping. We arrived home to the news on January 16 that Alberta had paid $800,000 to cover Stockwell's "Goddard" defamation suit. On the 18th, Stock apologized for the cost, but did not appear apologetic for the whole suit. He said during his press conference that he wouldn't "fake crocodile tears." Even if people agreed with the basis of Stockwell's original letter and sentiment, his attitude lost him more points than it gained him. Why is it so hard to say, and be, sorry for offending so many people with so few words? After that media storm hit, Stockwell and Valorie got away for a holiday in Mexico also. It was a good break for them, as they had just put in a frenetic year as well.

The 37th Parliament opened on January 29, 2001. We had a brief caucus that morning to prepare for the days ahead. I mentioned to Stockwell that the press had heard a rumour that I had bought back my service years for my pension. I told him this was true, and that I was prepared to address it with them, but thought I should give him a heads-up as it would likely turn into quite a story. Did it ever! The firestorm that arose was difficult to ride out. Although many of my colleagues had already bought back their past service (and all eventually did, with the exception of Preston Manning and Werner Schmidt from Kelowna), I was the poster girl for the pension because I was already vested—that is, I'd already reached my minimum six years to make me eligible to collect. I got pasted in the media and was labelled by Joe Clark as the "High Priestess of Hypocrisy." I was prepared to pay the price, but what surprised me the most was the virtual silence of my colleagues who quietly paid the required amount and let me get hammered day after day. I suppose it is easier to simply funnel in behind the water-skier and let her face the rough wake alone. I lost a lot of respect for those who seemed content to buy back, as I had done, but refused to step forward to face and share the accusations.

In late January and February, post-mortems were conducted across the country regarding the election. Riding presidents and campaign workers had discussions about what went right, what went wrong and how we could improve things for the next time. These were helpful meetings because this was a chance for the front-line workers to give input to the party leadership. I attended the Calgary and Edmonton meetings. In Calgary, one of the riding presidents stood up and said how hard so many people had worked on the campaign. He voiced concerns about the gaffes that occurred and thought we had not made use of all our good people. He then said in a loud voice, "Where the h-ll were Deb Grey and Preston Manning during the election? They should have been front and centre across the country. People know them and trust them. Why weren't they out there?" Stockwell stood up to the mike and replied, "You are absolutely right. And I am proud to say that Deb and Preston were a valuable part of our campaign. They were high-profile chief spokesmen and did a great job for us right across the country." He looked at me and smiled as he spoke. I could hardly believe my ears. I sat there, stunned. I wanted to stand up and yell to the crowd, "That is simply not true!" He sounded so convincing that I am sure many in the crowd thought they must have seen us on TV and just forgot in the interim. It was quite a lesson in crowd management, but one that made me feel heartsick.

At the beginning of the session, Chuck Strahl and I were in the leader's office for a meeting. Stock asked Chuck and me to remain in our roles as caucus officers, I as the deputy leader and Chuck as House leader. (I had been re-elected as caucus chairman at our December 13 caucus.) Jay Hill had been let go from his position as whip and John Reynolds replaced him. We reiterated our loyalty to the party and to him as the duly elected leader, and told him that we would do all we could to help him. He said he wanted absolute loyalty and then explained his definition and how it is perceived and communicated. A neutral statement of loyalty, as seen by the media, is considered lukewarm. A strong "over-the-top" expression would be viewed as merely neutral. Were we committed to the over-the-top expression of loyalty that he was asking? I, unsure what he was getting at, asked what that entailed (perhaps waving pom-poms like a cheerleader?). He responded that it meant "if I kill my grandmother with an axe, I want you to say, 'she had it coming.'" When you hear a really bad, inappropriate joke, you're not sure you actually heard it correctly or if anyone else thinks it is funny. Chuck and I left the room feeling somewhat sickened, hoping maybe it was a bad joke, but not quite able to convince ourselves of that. I am as loyal as a pup, but the first rule of loyalty, in my books, is, "you get 50 per cent automatically; the other 50 per cent, you have to earn." I was not able to blindly give 100 per cent immediately, especially the way it was being demanded. I also believe that if someone doesn't earn the second 50 per cent, then "slippage" starts to occur with the first 50 per cent.

Soon after the session started, Logan Day announced to some media that Stock's press secretary (who was Renee Fairweather) was about to be fired. This is always deplorable; surely whoever the person in question is, he or she deserves to hear such news in private, directly from the employer. The rumours were rampant, but in actual fact it was not Renee at all. It turned out to be our director of communications, Phil von Finckenstein. Phil had done the best he could, but was not given the authority to make decisions. Any advice he did give basically went unheeded. He was fired on February 6, only a few days into the new session. Right after that, I heard that Logan was making calls to various MPs, trying to solicit funds to "top up" salary demands by Ezra Levant to be hired as our new director of communications. Ezra was a long-time Reformer who was a very gifted communicator. He had come to work in the leader's office some years before, to "spice up" our Question Period team under Preston's leadership. Sometimes he got carried away with the "spice," straying from the hard, cold facts of the case, whatever it was at the time. He and Logan were best friends. Logan had left Ottawa for private life in Calgary, but still seemed quite involved in our affairs on the Hill. Aside from the fact that it was not acceptable to try to get around salary caps, I was frustrated by the way it was happening. I met with Stock on Valentine's Day and said, "You have every right to have Logan as one of your advisors, but I think he should show up in the chain of command somewhere, so nothing looks hidden or secret." Stock replied, "Thanks, Deb. I appreciate your advice. But trust me, although Logan is my son and of course I talk with him, he has absolutely nothing to do with our organization and is not involved in any way with calling MPs. The press is making it up." I left, feeling reassured that things were okay. That very evening, the whole thing blew wide open in the media. Diane Ablonczy and I were having supper at Yesterdays, close to the Hill. Stock called me on my cell and asked if I could come up to his office right away. It was then I heard that Logan had actually made some calls, but just "as a friend because he knows all these guys." I conveyed my concern to him about trying to do an end run around the press and us. It generally comes back to haunt you and this time it did. Nonetheless, Ezra began immediately as our director of communications and the first fire to be put out was his own hiring. His tenure would be short and explosive.

Within days of Ezra's arrival came word about a donation made by the Calgary law firm that had defended Stockwell in the Goddard lawsuit. It raised several eyebrows and naturally drew shrieks and howls about kickbacks. Apparently William Britton, a partner at Bennett Jones in Calgary (but with no personal involvement with Stockwell's defence) had made a contribution of $70,000 to the Canadian Alliance. However, the cheque was written not on his personal account but on the firm's account. This looked as if it might be a donation on behalf of someone else and, if it was, the party couldn't keep it. Glenn McMurray, our party's executive director, alerted the leader's office to this enormous donation. An investigation by the firm and members of our national council concluded that the donation was a personal one and should not have been written on the firm's account. Legally and technically the matter was cleared up, but politically it remained a hot potato. The easiest way to deal with the kickback charges would have been instructions from Stockwell himself to return the cheque. That did not happen. Worse, some of Stock's supporters on the national council tried to blame our national office staff. This was preposterous; they were the ones who sounded the alarm! When that didn't work to divert the media's attention, the old standby of blaming the "Manning-ites" on the council for conspiracy and leaking documents was tried. After that, the issue was declared "resolved." The money was kept and all that remained were more doubts and long shadows cast on the credibility of our party and our leader. At our priorities and planning meeting of senior caucus officers and a few chief critics (about a dozen people), there was a heated discussion about the Britton donation. Diane Ablonczy, during the course of the conversation said, "Ohhhhh," thinking about the potential long-term media attention. It was then she was challenged by Stockwell on the oath of loyalty. He repeated his "if I killed my grandmother with an axe, I want you to say 'she had it coming'" line. This was the second time I had heard it, and Diane's first. She was as shell-shocked as I had been. She challenged him and a heated discussion ensued. I remember looking over at Paul Wilson and watching the physical pain on his face. The same thing happened again to our shadow cabinet and the entire caucus over the next week or two.

By this time, it was almost impossible to put a good face on all of our problems. Relationships were fraying, morale was in the cellar and there was not much hope of a turnaround any time soon. On the heels of the Britton mess, Stockwell eventually apologized to Lorne Goddard on March 5. He said "Sorry," but it was noted that he did not look sorry. He took out a personal mortgage on his home for $60,000 to repay some of the $800,000 owing to Alberta under the Risk Management Fund. On the surface it looked as though we would be able to move forward. However, underlying the daily events was a current of mistrust and fear amongst the long-time employees. The frustrating part was that, on the surface, the comments were that everybody was a valued member of the team and nobody would lose their position. The reality was quite different. In January, Carolyn Stewart-Olsen, our press secretary, had been fired. Phil von Finckenstein had been let go in February. On March 6, Maureen McGrath, in our media monitoring office, resigned. Most of these people came down the hall to my office to tell me what had happened. It felt like my office had become a revolving door for so many that were either in tears or close to it. It got to be a pattern; Linda would come into my office and say, "So-and-so is here to see you." We would look at each other and know what it was about without even speaking. After Maureen came Sean McAdam, one of our long-time employees. Sean was a great guy who was very bright and capable and loved being part of the team. He worked hard and fought for basic Reform principles. He had been a candidate for us twice and was very committed to the cause. Sean had been working as our Question Period coordinator for some time. On March 7, he came through my office door to tell me he was resigning. I was very sad to see him go. He would be difficult to replace. The next one was also a huge blow. Paul Wilson, our director of research, handed in his notice on March 15. This would leave an enormous hole in our organization. Paul and his team of researchers had done such a great job of hunting down information on the HRD scandal and Shawinigate. That same day Chris Froggatt, another long-time employee, came to tell me he was resigning. His case was particularly disturbing as he was the victim of a whisper campaign insinuating that he was leaking documents and information from the leader's office.

Meanwhile, our caucus was also concerned over many other issues. Members called for a full-blown retreat to discuss some of the crises surrounding the leader and our whole situation. Frustration was palpable with Stock's relationship with the press, staff and the caucus. I tried and tried to bring it up at our priorities and planning meetings, but it did not seem at all urgent. We set a date for April 3 at a restaurant several blocks from the Hill. Every time I suggested working on an agenda, it got pushed aside.

Chuck Strahl told me that he had been invited to Stornoway and the caucus retreat was discussed. He asked why I wasn't present; as caucus chairman I needed to be there to discuss strategy and plan the agenda. He was told that I hadn't been invited. Terence Kowalchuk, the leader's assistant, told me later that it was just an oversight. Whichever it was I could handle, but getting told two stories and expected to believe them both was a bit of a stretch. Another incident I had with Terence was regarding the election post-mortem that was scheduled in Edmonton. The date had been picked and the place booked for late February. Terence told me that the date had been changed because the provincial election was underway. He said that the strategic thinking was not to mix federal politics with provincial, so the date was postponed to March 24. I accepted his explanation, but later heard from someone who was involved in the organization that Ralph Klein and the provincial PCs did not want Stockwell anywhere near Alberta during the election, as it would bring up the touchy subject of the $800,000 lawsuit cost. I felt bad for Terence; maybe he had no idea either. I suspect that I will never know the whole story.

In mid-March, we got embroiled in another grand mess. News came out on Saturday, March 17, that Rahim Jaffer (Edmonton Strathcona) had his assistant, Matthew Johnston, do a radio interview claiming to be Rahim. A listener called in and said that it was not Rahim's voice, but his staffer's. The station called back and asked if Rahim did the interview. He lied and answered "Yes." Ezra was in charge of dealing with the media plan. When Rahim flew into town and worked on the strategy with Ezra, it appeared that Matthew had acted entirely on his own. However, it turned out that, in fact, Rahim had been fully aware of what Matthew was doing. Chuck begged Ezra, Rahim and Stockwell to tell the truth and nothing else. If they didn't, it would surely come back to haunt us once again. On March 20, Rahim rose in the House and apologized to the talk show, his family, caucus and constituents. On the heels of this episode came the postponed post-mortem in Edmonton—what a fun go-around that was. It addressed the same frustration over the lack of use of Preston and me in the campaign, as well as Rahim's antics.

Back in the House, we were still putting the pressure on the Liberals regarding Shawinigate. Ezra thought we needed to spice up the story a bit. His specialty was "torque." I thought we already had plenty of torque and what we needed was a hard-hitting attack backed up by solid ammunition. We relied on our researchers to find the best information and facts. This would be tough as Paul Wilson, our director of research, was leaving at the end of March and morale was low. However, they were a professional bunch and did their best. On March 26, another employee of the leader's office, Kory Tenneycke, resigned. I wondered who or what might be next in our long saga of difficulties.

The long-awaited caucus strategic weekend retreat—which had been shortened down to a weekday retreat and then to a supper meeting off the Hill—finally took place on April 3. Chuck had been invited to Stornoway again with a small group and they drew up the agenda. I had virtually no input, but chaired the actual event. It was an evening of platitudes and glossing over our fundamental problems of communication and lack of truthfulness. By the end of the evening there was frustration with the leader for not wanting to get to the root of the problems. Nobody felt that his or her concerns had actually been addressed, sad to say.

I headed home to the riding, feeling somewhat discouraged. However, all was not lost. I had found a new motorcycle and bought it the previous week! On Saturday morning, Lew and I drove our truck out to the seller's acreage to pick it up. I was surprised when my cell phone rang that morning of April 7. Nobody knew my cell number except my family and a few friends. Imagine my surprise when I discovered it was a reporter from the CBC, asking what I knew about the "spy." At first I didn't know what to think; I thought it was a pal playing an April Fool's joke on me. I laughed and said, "Don't know anything about a spy. All I know is that I love my new bike that I'm picking up." The reporter asked if I had seen the *Globe and Mail* yet. I had not. When I got back to the city I picked up a copy of the *Globe* and groaned as I read it. The report said that Stockwell had approved hiring a spy to investigate some of the Shawinigan shenanigans. That afternoon, Stockwell denied that he hired the spy but said he had met with him. On April 8, Stockwell announced that he had not, in fact, met the spy. The next day, April 9, Stock announced that no job offer had been made to the spy, but that he had met him. This all arose through two of our MPs,

Myron Thompson (Wild Rose) and Darrel Stinson (Okanagan-Shuswap). An inseparable pair who have done investigative work into gangs and crime, they operate a bit like Frick and Frack. They, complete with cowboy hats, made it clear that they and the spy had met with Stockwell to get some sleuthing done. Two days later (during which time they were both nowhere to be found) their story changed again and they said they had not met with the man. Renee Fairweather, our press secretary, resigned on April 9, amidst the spy saga. The so-called "spy" turned out to be a Mr. James Leigh, who supposedly lived undercover, but conducted interviews and sent e-mails to several members of our caucus. Leigh, who met with our party officials, claimed that he had been hired to investigate "Preston supporters" as well. I remember going to bed that night wondering when all this foolishness would end. Sadly, I had no idea that it was only beginning.

On April 10, Stockwell accused a Quebec judge, Justice Joel Silcoff, of being in a conflict of interest after approving a search-and-seizure order on the home of Francois Beaudoin, the former head of the Business Development Bank. This was the same Beaudoin that Chrétien had talked into giving a loan to Yvon Duhaime at the Auberge Grand-Mère. Beaudoin's employment had been terminated in October 1999. Judge Silcoff had recently been appointed to the bench in June 2000. Before his appointment, he had been a partner for the law firm that represented the Grand-Mère Golf Club. It did raise eyebrows that this could be a possible conflict of interest. The media became suspicious and started sniffing around, trying to find more evidence of a cover-up. Instead of continuing to ask hard, solid questions about it all, Stockwell and Ezra opted for the "torque." Between them, they decided that the search-and-seizure order should be overturned and that the Alliance would file a complaint to the Canadian Judicial Council concerning Silcoff's conflict of interest. Instantly the media focus switched from Shawinigate to Stockwell. Instead of hammering the daylights out of the government, here we were, on the defensive again. Rumour had it that the judge was considering suing Stockwell and the Alliance. You might think Stock would know enough by now to steer clear of such activities, but it was questionable if any lessons had been learned from the

Goddard suit. Chuck Strahl, our member on the Board of Internal Economy, was told that Stockwell would not have any legal costs covered by the House of Commons budget. Ian Todd, chief of staff, flatly refused to proceed with any legal action. John Reynolds, our whip, tried to assure the press that nobody meant any offense and all was well. Another golden opportunity was lost to stay on the offensive. More media stories focused on us and our poll numbers were sinking fast, reflecting the public's opinion of our "Three Stooges" performance as the Official Opposition.

Thankfully, Lew and I flew to Taiwan on April 11 for an international women's conference. This was a most welcome break, as things were so crazy at home. We had a very wonderful trip, meeting international representatives and Taiwanese government officials. A highlight was meeting the vice president, Annette Lu. She had been imprisoned for several years in 1979 for giving speeches about democracy. Now, not many years later, here she was serving as the second-in-command. Wow. What an amazing woman. I enjoyed meeting with her and was awed by her resolve to continue pushing other countries to recognize Taiwan as a country independent from Mainland China. We also enjoyed touring industrial manufacturing plants, seeing how technologically advanced Taiwan was. It was also fascinating to experience a completely different culture. The density of population was overwhelming for us. We learned that there were approximately 600,000 scooters in Taipei, a city with a population of about three million. It was amazing to watch them all weave in and out of traffic. We did not witness one accident, much to our surprise. The maximum size of scooter allowed in the city was 150cc. I wondered how I would ever manage there on my 1200cc!

Observing the people and their style of life was fascinating as well. Our young host Henry and his wife could have purchased a very small apartment for a million dollars on their middle-class salaries. They were torn between that and living more modestly, saving money for their future children's education. And speaking of children: one day, while wandering through the Chiang Kai-Shek memorial, we passed a group of little kindergarten kids. They all had turquoise and yellow shirts on and were walking single file. When we went past them, we said "Hi." They beamed and said, practicing their English, "Hello. Good morning. Give me five." We laughed right out loud. They were so cute! Home seemed far away. I enjoyed every day, dreading what would happen next once we got there.

We arrived home on April 18, with the judge affair still in the news. I think the leader's office wanted to divert attention from the spy affair. They did it in spades with this one! I flew back to Ottawa on Sunday, April 22, and the next morning I attended a Question Period strategy meeting, the leader's strategy conference call and a full shadow-cabinet meeting. They were all difficult meetings because things kept getting worse rather than better. I did not like the direction the communications strategies were taking. It seemed that the press was being blamed for our woes and not us. Ian Todd showed up at my office mid-morning, asking to see me. Linda and I looked at each other, wondering if this would be another "visit" similar to so many we had already had. Ian sat down, sighed and said "Deb, I just pulled the plug." I couldn't believe my ears. Ian's last straw was being told to initiate legal proceedings in the Silcoff affair. He could not do it. I found out a few details about what was going on behind the scenes and realized it was worse than anyone had imagined. He had worked so hard to keep order, do things properly, encourage the staff and further the cause of the Alliance. But I knew how difficult it had been and realized this was the end. I couldn't stand it any longer, either. I was determined to talk to Stockwell as soon as I could. That chance came at 3:00 P.M., right after Question Period. He was on his way to speak at Kingston. I asked him when he was leaving and he said, "Right away. Is there something you need before I leave?" I replied that I could talk to him when he returned, but that it should probably be soon. He said, "Go ahead. What is it, Deb?" So there we sat, right in our seats side by side in the House of Commons, with the galleries full of people. I said, "Stock, I want to let you know that I am stepping down as your deputy leader. I cannot go along with some of your decisions and I look complicit. I won't mention this to anyone and we can have a discussion in caucus on Wednesday and come up with a communications plan." He responded, "I'm sorry to hear that, Deb. Maybe it is best, though. We'll talk about it on Wednesday." I felt relieved that I could now just move to another role in the caucus and not have to be so up-front about defending his actions and words. It surprised me to find out that Chuck had done exactly the same thing earlier in the day. It was interesting that our breaking points came at precisely the same time, unbeknownst to each other. Enough was enough. Neither of us could live the lie anymore.

I went back to my office and then Diane and I went for an early supper to get off the Hill. Soon her phone started ringing. The national press gallery had been told of our discussion and a feeding frenzy began, with reporters eager to get the scoop. I lay low that night and did not go back to the office as I usually did. My phone rang at 2:20 A.M. CTV had called Diane trying to find a number for me. She didn't give it to them. Next they phoned my assistant Linda and woke her up looking for me. She called me and said they were trying to find me. I called them and told them I was not prepared to go on "Canada AM." I was wild. I'd kept my end of the bargain about not telling the press about our so-called "confidential" discussion. Why hadn't he? The morning news broke the story. Reporters were camped out trying to find me for a comment. My policy had always been to say, "We are having a family discussion and it will stay at the family table." I tried that for the entire day, but it was impossible. On Tuesday, Grant McNally, our deputy house leader, stepped down also. Art Hanger (Calgary Northeast) and Val Meredith (South Surrey-White Rock-Langley) said publicly that Stockwell should resign. Caucus on Wednesday, April 25, was brutal. The first item of business was to replace me as the caucus chairman. Randy White was elected. Dick Harris was appointed whip and John Reynolds took over as House leader, replacing Chuck. Grant Hill was named deputy leader. Stock had asked him to fill this role out in the hallway on the way into caucus. Ted Morton, one of our Senators-in-waiting, was named director of research. Several people spoke up asking about the way this was made public. I certainly wanted an answer to that question as well. Some wanted Stock to resign immediately, and others wanted to see us thrown out immediately. It was heartbreaking for everyone. So many of us had worked for so many years to get to this point. It seemed that the whole thing might slip through our fingers that very day. Art Hanger suggested that Stock had better come up with a strategic plan by the next week so that we all knew where we were headed and why, or else he should resign. On Thursday, Stockwell dumped Art Hanger (Calgary Northeast) from his position as defence critic and also Gary Lunn (Saanich-Gulf Islands) was relieved of his critic responsibilities for being sympathetic to Art's concerns. On Friday, April 27, I was moved out of my office in the Centre Block to the Confederation Building and remained there for the rest of my parliamentary career. I flew home that same day and wanted nothing more than to be in the safety of Lew's arms after the most difficult week of my elected life to date. We went underground for the weekend and although the press was still trying to track me, I did no interviews.

I returned to Ottawa on Monday and tried to resume my normal routine. Stock was given an ultimatum by the caucus to come up with an overall strategic plan. I was looking forward to seeing that in caucus on Wednesday. On Tuesday, May 1, Preston Manning was moved out of his Centre Block office to the West Block, a move that was neither necessary nor ever explained. Lew had purchased a motorcycle from some friends in Kemptville, approximately an hour south of Ottawa. I needed to pick it up, so I asked Grant McNally if he would like to drive out with me in REFORM 1 and drive the truck home while I rode the bike. It was the best thing we could have done. Getting away from the Hill was terrific. We felt like a couple of kids playing hooky from Question Period. Not bad for a pair of schoolteachers who knew plenty about hooky! We stopped and had a hamburger at the Dairy Queen and drove out to the country. It was so good to get on the bike and clear my head in the breeze. I would be grateful to take the odd cruise in the upcoming days just to get away from the feeding frenzy of the press. But I was hopeful that things would improve. After all, Stock would be making a presentation the next day in caucus and surely things would improve after he realized the seriousness of the situation.

Wednesday morning arrived and I hoped we were going to be able to move beyond the last disastrous week. I went in to caucus with my usual "having a family discussion" line. The whole caucus waited for the leader to make his pitch. We all wanted this to work and improve our situation. At the beginning we were all told to turn off any tape recorders. This was bizarre. I had chaired the caucus for many years and never did I mistrust anyone and assume the meeting was being taped. This did not convince me that things were going to get any better. However, I still was cautiously optimistic that we had reached a turning point in the crisis. When Stockwell started to speak, I could hardly believe my ears. He began his "now or never" speech by saying, "I am a conservative." He then went on to talk about what a great country we have and why we should be the government. I felt like an ordinary citizen who had been taken by a friend to a political meeting against my wishes. I sat uncomfortably as Stockwell began to give a campaign-style election speech. He spoke of his heart's desire to see us as government, being a family man, knowing the value of a team, being a populist, being an open and inclusive leader, then proceeded to talk about Canada. He used a "light" motif, including everything from lighthouses to northern lights to lanterns to fibre-optics to describe Canadians and our accomplishments. And with that, he sat down.

There was stunned silence in the room. No one was quite sure what to say or where to start. Randy, the new chairman, introduced Dimitri, our pollster, who, along with Tom Jarmyn, Stock's new strategy person, gave a PowerPoint presentation that dealt with nothing more than election readiness. Why we were discussing this at all was a mystery; we had just come through an election and the next one would be at least three years away. They mentioned democracy, issues, wedges that could be used, the profile of the leader and our critics. And that was it. They then moved on to talk about staffing the leader's office, strategy and feedback groups, and the leader's upcoming tour of the country. Not one word about the crisis that we faced. Not one word about the spy, Rahim's radio lie, the judge. Stock had completely missed the point. We were not there as constituents to be persuaded of the merits of voting for the Alliance. We were colleagues who were desperate to see a leader lead. During the question and comment time, several MPs stood up and said this was no strategic plan at all, that Stockwell had lost the confidence of the caucus and should step aside. None of the questions they raised was actually addressed. Finally Jim Pankiw, our straightforward MP from Saskatoon Humboldt, got up and said, "What's going on here? That presentation didn't even touch on the problems we identified last week." Sadly, that question was ignored as well and we were told that we had to give unanimous approval to the "strategic plan" that had been presented. Art Hanger exploded and said he would do no such thing. He demanded Stockwell's resignation again. Shortly thereafter, a communications person came in the room with a prepared press release ready to go out, stating that "caucus gives unanimous support for the strategic plan." This touched off another firestorm and many MPs refused to give their endorsement. Val Meredith said that we had not even had a chance to read the document fully. A vote was taken and carried that caucus would be given the time to read it, discuss it and vote on it the next week. Nonetheless, Stock went out to the press after caucus and made this statement: "I am pleased to announce that the Canadian Alliance Members of Parliament unanimously endorsed the steps outlined in a strategic plan presented this morning."

I could hardly think straight when I left the room. What if one of the reporters asked me the simple question, "Is that true, Deb?" I was sick, wondering what I would say if they did. I thought of what Jordi Morgan, one of our communications team, said, "Never lie, never fudge, never guess." I knew what I would have to say if I got cornered. This was a dilemma, because I would be attacked for being a "dissident," as we were already being labelled. What a predicament. The saddest part was that Stock was continually making errors in judgment and then covering his tracks by issuing dishonest communications. This was another of a long string of events that proved it. I knew there would be a terrible price to pay for being a truth-teller, but I had no choice. I could not just gloss it over as so many often try to do.

The price started exacting itself with a group of people who began targeting my constituency with nasty messages, using a telephone with an automatic dialer. The first week in May people phoned my office, furious about the calls they were getting. My assistant, Averil Grant, was a tremendous help during those difficult days. My riding association filed a complaint with the National Office, but nothing came of it. My constituency board was very supportive of me and I kept them abreast of everything that was going on in caucus.

After the explosive "unanimous endorsement" caucus, Art Hanger again called publicly for Stockwell to resign. He was immediately suspended from caucus. On May 6, Gary Lunn did the same and faced the same fate. On May 7, there was another flare-up. Stockwell gave a speech to the Canadian Jewish Congress in which he blamed the Palestinians for the Middle East crisis. Monte Solberg (Medicine Hat), our foreign affairs critic, knew absolutely nothing about the speech or the position Stockwell was taking. The National Council on Canada-Arab Relations denounced his comments and threatened a lawsuit. Days later, Stock backtracked and offered an apology of sorts in the House. Consequently he had now offended and alienated both groups. Stock carried on as if nothing had happened and left Monte holding the bag, trying to repair the damaged relationships.

The May 9 caucus was just as explosive as the one before it. However, at this one, after many agonizing comments from much of the caucus Randy White said, "Support the leader or get the h-ll out of this caucus." This was a pretty clear ultimatum. Those of us who raised concerns were hardly trying to cause trouble. We were only trying to address the root causes of the trouble we were already in. But some refused to listen. The next week, May 15, a group of eight MPs held a press conference voicing their concerns about the situation. They were an impressive bunch. Among them were several members of the Class of 1993. One was Jay Hill (Peace River-Prince George), who had run in the 1988 election and was as faithful to the Reform cause as anyone I have ever met. He was a no-nonsense kind of guy and did not appreciate anyone trying to hoodwink him. Also there was Val Meredith (South Surrey-White Rock-Langley), another first-generation Reformer. Stockwell's group always referred to us "dissidents" as "Manning-ites," but Val had been a staunch supporter of Tom Long in the leadership race. She had run for us in '88 as well, and been a member of our National Council. Chuck Strahl (Fraser Valley East) was a senior member of our caucus and had given strategic guidance to caucus and the party over many years. He was also a committed Christian and agonized over the dishonesty that he saw in the leader's circle. Another straightforward guy was Art Hanger (Calgary Northeast). Art had long been a detective with the

Calgary City Police. He was rough, tough and afraid of nothing. He could smell a con job from quite a distance. Jim Gouk (Kootenay-Revelstoke) had voiced concerns but felt that nothing was being addressed at the root. Three members of the group had been elected in the Class of 1997, including Jim Pankiw (Saskatoon-Humboldt), who was black-and-white about everything. He never shied away from a controversy and wanted no part of tinkering with symptoms. He wanted the root causes dealt with. Grant McNally (Dewdney-Allouette) was a sensitive guy who had been through his own personal trials. His son Graydon had been diagnosed with leukemia and he was not well. Grant had that to deal with and this pain was almost more than he could bear. And Gary Lunn (Saanich-Gulf Islands) was the one who had supported Art Hanger in calling on Stock to resign in late April. I had been invited to join them, but I felt I should stay in the caucus as long as I could. For one thing, I hated to leave. For another, with my history as the first Reformer, it would be seen as an enormous indicator of what the true situation was. Everyone knew it was bad, but "if Deb Grey left, it would be huge." At the press conference, Chuck was the spokesman. He read this statement, "Today, a few more of us have made the difficult decision to speak out about one of the major impediments to fulfilling [the Alliance] dream, which is the leadership of the Alliance itself. We realize that by speaking out, there are implications, including the fact that we will be suspended from caucus. But we are convinced that over the past few months the current leadership has exercised consistently bad judgment, dishonest communications and lack of fidelity to our party's policies. Since we do not want to be associated with such practices, we have chosen to speak out today in an effort to bring about change." Ezra took great exception to this and immediately threatened to sue Chuck. He issued a letter that, true to form, went completely over the top. Stockwell did not reel him in and ask him to withdraw the letter. However, some of Stock's staff and supporters realized this was ridiculous and that Ezra's time had expired. He resigned on May 17, three months and three days after his arrival.

During this time a group was formed, calling itself "Grassroots for Day," under the leadership of George Bears, a man from Calgary. The group was very supportive of Stock and issued statements to that effect. When asked about them, Stock said that he was grateful and mentioned they could say whatever they liked as long as it was "positive and respectful." They mobilized and targeted Bob Mills's annual meeting in Red Deer on the weekend of May 18. He represented the federal riding that Stockwell had provincially. He was having great difficulty in supporting Stock and this made things difficult because many of his own supporters had supported Stock as well. Several people showed up at his meeting. They were not allowed in, so they stayed outside, causing a disturbance. The *Edmonton Journal* published a big splash about what had happened and in it the Grassroots for Day bunch said that they would be targeting my town hall meeting the upcoming Tuesday night, May 22. I thought about cancelling it because I knew it would turn into a brouhaha. But then I got angry thinking that if I did that, the constituents of Edmonton North would be short-changed and G4D would claim victory. So I went ahead with it. What a night! There were at least 250 people there, some wearing masks, some handing out buttons, many being very disruptive. Several of the national media outlets were in attendance and the meeting was covered live. Several of the G4D conducted media interviews at the back of the hall, out in the foyer and outside on the grounds. Peter Schalin, a real estate agent and the son of my board member Garry, was their chief spokesman. He held court with the media for most of the evening. At the actual meeting, I held my own, but it was nothing more than a circus and a publicity stunt. When Stock was asked about it, he said that he thought they had been "positive and respectful."

The next weekend was a meeting of our national council in Calgary. I was a member of the council because I was on the transition team when the Alliance was formed. This was sure to be a live-wire weekend. And it was. They spent the first part of the Friday meeting venting, expressing frustrations with all that had gone on. They then went on to talk at length about reconciliation and how we could achieve that. Right on the heels of that long discussion came a vote to throw Rick Anderson off the council. I believe that Rick was the best strategic thinker our party had ever seen, in fact one of the best in the entire country. He was terrific at issues management, foreseeing difficulties and devising a strategic plan that would, if followed, see our party make great gains. And we had; because of his strategic thinking and that of Cliff Fryers, our party had grown in the '93 and '97 elections, and they had both been extremely instrumental in the birth of the Canadian Alliance. Rick had predicted that the "freedom train" Stockwell had talked about so much during his leadership run would eventually have a wreck. He was bang on. Rick always called things as he saw them. And given my many years of working with him, I realized he saw them pretty clearly. On this Friday, May 25, pandemonium erupted after Rick was expelled from our national council. It degenerated into a shouting match in the corridor at coffee break.

I was so distressed by the fiasco, I went out the back door, found a staff person in the hallway and asked her to show me to the freight elevator. She put me on it and I went straight down to the parking lot and left town. I phoned the hotel and checked out, then drove straight home to Edmonton. That night on the news I was quoted as saying that it felt like witnessing a lynch mob in the meeting. When I flew back to Ottawa, the media was swarming the airport and accosted me upon my arrival. Somehow I staggered through the scrum and reiterated my concern about the lynch-mob mentality.

The months of April and May had taken a huge toll. I had hardly slept. Every night I would lie awake in bed, thinking that the worst must be over. And yet, the next day something horrible would happen. I am a "tomorrow person," always optimistic that things will get better. I tried to encourage myself that this would pass and the caucus and party would come out stronger. In reality, however, it did not seem possible. Soon, a "Yes" committee was struck by several individuals to try to make sure the leadership review passed at the next Assembly, scheduled for April of the following year. People were mobilizing to get our party back on track.

In early June, the annual staff and media barbeque was held at Stornoway. This year the party took place, but the next night, the media event was abruptly cancelled. The leader's office issued a press release saying that the leader had to cancel the event and go to be with his father who was in critical condition at a Calgary hospital. Within an hour, another press release was issued with a correction. In fact, Mr. Day Senior was in critical condition, but in an Edmonton hospital. The press were suspicious. Anne Dawson, from the *Ottawa Sun,* called out to Grande Prairie, Alberta to the senior Stockwell Day's home. He answered the phone! She told him the story and he responded, "Oh, I was in as a day patient here in Grande Prairie, but I'm home now." This touched off another furor in the news. Stock and Jason Kenney blasted the press, referring to Dawson as a "scumbag." I'm not sure what this was supposed to prove. She had not told a lie; she had made a phone call. Once again I realized that until the root was dealt with the symptoms would never change. I went for a long motorcycle ride that evening, thinking that was the best thing I could do with my time and my broken heart.

On June 2, Chuck Strahl received an e-mail with the following text:

From: **stocksangel**
To: **chuckstrahl**
Subject: Treason

I know where you and your backstabber friends live because
I have the membership lists for your area, Duncan [Chuck's
riding president]. Knowing that I invite you to speculate as to
what I might do with that information. The possibilities are
very interesting (family, etc). I won't make any direct threats,
I don't think I have to.
Stop trying to destroy Stock! You have been warned!

Grassroots for Day

Chuck showed this message to me on June 5 and it caused us both great concern. Surely this was escalating past the point of political discourse and disagreement. I was afraid of what might happen next. That afternoon I did an interview with Don Newman on the CBC *Politics* show. He asked, "Will you be working on the 'Yes' committee to call for a review of the leadership and a leadership vote?" I responded, "Yes, I will…the 'No' side certainly seems active right now. The G4D bunch (who) swamped my meeting have done some miserable demon-dialing in my constituency and Stockwell said he goes along with these folks as long as they keep it 'positive and respectful.' Well, showing up and swamping meetings or causing a disturbance outside Bob Mills's meeting or running radio ads against Chuck Strahl…. Today an e-mail came out to Chuck from G4D, saying 'we know where you live and your family.' This is out of control, Don, and if that's what the 'No' side is up to, you can guess that people are going to get involved in the 'Yes' side." Forty-eight hours later I heard on the CTV "National News" that G4D, in the name of "George Bears et al v. Deborah Grey," had filed a lawsuit at the Alberta Court of Queen's Bench against me. They were demanding $450,000 for defamation of character on behalf of all members of G4D because of my comments in the Don Newman interview. They claimed that G4D had no idea who the sender of the e-mail was, and that he was not a member of their group. All I knew was what the e-mail said. It was up to them to figure out if he was a member of their group or not. Again, I wondered whatever could be coming next.

Lew came down to Ottawa so we could drive his new motorcycle and REFORM 1 home for the summer. The House hadn't recessed yet for the summer but it was pointless to stay around. We headed out on June 13 and drove to Toronto to stay for a couple of nights with some friends. It was peaceful and we did not watch the news to see what new disaster had occurred.

On June 14, Stockwell gave a speech to the Empire Club in Toronto about conservatism and how we needed to work together. Much of the speech denounced Joe Clark and his attitude toward the Alliance. He then announced that our national council (which had nearly eaten itself whole only two weeks before) would set up a "Dialogue Group" that would form a "Unity Committee," and then a party referendum would be held to give the Unity Committee a mandate to enter formal negotiations with the PCs. This seemed a bit much. Over the last few months there had been casual supper meetings between various members of the two caucuses, but it was hardly dating time, let alone the moment for an offer of marriage. I likened Stock's announcement to a groom proposing to someone, but not exactly in the form of a question: "I have just kicked the slats out from under you, sweetheart, but now I am going to marry you, you lucky thing!" Surely this was not the way to win someone's heart. The reaction was swift and uncharitable. The "bride-to-be" was not receptive to the advances of her suitor. Stock's comments would get their backs up like nothing else could. Nobody in our caucus knew this was coming. He had freelanced the whole speech and taken the caucus and the party by surprise. Instead of bringing the two sides closer, he had made them both furious. I soon heard that Monte Solberg had left the caucus because of his frustration with Stock over his May 7 speech to the Canadian Jewish Congress and the divide this speech would create with the PCs.

It felt so good to cross the border into the U.S. We would be spared any Canadian news, and could try to forget the whole sorry spring for a few days. By the time Lew and I got back into Canada, Brian Fitzpatrick (Prince Albert) and Andy Burton (Skeena) had joined the group. This was significant because these two were rookie MPs from the Class of 2000.

We arrived home on June 25 and I had a busy week with constituency business, meetings and events. I wanted to have a personal chat with Peter Schalin and a pal of his, Roy Beyer, who was involved with the Canada Family Action Coalition, which had been instrumental in forming the group "Families for Day" in the leadership race. I had known them both for some years and wanted to tell them a few details in order to let them know a bit about what was going on. They were both considered to be influential in the Christian community and I thought they could benefit from having some behind-the-scenes information. Interestingly, on the day of their visit, June 28, I received an anonymous phone call from a woman who had been sitting in the booth next to them both at lunch the day before. She told me she didn't pay much attention to politics, but that she had heard my name before. At the Red Lobster she had overheard the two of them strategizing about their visit to my office the next day. I was very amused and grateful for her call. I was ready for their visit at 1:30 that afternoon. I told them about some of the errors in judgment that had occurred and the disturbing trend of covering them over, using dishonest communications. I discussed money and lawsuits (bearing in mind, of course, that I was the defendant in Schalin's lawsuit against me as he was a member of G4D, allegedly getting information from my board meetings from his father, Garry, one of my directors). I then asked them a few questions about their G4D lawsuit against me. Did they know what I had actually said on Don Newman's show that was the basis for their defamation suit? "Well, no. We just assume that George Bears does." "But," I replied, "Peter, you are a member of G4D. You are a plaintiff. You need to know what I actually said if you are suing me." He admitted that he had not seen the tape nor read the transcript. I told them that I had a video of it and invited them into the boardroom for a showing and popcorn. They declined, as they seemed in quite a rush to leave. I wished them well and smiled as I watched them hurry out of the building.

The next day I had a meeting with my lawyer, Fred Kozak, who would be representing me in the defamation case. I felt comfortable with him and his articling student, Paul Eastwood. They assured me that they thought the case would go okay, even though it might take a while and get messy. Sad to say, I now understood "messy."

A couple of days later, I celebrated my 49th birthday on July 1. The present situation was so troubling that it was a nice diversion to have friends and family over for a barbeque and enjoy a gorgeous summer evening. I had witnessed enough political fireworks over the past several months, but it was fun to watch some real ones. We rode our motorcycles downtown to enjoy the display. I had a few birthday calls from some of my pals who were outside the caucus. They were concerned about me because all eyes were on me. I really appreciated their love and genuine friendship. They knew how tough this was for me. The media kept intimating, "If Deb Grey bolts, we know things are going to implode."

The next night I went to bed, then lay awake for hours as I had every night for almost three months now. In the middle of the night, I got up, went to the desk and wrote out a statement, stressing my take on the whole mess we were in. I went back to bed and somehow got a little sleep before morning. When I woke up, I went straight to the desk and picked up the paper. I knew in my gut this was it. I took the paper to Lew in the kitchen and said, "This is the day, sweetheart." He knew exactly what I meant and hugged me for a long time. I called my staff, told them to hook up on a conference call, read them my statement, then said, "Please book a press conference at my constituency office for two o'clock this afternoon." I was ready to speak.

CHAPTER 20

———————

Bridge-Building

THERE WAS A HUGE ARMY OF MEDIA GATHERED at my office. It was evident that this was going to be a big story, as many had predicted. My phone rang off the hook with people who were full of conjecture and advice. I did not take any of the calls before the press conference. I visited with the media when they arrived to set up; I had known all of them for a long time. Many of the media people actually sympathized with me because they knew how agonizing these last months had been. My text for the press conference was the one I had written in the middle of the night, verbatim. I read it aloud:

> One year ago this week, our party chose a new leader, Stockwell Day. He asked me to stay on as his deputy leader and I agreed. I have tried to support, advise and participate as best I could. By this April, I realized I could no longer do this job. I did not agree with certain actions of the leader and his team. Therefore, on Monday April 23, I told him, confidentially, I would step down as deputy leader and we would discuss it in caucus on Wednesday and develop a communications plan. At 2:20 that same night, *Canada AM* called because they had already been told of my decision. I did not tell anyone else I was stepping down, and yet I was criticized for making it public. The group

"Grassroots for Day" has launched demon-dialer messages into my constituency and others, swamped meetings, sponsored radio ads attacking MPs and initiated a $450,000 defamation lawsuit against me. This all appears to be with the sanction of the leader, as long as it remains "positive and respectful," as he told me. I have been accused of not honouring the constitution. I respect our party's constitution and fully acknowledge that Stockwell can claim the right to stay on as leader until next April, when our members are guaranteed a leadership vote. However, I do not believe he has the ability or the substance to fulfil that role. There is nothing in our constitution that does not allow him to resign and call a leadership review. I believe he should do that now. I find it incomprehensible that our national council acted contrary to our party's constitution by removing a fellow councillor, Rick Anderson, without the required percentage and consultations that are called for. This sets a dangerous precedent. Also, just last week, Stockwell announced he is going to revoke party memberships of the so-called dissidents. Today, the media is reporting that Stockwell may also be considering revoking the memberships of riding executives who support those "dissidents." This is absurd. The leader should know that there is a lengthy consultation process in place and revoking memberships is not an easy thing. Besides, it is hardly a constructive, bridge-building exercise. It is time our national council looked after the interests of our party and worked toward resolving this crisis of leadership. Suspensions or revoking memberships are not the solution; they are only the sign of deeper problems not properly addressed. Since April, I have tried to work things out behind closed doors at our family caucus table. However, any debate, discussion or disagreement is simply not allowed. We have been told to support the leader, express confidence in him or leave caucus. Unfortunately, there is only one of those options left for me.

I finished, breathed a small sigh of relief and then opened it up for questions. Here is a sample of my responses to some of them: "You can just guess how painful it is to come to this stage for someone who has the longest history of election in this party"; "I just do not see him as prime ministerial material"; "Stock, there is no shame in admitting you're not a leader. For the good of the party and the good of the country, resign and call a leadership review."

I spent quite a while doing interviews over the phone that afternoon. When I got home, I felt like a huge weight was finally off my shoulders. On my fax machine was my letter of suspension from the caucus. I was sad, but felt so relieved that I had finally come through the door that had been ajar for such a long time. It was one of the most difficult decisions I had ever made in my whole life. I went home and was so glad to see Lew, who was as steady as ever. He knew that I had just gone through a very difficult ordeal so he suggested we go for a motorcycle ride. That was just what I needed. Away we went, enjoying the smells of the canola fields coming into full bloom and the magnificent, cheerful song of the redwing blackbirds, one of my favourite summer sounds. On Saturday, July 7, we were booked to spend a week at our time-share unit in Canmore, Alberta, riding our bikes in the Rockies. It couldn't have been any better timing. After I had completed every last media request, we loaded our bikes and away we went. The mountains looked more inviting than ever. Their rugged majesty begged us to forget what was so temporal and enter into their timeless silence.

However, the day after we arrived, that silence was shattered when we got word that Stockwell had found out the caucus was planning a vote of non-confidence at their meeting scheduled for July 17 in Calgary. On July 8, exactly one year after he had won the leadership, he made a counter-proposal of his own. He offered to take a leave of absence until the next Alliance assembly (scheduled for the following April). His conditions were: "terms of reconciliation" would be offered, asking suspended MPs back to the caucus; Grant Hill would serve as the interim leader; Ken Kalopsis (a long-time Reformer whom Stockwell accused of being a 'Manning-ite') would have to resign as party co-chairman; and the work of the Unity Committee would carry on.

Chuck was asked to be on a conference call on behalf of the suspended MPs and, as I still sat on the transition council, I was on it as well. The conversation went fairly well for the first while. Chuck and I thought the proposals were reasonable and that the entire caucus would likely accept them. Grant Hill would do well as interim leader. He was a very calm and reasonable man; all of our caucus respected him. I asked one question about whether he would be given the full power and authority to name his caucus officers, critics, et cetera, or if he would merely be a stooge acting on someone else's orders. It was an important question that would be uppermost in the caucus members' minds, both those who were suspended and those who were not. Someone on the call reacted strongly and negatively to my comment and said, "Of course." As the discussion continued, I turned to the TV and saw John Reynolds come on live and say, "Stockwell's offer is off the table. The dissidents are demanding their original positions back." This was a lie. I asked the group on the conference call what in the world was going on. The call was still in progress, but here was Reynolds on live TV. Needless to say, pandemonium broke out on the call and it ended abruptly.

Every day brought a new reason for another conference call for the council. One day I called in from a phone booth at Emerald Lake, another time from Radium Hot Springs. By day three I was "voted off the island" and expelled from the group. I could see this coming, obviously, and although I was sad, I also felt a sense of relief that it was actually over. I was at least glad to have a few days left of our getaway week. Each day we would look at the map and decide which direction to ride in. We experienced a new road, a new destination, a new discovery. It was magic. Riding for me has always been a catharsis, but never so much as it was that week. I loved every minute, every smell, every bird's song.

We returned home somewhat refreshed and hoping to be out of the painful loop of the caucus's upcoming get-together in Calgary. It turned out to be another "Keystone Cops" affair. Apparently Stockwell had informed his inner circle that he had no intention of resigning. They blew up, especially Randy White, who had been telling caucus that he had convinced Stock to resign ninety days before the leadership vote. This would negate the need to have the vote of non-confidence at the

July 17 caucus. (It was rumoured that forty-two of the remaining fifty-three members of the caucus were prepared to vote him down.) Stock vacillated back and forth from his offer of taking a leave, to the caucus officers' plan to step down ninety days prior to a vote, to giving the caucus the choice. Moments before walking in to the caucus, he made his decision and told the caucus and the media he would resign ninety days before a leadership vote. The national council would set the date and details of that race. They, also, were virtually paralyzed by various factions and at the end of the day, they announced a leadership vote to take place on March 20, 2002, which was almost nine months away. Some members of caucus were pleased that he was resigning, but many saw it for what it was—a huge delaying tactic that left Stock still at the helm for many months to come. During that time, the polls remained low, public confidence eroded, funding dried up and the entire blame was put on a symptom, the "dissidents" with no attention paid to the root cause.

The suspended MPs had a caucus of our own in Ottawa on July 19 to make some decisions and strategize. Inky Mark (Dauphin-Swan River) had joined us in early July and was in Ottawa with us. Brian Fitzpatrick came to the meeting but decided to return to the Alliance caucus the next day. We were still a dozen, a sizeable group with considerable experience and we wanted to do something productive after such a difficult year. We were also tired of being called "dissidents" so a new label was essential. One person that I got a kick out of, though, was my dear pal Jay Hill. On occasion, he would introduce himself to someone saying, "Hi, I'm Dissi. Dissi-Dent." That would throw us into gales of laughter. The way he smirked when he said it and the obvious mischief in the middle of such a painful situation was just what we all needed from time to time. However, we really did need a proper label. We discussed it at length and eventually came up with the name "Democratic Representative Caucus." Even though we faced howls of scorn and ridicule, we felt this at least represented what we were attempting to accomplish. One of our main strategies was to form stronger bonds with our PC colleagues, which was one of the primary mandates of the Alliance. It had gone seriously offtrack with Stock's June shotgun-wedding approach. Consequently we tried to build bridges with the Tories and managed to organize a meeting of our two groups at Mont Tremblant, Quebec, scheduled for August 17 and 18. Cliff Fryers was involved in the organization and negotiations for the conference. He said he thought it would be beneficial for me to be there as one of our group's representatives. I had a long history with the PCs and I would be a good bellwether as to whether closer cooperation would work at the ground level. I talked it over with Lew and my board of directors and agreed to go.

During the remainder of July and August, though, I was determined to spend some time with family and friends who had been so faithful to me during this almost impossible year. Lew and I hosted our Larson relatives for barbeques at our home. Nothing takes the blues away faster than having a house full of energetic, playful kids. Our great-nieces and nephews provided no end of fun and laughter for us. Mom and Dad Larson were a great source of encouragement and conversation to us as well. I loved Dad's stories; he had a never-ending supply of them. We visited with Lew's siblings, kids, nephews and nieces as much as we could. I also got a chance to get to the coast and visit my family. During our difficult spring, Mom and my sister Alison had gone on a wonderful walking tour to Italy. Unfortunately for me, it occurred exactly during the hardest part of our spring—early April until early May. On those days, I wanted so much to be able to call my mom and cry on her shoulder. It would have felt so comforting. Instead, I would try and pour my heart out typing an email and Alison would retrieve it at an internet café somewhere in Rome or Tuscany! I was thrilled that they had a chance for such a great holiday but I yearned to talk to them almost every day. It was good to spend time with them that summer and feel completely safe, knowing that they loved me, no matter what.

The unconditional love I experienced from so many friends was a real encouragement. Our friends, Lorne and Rita Penner, and their kids loved us up lots that summer. Rita is the daughter of Len and June Perry, full-time staff members at Camp Homewood. I had babysat Rita when she was two years old and now she was a grown woman with four wonderful kids of her own. We loved their energy and individual personalities. They were fun to be around and we always laughed a lot when we were together. Many evenings were spent around the campfire roasting hot dogs, enjoying good conversation and being entertained by the kids' skits and stories. I loved it. One night that summer, we adults went motorcycle riding. Rita had bought Lew's old Goldwing for Lorne. Away we went, just to get out in the country. On the way, we dropped off their eight-year old son, Luke, at his soccer practice. I took him there on the back of my bike. When we got to the soccer field, he took off his helmet and walked toward his team. When he got up right beside them, he turned around and hollered, "Thanks for the ride, Deborah Grey!" We all laughed right out loud. Luke had known us all his life and to him we were just Deb and Lew. The fact that I was a celebrity never entered his mind. Or so I thought! That evening, he took the opportunity to name-drop to his pals. It felt so good for me because many people were shunning me these days, but not my pal Luke. Thanks, bud.

My good friend Maxine Hancock was such a help during this time, too. She and I had talked a lot over the last months, trying to process what was going wrong and what the solutions to our problems might be. I appreciated it when she wrote an article in *ChristianWeek* newspaper entitled, "What Makes Deb Grey Tick(ed)." In it, she spoke of our long friendship and experience of working together in our community and church, as well as being a close friend to her and Cam and their children (*ChristianWeek*, September, 2001). I will always be grateful to her for going out on a limb in her professional capacity by writing that article. Thank you, Maxine.

We were also glad for our friendship with Doug and Polly (Marks) Torrance. Lew and I had met Polly two weeks after we were married in '93. She was a single pastor who was the guest speaker at a family camp that Lew and I went to visit right after we returned from our honeymoon. The preacher called us up to congratulate us and we said a few words to the group. Polly stood up to give the message. She is quite a character. She pointed down at me from the pulpit and said, "How old are you?" I replied, "Forty-one." "Have you ever been married before?" "No." With that, she lifted her arms in the air and bellowed, "Well, praise Jesus, there's hope for me!!" The crowd erupted in laughter. And so was my introduction to Polly Marks. We have had a wonderful friendship through all these years and we were delighted (as she was!!) when she met and married Doug Torrance three years later. They now pastor a church in Yorkton, Saskatchewan and we get to see them occasionally. I appreciated Polly so much through the difficult days of 2001 because she helped me work through the pain of the very public "battle of the born-again." Surely Christians ought to be able to keep their disagreements to themselves and get along, right? Surely they ought to be mature about their involvement in the political realm, right? I agree with that thinking. Unfortunately, I believe that the Christian community is somewhat naïve regarding the political arena and issues. For instance, many churches think that if they can get a Christian believer in to a place of political leadership, things will automatically improve. This is nonsense. A society will only change as individual hearts within it change. You cannot purify it from the top. Constantine tried that centuries ago and it was an abject failure. When the church gets caught up in the excitement of electing one of its own, that is noble, but it must remain faithful to its original mission. When the church becomes the selling-place for memberships for a party or a person, it runs the risk of pitting Christians against other Christians. This is dangerous. We watched it play out in spades within our party. The ultimate test is to ask the simple question, "What is the truth?" and then look for evidence to back it up. Those who support something will shine the best light on it, presenting it persuasively. Those who oppose will try and expose its worst side and present it equally persuasively. Neither is wrong. They both put "spin" on it, to use a political word. But, deep down, every communicator knows when spin crosses over the unseen, unspoken line and it becomes a lie. It is then that our integrity becomes threatened. It is then that the damage is done. It is then that the Christian community must learn to read the signs carefully and measure up words and actions. I appreciated Polly and her insights as a senior pastor.

In mid-August, a few of my DRC colleagues and I headed to Mont Tremblant where we met many people who had traditionally been our political foes. We started a helpful dialogue and spent a rewarding weekend together. We heard from Andre Turcotte, president of Feedback Research Corporation. Andre had long been our Reform and Alliance pollster and was very capable. He had an uncanny knack of predicting election results within a slim percentage of the actual result. His research showed that a majority of Canadians were hungry for a change of government in Ottawa, and when asked the question about "uniting the right" 59 per cent of Alliance voters thought it was a good idea and 41 per cent of PC voters thought it was a good idea. A majority of Canadians agreed on the following strategic imperatives; it is time for a change, the lack of a competitive alternative to the Liberals is a serious problem, they are ready to support a party that can demonstrate a principled opposition to the Liberals. (Feedback Research Corporation, survey conducted August 3–8, 2001.)

Another discussion was about democratic reform. Northstar Research Partners, the PC pollsters, presented polling research. When asked, "Our federal system needs to be overhauled so that citizens have a much bigger say in how things are done" vs. "Our system has flaws, but encouraging more citizen participation isn't that big a priority for me" 73 per cent chose the first statement. Regarding more free votes in the House of Commons, when the option was "according to the wishes of constituents" 49 per cent said it was "something I support." When the option was "allowing MPs to vote according to their consciences," 46 per cent said it was something I support." Regarding referendums on major issues, 49 per cent supported and 19 per cent found the idea "very appealing"; regarding an elected Senate, 36 per cent supported it and 30 per cent "very appealing"; regarding having an Ethics Commissioner report to Parliament, 45 per cent supported and 30 per cent "very appealing"; and regarding MP recall, 34 per cent supported and 29 per cent "very appealing." (Northstar Research Partners, August 2001.)

We then had long discussions about the possibility of working together in some form of parliamentary cooperation. There was a recognition that it would be beneficial for DR and PC MPs and Senators to cooperate with each other. It was suggested that we could set up joint working groups to establish common positions on issues of importance and additional working groups to coordinate Question Period, debates, media and research. Obviously a key to that strategy involved building personal relationships. We would build trust and understanding and demonstrate to our respective party memberships that we can work together on issues of interest. Finally, we would need to decide on whether we would have separate leaders, caucus officers and critics, or a joint caucus with a caucus leader, deputy leader, caucus officers, critics and caucus meetings. We decided to mull on these options and discuss them again at our next meeting, which was set for Edmonton on September 10, 2001. We left Mont Tremblant knowing each other better and trusting each other more. Isn't that usually the way when people can sit down face to face in a spirit of complete honesty?

At the end of August, the DR had a caucus meeting in Castlegar, home of Jim Gouk. Our days were filled with meetings and strategizing about entering into a full parliamentary coalition with the Tories. Some had reservations and by the end of our retreat, Art Hanger, Jim Gouk, Gary Lunn, Andy Burton and (later) Monte Solberg decided to go back into the Alliance caucus. We were now seven and made a commitment to each other that we would remain together and see this whole project through, no matter what came along. We would form the coalition and work with the PCs to try and build the bridges that were necessary and that the Canadian public was demanding.

The PCs had their pre-parliamentary caucus in Edmonton on the weekend of September 8 and 9. We joined them for a PC/DR coalition caucus meeting at noon on the tenth. We spent the afternoon hashing out details of how an actual coalition would work in Parliament. Most people accepted the concept but Elsie Wayne was not happy. Nonetheless we persevered, hoping she would come onside. By the end of a long afternoon, we had agreed on a full caucus coalition. On the first day of our upcoming fall session of Parliament, September 17, we would apply to the Speaker of the House for formal recognition as the "PC/DR Coalition." We all left the Westin in Edmonton the afternoon of September 10, 2001, officially expelled from the Alliance caucus yet pleased about our decision. We wondered how tomorrow's news would report the formation of the coalition. We had no idea....

The next morning, I was speaking at a breakfast meeting to some people at our area office to update them on the proceedings that led to the coalition. I left home a few moments before 7:00 A.M. I turned the news on in the truck and caught the words, "…smoke coming out of the building." The cell phone rang and it was Lew asking if I had the news on. I replied, "Yes, it sounds like a warehouse is burning somewhere in town." He had turned on the TV and told me a plane had crashed into the World Trade Center. We assumed it had been a small Cessna. We listened together and then, moments later, he said, "Here, they're showing a replay." Then, astonished he said, "Wait! This is not a replay. Another big plane is flying into the other building and the other one is already burning! This is live!" Instantly we knew this was a terrorist attack. He kept relaying updates to me all the way to my meeting. Nobody there had heard the news. We tried to carry on with our information session, but soon gave up as Lew called to tell me that one of the towers had collapsed and then again, soon after, to say that the other one was going down. It was surreal and very frightening, almost like everything was happening in slow motion. We then got word of the Pentagon crash and the jet that crashed into the field. It seemed like reports would keep coming in of more attacks. The meeting ended and my staff called me to report what they were hearing. I immediately called the Prime Minister's Office to lend my support to whatever emergency measures were being taken. I then called my Ottawa staff and told them to vacate the Hill immediately. The U.S. Embassy is just a few blocks from Parliament Hill and I was afraid it would be a possible target. I went to my constituency office and we watched the horror live for some time. All airports were shut down right away and none of our caucus could get out of town. I was scheduled to fly to the West Coast that afternoon. That would now be impossible. I talked to Lew and he said we could drive and maybe take someone along if they were stranded. I called Chuck on his cell phone. He was at the airport and caught a taxi back to our place. Jay Hill and Val Meredith and Gary Lunn managed to get a rental car and they took off a couple of hours ahead of us. Our drive was spent talking non-stop about what had happened and what it might mean internationally. It was a time of great apprehension. It felt like we were sitting on a tinderbox that could explode at any moment. Surely this was the most brutal, hateful attack that had ever happened. (Later

I spoke with an older woman and asked her if it were similar to the Second World War. She replied, "We knew terrible things were going on there, but we only received news of it after it happened. Watching it live has far more impact than anything we ever heard about then.") Strategically, it was brilliant and well calculated. An attack on a specific people or group or an area is one thing. This screamed hatred at capitalism and the whole free world itself. After listening to the commentary and realizing that it was likely the work of Osama bin Laden, I could just picture him holed up somewhere with a gas-powered generator watching the whole thing live on CNN. The devastation was so incredible; I wonder if even he thought it would be this perfectly executed? We arrived at Chuck's place in Chilliwack well after midnight and then sat up for hours watching the images on TV. We went to bed feeling sick for the many families who had lost loved ones and wondering if the next day might bring more attacks somewhere else. It was a terrifying and eerie time for everybody.

Later in the week, on September 15, my sister Skip had her first-ever one-woman art show. She had been an artist for many years and put lots of her work in shows but never hosted her own. We were excited for her and went over to Victoria to support her in this adventure. September 11 certainly put a cloud over the event, but all in all it went very well. Dad came down from his home in Hay River, Northwest Territories and we all enjoyed a family visit. It was especially comforting to all be together when we thought about how many families had just been literally blown apart in 9/11. We all love each other's company anytime; even more so this visit in light of the horrible circumstances. Even though everybody in our family is as different as night and day, we complement each other very interestingly. Mom is a quiet, consistent woman who is very comfortable with who she is. Her passions are reading and walking. She is seventy-nine years old and walks miles every single day. She lives in Oak Bay in Victoria, one block from the ocean and volunteers a lot with seniors. If she takes someone for a walk, she would like to think they could go as far as she does. There is usually no hope of that. She says, "If they start looking homeward after half an hour, I know they are not serious walkers," and she takes them home. If it rains, she simply puts on her slicker and away she goes. I am so thrilled that she is so healthy, so alive and so easy to be with. Leslie is an administrator for a co-op student program at Camosun College in Victoria. She worked in retail for many years and then went back to school for retraining in her forties. I really admire her for that. Her kids were grown and gone and she thought it was time to open a new door. She learned keyboard skills and how to run a computer; no small task for someone who had no inclination for such things. She has been at Camosun for several years now and I am proud of her accomplishments. Her two adult kids are Kate, who lives in Victoria with her infant daughter, Niya, and Doug, who is single and lives with his father, Dick, in Bellingham, Washington. Skip (also known as Alexis) has also lived in Victoria for many years with her husband, John Celona. Her daughter Shane and her partner, Doug, also live in Victoria. Skip has been an artist for most of her life and makes a living between creating art and teaching it. She is an expert in sixties tunes and any time I can't remember the words to a song from that era, I call her, sing a bar or two and she instantly picks up on it and sings the whole verse and chorus as well as telling me who sang it. She is a champ! Alison and her husband, Michael, live in Surrey, near Vancouver. She was a real estate agent for many years. She loves people and is a very competent saleswoman. She has two daughters from her first marriage: Tanya and her husband, Lonnie, who have three children, Kamron, Ryleigh and Madysen; and Kirsten, who is married to Rob. Michael is an engineer and they have a company that makes water purification systems. My younger brother Shaun is married to Cheryl and they have no children. They also live in Surrey. Shaun works at a furniture manufacturing plant in the area. My dad, Mansell, has lived for many years in the North and has been involved in AA and counselling. He has lived out on a trap-line in the bush and provided the alcohol-counselling component for Native fellows when they get out of jail. I am very proud to see him helping others try to overcome the addiction that haunted him for so many decades. I am so proud of him.

After the art show and late-night Starbucks coffee visits, Lew and I had to get back to Edmonton. We arrived late Saturday night and celebrated Lew's birthday on Sunday, September 16. I was booked to fly to Ottawa late that afternoon, but called the airport beforehand as the flights were still not back to normal after 9/11. The lady asked me where I was right now. I replied, "At my kitchen table at home in Edmonton." She laughed and said, "That's a perfect place to stay for today. Your plane can get out of Edmonton, but you will get stranded either in Calgary or Toronto. Planes are ending up with no crews and crews with no planes. I can book you for tomorrow morning." That was just fine with me. I found Lew outside and said, "Happy birthday, sweetheart. Guess what? Your present is me!" Having to travel so much is hard because inevitably you miss some special occasions. This was a gift of time for both of us.

I flew to Ottawa without incident the next morning. Our PC/DR coalition sat in the Chambers together for first time. It felt good to have a home, but I missed many of my Alliance friends. It was hard to be in the lobby passing by Diane, Monte, Art Hanger and several others who had become true pals over the years. We visited when we could, but it was awkward. But there were some who would neither talk nor even grunt when we passed each other. What is it about a person that bars them from the basic courtesy of saying "Hello" even though they may have major disagreements over issues? I have always found this impossible to understand. And so, I got used to being completely ignored by several of my long-time colleagues, mostly "Stockaholics" as they referred to themselves. I had always believed that if you work hard enough at something and have a will to succeed, you can push through the tough times and still come out the other end as friends. I had always managed to work things through with people, at least to a degree. I can't stand unresolved conflict and will do almost anything to find a way of reconciliation, no matter what the issue or relationship. It is essential to have some degree of willingness from both sides. Sadly, this was not the case in this situation. It was during this time that I learned one of the most valuable lessons of my life. I probably should have learned it by the time I was seventeen and ready to finish high school, but at least I learned it before I turned fifty. That lesson is: "Not all your colleagues will be your friends." It seems so basic, but I had never really grasped that before. Granted, you will always gravitate toward some that you "click" with and become closer to them. But, still, I had always maintained a warm relationship with all, regardless of whether I considered them "bosom buddies" or not. This doorway was extremely difficult and painful for me, as I realized that, perhaps for the first time in my life, there was something I could not "fix." The pain was deep on all sides and it looked as though the scarring may be permanent. Through those days, I learned a second part to that valuable life lesson: "Not all your colleagues you want for friends." When I grasped that concept, it was truly one of the most freeing experiences of my life! I had always wanted to please, wanted to accommodate, wanted to resolve. Although my basic character is still exactly the same, I now realize that sometimes people work together and the relationship remains at a strictly professional level. I found that concept such a relief (and probably so did many who have worked with me for years that never could stand me!)

This was an interesting concept to grasp in the light of our little coalition. We all entered into it with so many pre-conceived ideas about each other. I was "Deb Grey, that Reformer who stole Beaver River away from the PCs." Although that had been over twelve years ago, the wounds were still fresh as my entrance on the federal scene signalled the fragmentation of the conservative movement in Canada. From the PC perspective, I was the thin edge of the wedge that led to the pounding they took in the '93 election. I could understand their disdain and genuine dislike, not of me, personally, but what I symbolized to them. On the other hand, I had witnessed Joe Clark for many years and he had symbolized everything that was disdainful for many Westerners; a "sell-out" to the East with no defense of Western issues that were so important to us, such as Senate reform and the agony of the National Energy Policy. Joe had also referred to me as an "enemy of Canada" during the Charlottetown Accord days. Needless to say, if this coalition was going to work, we all had to bury the hatchet and agree to move forward together, not lick old wounds from the past. Elsie Wayne was an outspoken critic of what we were attempting to do. She had been in a somewhat similar position as I had; holding the fort under the PC banner during the '93–'97 Parliament when she and Jean Charest were the only PC members. It was understandable that she was not keen about this coalition, but we all determined to make it work. And so, we did just that. Joe Clark was our parliamentary leader and Chuck Strahl our deputy. I became our caucus chairman, Peter MacKay was named our House leader and Jay Hill was our whip. Not only were we eighteen MPs in the caucus, but were complemented by the thirty PC Senators. This made a fair-sized caucus. Many of the long-time Tory Senators wanted no part of this coalition, but several had advocated a uniting of our two parties for some time. This seemed like a natural progression in the bridge-building phase to them. Some of the Senators stayed away from our caucus for some weeks and then joined in when they witnessed how well it was going. Others stayed away completely and continue to do so, even now. Of those who participated, MPs and Senators alike, the coalition surprised us all that we got along so well. This was living proof that people can get along if both sides put their mind to it and their shoulder to the wheel to get something done. It was remarkable to see long-time "sworn enemies" laugh together and truly get along. The will was there to make it work; that is really all you need in any project in life, it seems to me. Peter MacKay and I spoke at some functions together, making an incongruous, but very effective, pair. Several riding associations in Ontario had already agreed to work together, regardless of whether their party brass endorsed it or not. There was a hunger to move forward and once that seed is sown, not much can stop it. Many party members from the PC and Alliance sides were demanding that we all become one, sooner rather than later, to form a single, credible, principled alternative to the Liberals. Many ordinary Canadians, who were not political activists, were also demanding the very same thing. We hoped that we would be able to take the first step in this evolutionary process.

On September 19, our coalition House leader, Peter MacKay, rose in the House on a point of order, requesting that we be recognized as the fourth largest entity in the House. As well, he asked that the Speaker rule on the location of our seats, precedence of questions in Question Period, speaking times during debate, financial resources (research and communications capabilities) and the allocation of supply days (where the opposition party can allocate the topic of debate). (*Hansard,*

September 19, 2001.) On September 24, the Speaker granted us official recognition in the House, but we were not given any extra research and communications budget. We thought that the per-capita dollars granted for each of us seven members of the DR should follow us, but that was denied. Nonetheless, we had been granted status, so we accepted that. Strangely, the group that protested the most vigorously in the House was the Alliance. Pity. We did receive more questions in Question Period based on our increase, so that was helpful. Each day we got in the rotation and joined our voices with the opposition parties, questioning the Liberals about their incompetence, scandals and lack of integrity when it came to boondoggles and the like.

During that fall, I was embroiled in the G4D lawsuit. My lawyer and I wondered how many people were part of this group that George Bears said he represented. The suit had been filed as "George Bears et al v. Deborah Grey." We made a request for the names and addresses of the entire membership of G4D. I asked for the names because if I won my lawsuit they would each be responsible for their share of paying the legal costs. When asked to provide actual names, the response came back on October 23, 2001, "Grassroots for Day has three members: George Bears (of Calgary) Peter Schalin (of Edmonton) and Kari Simpson (of Vancouver)." (Although, when contacted, Kari Simpson appeared to be uncertain that she was involved at all.) Originally, they had insisted they had more than seven thousand members, but now these were referred to as "supporters." My lawyer said, "Politically, I would think that's very embarrassing and I think that's why they didn't want to give us this stuff." Schalin responded that even with the low membership, G4D has plenty of support. "The members are the ones who are the public face of the movement and leaders of the movement. We decided in our group who the members would be and then every-body else is supporters." (*Edmonton Journal*, Wednesday, October 24, 2001.) Gotcha!!

One of the best parts about serving in the coalition was the oppor-tunity to work with a task force on democratic reform. This had always been one of my keen interests and I was happy to participate in it. It was made up of MPs and party activists and officials from both sides.

Senator Lowell Murray and I were named the co-chairs. This was hilarious because Lowell had been one of the most vociferous critics of the Reform Party and me since our inception. He had attacked me at length during Charlottetown. Now, he was being asked to work hand in hand with me chairing a task force. He agreed and it was one of the best experiences I have had. We got on like a house on fire and enjoyed each other's company and styles. Discussions were vigorous, debate productive and conclusions generally unanimous, but if not, consensus reached agreeably. What fun!! In January 2002, we had a face-to-face meeting with all the members of the task force at the Vancouver Airport Fairmont Hotel and put together our final draft of the document. It was discussed and adopted by the coalition caucus, then forwarded to the PC party for their endorsement at their summer convention in August in Edmonton. Since the '93 election, the Tories had done a lot of serious work on rebuilding their party. After their '95 convention, democratic reform had become a key issue. We were pleased to see it have such prominence and were comfortable with virtually all the items included in their policy manual and in our task force report, which deepened and broadened their existing policies. Our report included proposals under the headings of Political Reform (Parliamentary Reform, Broader Citizen Involvement), Electoral Reform and Party Reform. It made particular proposals and recommendations on free votes, confidence votes and party discipline; commons committees, code of ethics and discipline of Parliamentarians; relationship between Parliament and the Courts; Senate reform; citizens' initiatives and referendum; electoral systems; fixed election dates; party end election financing; and party governance and policy process. It was a very worthwhile project and we were extremely pleased with the reception it received.

We were all very pleased at how things were going in the coalition. We were living proof that it really could work. The tenor of our relationship with the Alliance MPs improved generally throughout the fall, with the exception of a small group of Stock supporters. One glaring exception, however, was Randy White, who remained particularly vicious, especially towards Chuck. Their ridings were side by side, thus they shared a border, common interest groups, media outlets and saw each other at public events. Randy, I believe, was still angry that Chuck had replaced him as House leader in January, 2000, thinking that Chuck had been angling for that job. That was so far from the truth it is laughable. Preston had moved Randy out of that position and Chuck had been the whip. When Preston had replaced Randy with Jay Hill, a discussion ensued about which role Jay and Chuck should fill. It was thought that Chuck might better fit the role of House leader as it involved meeting with the other party House officers. Chuck knew them already in his capacity as whip and this would be a smooth transition. Thus it was that Chuck became House leader for the Alliance so long ago. But Randy held an ugly grudge and seldom missed an opportunity to take a swipe at Chuck, especially in their local press. This was unfortunate and served no purpose for the public or our party's good.

The Alliance had gone through a difficult fall, although things had calmed down somewhat after Stockwell agreed to resign. He announced in mid-December that he was stepping down as leader of the Alliance, but that he would be a candidate for the upcoming leadership race, which was to culminate on March 20, 2002. He had been organizing for months and had all the tools and resources of the Leader's Office at his disposal. This included a feel-good video that was sent all over the country to all ridings and many individuals. Right after his departure, the seven DR members had our party memberships revoked on December 13. Interestingly, this went completely against the constitution of our party. It stipulated that such a decision could be made only after "consultation with the executive in the riding." My guys were ready for the call, but it never came. My party membership, number "000002," was gone with a council vote and the stroke of a pen. Merry Christmas and Happy New Year, everybody!

After 9/11, travel became increasingly time-consuming. Security was tightened up to the point of the absurd, but understandably so. In real terms, it meant that I had to go to the airport much earlier than I was used to and everyone was subjected to long lineups and security checks. Lew and I had lived for some years in a small, two-bedroom bungalow about 25–30 minutes from the airport. Over the last couple of years, we had neighbours who played loud music in their yard until late at night and their cigarette smoke drifted over to our yard, something which we had not ordered and were not able to "return to sender." During the summer, we had looked around for a new place, but not seriously. After 9/11, we did step up our search for a place closer to the airport, with three bedrooms and a parking pad with room for the big trailer we had bought that spring to haul both of our bikes. We looked at a couple of places and were not interested enough to put an offer on them. In late September, after Lew had picked me up at the airport, we drove around to find a place he had seen while I was away. On the way to find it, we noticed a big place that had a large parking pad beside the house. I said, "Whoa, back up. There's a lot of parking at this one." He did and we sure liked the looks of it. The house was large and we figured it must have three bedrooms. It fit the requirements (as long as the neighbours didn't blow smoke over to us!), but was probably out of our price range, judging by the neighbourhood. We went home and I looked it up on the internet. It was more than we were planning to spend, but the interest rates were only 3.59 per cent. We went there the next day with our Realtor pal, Marvin Winch. We fell in love with it, offered full asking price and owned it within the hour, just like that! Selling our old house for a fair amount more than we had paid for it nicely offset the cost of the new one. We moved in on November 30, during the first full-blown blizzard of the season. It was a great project to have, not just because we loved the place, but also because it gave us such a wonderful diversion from our *annus horibilus*, as Queen Elizabeth II had referred to one of her recent horrible years.

The year 2002 looked to be far more promising. I entered it more peacefully and hopefully than I had the previous year. As I mentioned, in mid-January the PD/DR's Task Force Report on Democratic Reform was adopted, the Alliance leadership race was underway and Lew and I were in our new home and did a lot of entertaining. The place was built in 1976, but in 1982 the owners built an enormous family room off the back, totalling about 750 square feet. We have a pool table there and also lots of room for good old Gospel singsongs. We have enjoyed many nights there with my friend Joanne on the guitar and a keyboard available for anybody that could play it, usually Lew's cousin, Ruth and her husband, Eldon Langerud, who joined in with his guitar.

The Alliance leadership race was now in full swing. Besides Stockwell and Stephen Harper, Grant Hill and Diane Ablonczy entered the contest. Diane was running as the "unity" candidate. She had done a lot of work trying to build bridges with the PCs over the years. She had almost joined the DR, but felt that she should remain in the Alliance and work through it. Her campaign slogan was "Strength through Unity" and her platform fleshed out proposals for cooperation between the Alliance and the PCs. They included: a) discussions, meetings and events at all levels to build working relationships and bridges of better understanding; b) a draft statement of principles and key policies for governing the country, prepared by activists and elected representatives working with grassroots members, as soon as potential coalition partners could agree on a common vision; c) a "new partnership" convention based on equality, to which each CA and PC constituency would send three voting delegates, that would democratically debate and adopt principles for governing the country, key policy elements, a party constitution, a party name and an overseeing council. Diane's ideas were ahead of their time, offering a platform to discuss the idea of a full-blown merger of the two parties. It was a terrific opportunity for her to discuss the merits of these proposals with the party membership.

Stephen Harper's campaign slogan was "Getting it Right." He had watched the implosion of the party and been drafted by several of the Alliance caucus and other party activists. He offered to reunite and rebuild the party and expand its electoral base. He received the public support of more than half of the Alliance caucus and proclaimed that under his leadership, the grassroots members would again control the party. This was a comfort to many party members. He mentioned during the campaign that he was committed to working with the Tories, but not at Joe Clark's behest and not at any cost.

Stockwell's campaign slogan was "Standing for What's Right." In his brochure, he said, "In 2001, the caucus and grassroots prevented the party from being torn apart by 'backroom elites.' Last summer, the caucus dealt with the internal rebellion in a fair and firm manner." Regarding unity with the Tories, he said, "I stand strongly by our grassroots principles. I won't compromise them just to cut a quick deal with the Tories. Unity, yes, but not at any price."

It was clear who I was quietly supporting in the race. Diane was offering not only the concept of unity, but also a clear set of proposals and actions to bring it to fruition. My DR colleagues and I were not party members and did not involve ourselves in the race, but spoke about the unity option when we had a chance. When the ballots were cast on March 20, 2002, Stephen Harper won a convincing first-ballot victory, receiving 48,961 of the 88,625 votes cast, or 55.04 per cent. Stockwell placed second with 33,074 votes, or 37.4 per cent, Diane got 3370 for 3.8 per cent and Grant Hill got 3220 for 3.6 per cent. He, too, had run a pro-unity campaign.

The membership had spoken. I believe that many party members were quite interested in the unity proposals that Diane offered, but were more concerned with securing a new leader and putting the disasters of the last year behind us, once and for all. They did not want to risk a repeat of 2001, ever again. Stephen had won the race and made it very clear that the Alliance was moving forward, and I think the entire party breathed a huge sigh of relief. I was pleased that he had won a majority, but still did not know how this would play out in our lives. Stephen had not spoken positively of us during the race and we would have to wait and see what happened. During the race, my board had asked me if I would go back to the Alliance if Harper won. I needed to think about that, but I intimated that it might be difficult to return under any circumstances.

On April 3, a couple of weeks after Stephen won the leadership, the PC/DR coalition met at the airport in Calgary. Over the months of the coalition's existence, increasing pressure was put on the DR to buy PC memberships. There was a sentiment that this would answer everyone's concerns. However, when Elsie Wayne continued to say, "We just want all you Reformers to come home to the PC family," it didn't address the situation correctly. Many Reformers and Alliance supporters, like me, had never been PC members, consequently it never had been "home." The invitation seemed moot to us, and it certainly would not help the vote-splitting problem across the country simply because seven former Reformers bought a PC membership. With Stephen's recent victory, there were concerns raised about what would happen now. Some of the PC members, particularly Elsie Wayne and Greg Thompson, were feeling increasingly uneasy about the coalition. A long discussion ensued, but it looked more and more evident that our group might splinter. I headed home wondering how this whole thing would be resolved. The Alliance assembly was coming up in a few short days in Edmonton. We would all be watching any signals that emanated from the gathering.

On the Friday night, a farewell was held for Preston and Sandra Manning. I wanted so badly to be there with them. That was one of the most difficult parts of being outside my real political home. Preston and I went back so far together and had so many shared memories. Stephen had asked to speak and he gave a heart-felt tribute to Preston. That was a great comfort to me; they had also been through some rough waters in their relationship, and this was a well-timed reconciliation. Lew and I had been asked to be special guests that weekend down at Rosebud Theatre, on the edge of the badlands of Alberta near Drumheller. Years before, an enterprising family from the Peace River country in northwestern Alberta had become involved in the arts and, over the years, bought the entire town of Rosebud. It was a small hamlet that had virtually become a ghost town. The Ericksons had bought the buildings and rebuilt the entire place, re-creating an old-fashioned Western town. It has become a full-time theatre training facility, known as "Rosebud Theatre of the Arts." It offers live dinner-theatre productions in a wonderful ambience. Each year, young people receive professional training, then put their training to use on stage, delighting audiences that come from near and far. Before the production, the theatre-goers enjoy a fabulous meal, serenaded by the actors who wander through the dining hall, singing to the guests. It is always a terrific time and Lew and I were glad to be there on this weekend instead of back in Edmonton where the Assembly was going on.

As we were driving south, heading to Rosebud, the cell phone rang. It was Chuck Strahl and he said, "The coalition has fallen apart." I was silent for a long time after I hung up. After several minutes of silence,

Lew spoke up, "Maybe it's time to go back to the Alliance and finish your career in peace." I found myself agreeing with him, but had no idea how that would, or could, come about. What would happen next? I found out because the next day, during the intermission of the production of *Shadowlands* (the very moving life story of C.S. Lewis, a renowned Christian writer), my cell phone rang again and it was my riding president, Greg Nicholson. He was at the Assembly and said that Stephen wanted to talk to me personally. We set up a time later that afternoon. One of my other board members told Stephen that I would not go back to the Alliance under any conditions. Since his leadership victory, however, he had sent signals that if we came back, we would be given a chance to re-enter the caucus without grovelling, like the return of others had been in previous months. I have never minded apologizing for anything I have done wrong. However, the stipulations put on some of our other colleagues had been more about punishment and power than simply reintegration. I appreciated Stephen's willingness to talk to me directly and we had a very positive, productive chat. He asked me what my thoughts were about coming back to the caucus. I told him, "Stephen, you know I have always been a Reformer and always will be. That is where my heart is." We set up a meeting for the next Monday at his office in Ottawa. He had to run as he was giving his keynote address in less than half an hour. I always appreciated him coming to source and talking directly to me, especially when he was so busy and could have had someone else call or just simply not bothered. Thank you, Stephen.

On Monday, most of the DR met with Stephen and had a good chat. He said that it would be the best if we could all go back together and the sooner the better. There would be a window of opportunity, but it would not last long in order to put the crisis behind us. Stephen told us that the criteria would be to re-apply to the caucus for admission, provide a letter of support from our board and enclose $10 for the membership fee. We then met with Joe Clark and told him that the coalition was likely dead, not just because of Stephen's win, but as much because of growing public criticism of it coming from some of his PC caucus. We had all learned to work together and appreciated each other's perspective, but as time went on, it looked more and more unlikely that the coalition would remain intact. Jay Hill had decided over the weekend to return to the Alliance caucus and most of us agreed to return as well. Thus, on Wednesday, April 10, 2002, the DR attended its last PC/DR coalition caucus and said our goodbyes. It was bittersweet. We had enjoyed our time together and built some incredible relationships and bridges. We hoped that one day we would all be able to work together again. Who knew if that would ever be possible?

We left the coalition caucus and held a press conference. In it, I made this statement: "Since the recent leadership change of the Canadian Alliance, I have received overwhelming feedback from my constituents. I have been privileged to work as a member in the PC/DR Coalition caucus for the last seven months. However, the end game must be electoral cooperation, not simply a parliamentary arrangement. I am committed to helping build a national political alternative to the Liberal government." Five of the seven DR members returned to the Alliance. Inky Mark (Dauphin-Swan River) remained and became a PC and Jim Pankiw (Saskatoon-Humboldt), who was not readmitted to the caucus, became an independent.

We returned to the Alliance caucus on April 17, 2002. Chuck and I both made a short statement at the beginning of the meeting and everything carried on without any further mention of it. For the most part, caucus was glad to have this all behind us. Now we could all move forward as a team again. There were a few who were not one bit happy, but I have noticed a consistency in them—they don't seem totally happy about very much in life. Nonetheless, we were home again and I was pleased to receive my reinstated party membership: #000002.

CHAPTER 21

Chronology of a Courtship

A FTER THE DEMISE OF THE COALITION, Stephen had a private, ninety-minute meeting with Joe Clark. At it, they both put proposals on the table. Joe offered three proposals for closer ties: a parliamentary coalition with two leaders, policy review committees and another study on how to prevent vote-splitting. Stephen thought that the proposals were too weak; surely enough committees had been formed and studied the problem for years. Instead, Harper proposed that Clark and the twelve members of his caucus form a full parliamentary coalition with the Alliance in the Commons. Despite Harper's argument that his model was based exactly on the plan of the PC/DR coalition we had just participated in, Joe was not anxious to join. The offer was for him to serve as the deputy leader of the Official Opposition. He rejected it out of hand, claiming "he did not want to assume the role of a junior partner." (*Edmonton Sun,* April 10, 2002.) This was unfortunate; if he had agreed, we could have built on the strengths of our coalition and moved forward together, hardly missing a beat. Sadly, that opportunity was missed, and Joe said, "My conclusion is that Mr. Harper thinks he has enough wind in his sails that he can do this on his own. We will get on with building the strength of the Progressive Conservative Party in Canada." Harper's response was that any unity talks between the parties were "dead on a day-to-day basis."

(*Edmonton Sun*, April 10, 2002.) One step forward, two steps back…as in any courtship, there was conflict and competition.

Our Alliance caucus returned to its former strength, united in its resolve to move beyond the painful year of 2001. It was encouraging to mend fences and rebuild relationships with each other. Stephen had told us that we would be required to spend the spring session building bridges and by the fall would be re-integrated into expanding areas of responsibility. We participated in debates in the House and enjoyed cheering on our colleagues in Question Period. It was a much more pleasant and productive spring session than the one we had all lived through the previous year. Stephen gained the respect of our caucus. Many of them (those elected in 1997 and 2000) had not known him or worked with him before. This was a chance to see him in action and get familiar with his leadership style. It was very different from either Preston's or Stockwell's. Preston was always the democrat, wanting people's input, almost to a fault. He wanted to weigh every side of every issue, study pros and cons, look at the short-term and long-term consequences, give strategic consideration to and communications possibilities for each new initiative that we undertook. He was a multi-dimensional thinker, drawing up enormous flow charts to encapsulate his vision and thinking. I loved watching him and learning to understand how his mind worked. He was always able to make a decision, but not until he had heard from all sides. The Reform tradition was that "you will always get your say; you may not always get your way."

Preston, although very friendly and involved with so many thousands of people across the country, was uncomfortable with the intricacies of interpersonal relationships. This created difficulties over the years. By his own admission, he "made the mistake as leader during those early years of not paying enough attention to members and co-workers when they did well, or when they were discouraged, or when they needed help in defending themselves from unfair attacks from others. I was intensely proud of how far each of my MPs had come…but I rarely communicated this to them in any meaningful way. If someone was doing a good job I tended to leave him or her alone, while spending too much time on a few 'high-maintenance' members. And when my colleagues were the subject of personal attacks from our political opponents, I tended to treat such attacks with the same icy indifference with which I treated attacks on myself." (*Think Big*, McClelland and Stewart, 2002, p. 108–109.) In the political realm, as in any other, people want to be noticed, appreciated and recognized. We had operated as a good pair because I naturally am drawn to people first and policy second. Preston regretted that he did not possess those characteristics. But he realized that and made sure he complemented his own skill set with people who did.

Stockwell was an energetic person with a penchant for visiting with people. The larger a crowd was, the happier he was. This is very helpful in the political arena. He made people feel comfortable and that he was interested in them personally and in what they had to say. Stock had an amazing memory; this also is helpful in the political arena. He could remember facts and figures as well as people. It was reported that he presented Alberta's budgets, complete with statistical information, completely by memory. He had a knack for the theatrical, which, although not a weakness in itself, can lead to difficult consequences if unchecked (see Chapters 18 and 19). It was necessary to complement his style with people who could provide the balance needed to offset his strengths and weaknesses. Sadly, that didn't occur.

Now Stephen took on the role of leader. He is extremely bright and a gifted strategic thinker. For years he had provided the party with policy background, strategic advice and sound research on the Quebec issue. He is intense and sometimes brooding; not necessarily desirable characteristics for someone in the political realm. Stephen is not afraid of making decisions, whether people agree with him or not. This looked autocratic, but it shows he has confidence in his own judgment. His marriage to Laureen Teske and the birth of their two children, Benjamin and Rachel, have been "humanizing" elements in his life. I mentioned this to the press about the time we were coming back into the Alliance caucus. The media reported, "Told later of Grey's comments, a smiling Harper decided not to take issue with her analysis. 'Well, some people have said that my wife and children have humanized me a bit. And I guess that's what wives and children do to all men.'" (*Edmonton Journal*, April 11, 2002.)

As a wife myself, I was amused by his answer. I am sure, in some respects, I have humanized Lew, but I am also grateful for the humanizing effect he has had on me. No matter what the institution, organization, political party or personal relationship, feeling connected and being able to communicate are the most essential criteria for success. I am reminded of one of my all-time favourite pieces of literature, *The Little Prince*. In it, a small prince arrives on earth from his home planet of Asteroid B-612. He discovers many people and ideas, most of which he does not understand. It is a profound work that gives amazing insight into human relationships. My favourite section is Chapter XXI, about the little prince and the fox. When the little prince sees the fox, he asks if they can play together. The fox replies that he cannot do that as he is not "tamed." The prince asks what that means and the fox replies:

> "It's something that's been too often neglected. It means to create ties'....For me, you're only a little boy just like a hundred thousand other little boys. And I have no need of you. And you, on your part, have no need of me either. For you I'm only a fox like a hundred thousand other foxes. But if you tame me, we'll need each other. You will be the only boy in the world to me. I'll be the only fox in the world for you....If you tame me, my life will be filled with sunshine. I'll know the sound of footsteps that will be different than all the rest. Other footsteps send me back underground. Yours will call me out of my burrow like music. And then, look! You see the wheat fields over there? I don't eat bread. For me wheat is of no use whatsoever...But you have hair the colour of gold. So it will be wonderful, once you have tamed me! The wheat, which is golden, will remind me of you. And I'll love the sound of the wind in the wheat... Please...tame me!" "What do I have to do?" asked the little prince. "First you'll sit down a little ways away from me, over there, in the grass. I'll watch you out of the corner of my eye, and you won't say anything. Language is the source of misunderstandings. But day by day, you'll be able to sit a little

closer....". (*The Little Prince*, Antoine de Saint-Exupery, Harcourt, 1943.)

I think this is the best description of what human relationships ought to be about, and truly the best definition of a good, stable marriage. Once you are "tamed," life is never the same again.

Lew and I were more able to relax after I returned to the caucus. We enjoyed the spring and our new home. It gave us the chance to entertain friends and family outdoors for the first time since we had moved in. In late April, our church hosted a large, international conference in Edmonton. I flew home from Ottawa on Thursday morning, April 25, and took a taxi straight to the hotel to attend the women's luncheon. I saw Lew after it was over and he told me that he had invited some of the relatives home for coffee. He had no idea how many would be there. I said that was fine and that I would catch a ride home with Mom Larson. We got there at 2:30 and started grabbing what we could find in the cupboards to put out for a snack. At 2:55, Lew got home with twenty-seven people in tow! They were all relatives but two, a couple named Gary and Judy Duhachek from Nebraska. Lew's cousin, Bob Forseth, knew them and invited them along because they didn't know anyone else there. What fun we had! I had just arrived home myself and had no chance to go to the grocery store. I made coffee and tea and put out every cracker and cookie that I could find. Everyone had a great time; some played pool, others visited in the large rec room, others in the kitchen eating area and still others in the living room. We were thrilled with our new home and glad to have it filled with love and laughter. That same group, plus or minus three or four more, ate at our place on Friday and Saturday night as well. On Sunday many had left town, so the group was whittled down to a dozen or so. I did laundry, packed and flew to Ottawa early Monday morning. What a whirlwind weekend—but what a great house for a whirlwind.

The next major event was the celebration of my 50th birthday on July 1. It was dubbed, "July 1st 1952 + 50 = YIKES!!" During the afternoon, we had a public reception at Mom and Dad Larson's church hall. It was attended by about four hundred people. Was it ever fun to see the collection of people that had become such a special part of my life. The cross-section of guests, from relatives to church folk to political activists, was rich and varied. We had a great time of visiting and the open-mike session was particularly entertaining. My dad came down from the north and gave a moving tribute to the crowd, talking about his absence when I was a child and how proud he was to be my father. After the open house, we had seventy people back to our home for supper. Thank goodness it was a beautiful day; several people ate outdoors around the fountain on the deck. It was a busy day and that night I flopped into bed feeling grateful and loved. The next weekend, my mom and all my sisters came and we had a "girl weekend," touring the Edmonton-Jasper-Lake Louise-Banff-Calgary-Edmonton loop. We laughed a lot and it was magic to see their faces filled with wonder as they saw the Rocky Mountains close up. None of them had done the full loop before. It was a great trip to store on our "memory-bank movies."

July saw the lead-up to the PC convention that was to be held in Edmonton. Since the spring, commentators had been speculating as to whether Joe Clark would be able to hang on to his leadership. Political observers noted that he had been badly tarnished by not being able to keep the coalition together. In fairness, it had nothing to do with Joe that Stephen won the Alliance leadership and was able to rebuild it. Joe had spurned the idea of a full coalition, however, and there was speculation that he might get battered at the convention. On August 6, 2002, just before the convention was set to get underway, Joe Clark announced that he would step down as leader, provided the prime minister did not call an election before a new leader could be chosen. This amused many commentators, because how could the Tories set a date for a leadership convention with an unclear signal like that being sent? Nonetheless, during the fall, several possible candidates tested the waters quietly. The "non-race" race officially got underway around Christmas and a number of candidates stepped forward. Among them were Peter MacKay, the most high-profile figure and the front-runner on the slate, and Scott Brison (Kings-Hants), another Tory MP from Nova Scotia. Scott was bright, articulate and capable. He had quite a sense of humour. I had enjoyed working with him in the coalition. His main focus in the campaign was the economy. Another contender was Jim Prentice, a lawyer from Calgary. He was a long-time Tory who had advocated cooperation between our parties for some time. I had met him in our coalition days and thought that he brought the unity message to the campaign. Next was Craig Chandler, a long-time Reformer who loved to stir up the waters. He was pro-business. One of the old stalwarts of the PC party, Howard Grafftey, also ran. He was in his eighties and his platform was "the good old days," as nearly as I could make out. Last but not least was the perennial candidate David Orchard, a long-time party activist who had challenged Joe Clark in the last leadership race in 1998 and come second. I believe that David is really an NDPer at heart. Ideologically he is far more aligned with them; for instance, he is dead set against free trade, which had been the central plank of the PC platform in the 1988 election. I am not sure why Orchard remained with the PCs, but he threw his hat in the ring again for the upcoming race.

While that contest was gearing up, I was a delegate from our party to attend the NATO Association of Parliamentarians meeting in Istanbul, Turkey. I was able to use air miles and take Lew along as well. We left right after Remembrance Day in 2002 and were gone for approximately ten days. We were amazed at the size of Istanbul and marvelled at the city's "sense of the ancient." It was originally called Constantinople and dates back to 300 A.D. Its ancient walls can still be seen in many places. The present city boasts a population of close to fifteen million people and it spans two continents, Asia and Europe. The Bosphorus Strait bisects the city and separates the continents, with only two bridges for commuting purposes. Several small ferries go back and forth constantly, as well. We were somewhat surprised to see such a strong military presence in the Strait and in the city. However, this was not many months before the Iraq invasion and the Turkish Army was on fairly high alert. A British warship was a constant presence in the Strait.

The conference was attended by members of every NATO country and also had representation from several other countries that were lobbying for admission—Bulgaria, Estonia, Latvia, Lithuania, Romania,

Slovakia and Slovenia. (They were officially admitted to NATO on March 29, 2004.) There were four areas of debate and resolutions were agreed to and brought forward by committees on the Civil Dimension of Security, Defence and Security, Science and Technology and Politics. I participated in the Defence and Security meetings. It was fascinating to be part of discussions about 9/11 in an area so close to Iraq and during the months leading up to the invasion. From our conference, these resolutions were forwarded to the general NATO assembly, held soon after ours in Prague, Czech Republic, where they were debated and voted on.

We were able to do some touring of the city and it was truly magnificent. The highlight for most tourists is the Grand Bazaar, an ancient shopping area boasting five thousand shops. It winds along street after street, but much of it is underground; a virtual labyrinth of businesses. I loved the bartering! It was great fun to haggle back and forth, doing the "dance of the deal," turning to walk away and being chased by the vendor. Turkey is known for its beautiful handmade carpets, textiles and gorgeous leather products and we loved looking at them in the shops. We were also thoroughly entertained by the traffic in Istanbul. There were thousands of cars swerving in and out of lanes, around buses and trucks, looking as if they were moving to the sounds of a finely tuned symphony. We were breathless as our taxi drivers virtually flew through the streets, honking and waving others out of our way. We didn't even lose a rear-view mirror, much to our complete surprise.

When we arrived home, Mom and Dad Larson were thrilled to hear stories about our trip. Dad loved to listen and share in our experiences. He was glad when I gave him a couple of pens from Istanbul; he had a collection and was always happy when I brought him pens from my travels. We gave him some maps that we had received while there. He took them home and enjoyed poring over them for a couple of weeks. On Saturday, December 7, they came by our place to drop the maps off. I had arrived home from Ottawa the night before and invited them in for coffee. They said they wouldn't bother as they were heading over to their church to look at the Christmas decorations. I told them I was just going over the mail and asked again. Mom went out to the car and got Dad. We had a nice visit over coffee for about an hour and they headed out. A few minutes after I shut the door, I heard a knock. I opened the door to find Mom holding Dad up, his face covered with blood. He had tripped and fallen in our driveway and cut himself badly. I hollered for Lew and he ran downstairs. We got Dad a chair and I went to call an ambulance. He said he was fine, so Lew drove them in their car and I followed in ours to the hospital. We waited for a while for him to be seen and get stitched up. I had my Edmonton North Christmas supper that evening, so Mom said they would be fine and she would call when they got home from emergency. She called around suppertime to tell us that they had done a CAT scan on Dad and discovered that his brain was haemorrhaging from the impact of the fall. They would keep him in for the night and try to reverse the swelling. By nine o'clock they told her there was little hope of getting it under control. We got to the hospital by 10:30, just as he was being transferred into a room on the ward. He faded into unconsciousness soon after we arrived. He remained that way for just over forty-eight hours and passed away on Tuesday, December 10, 2002, at 1:00 A.M. It was such a shock for us all. One moment he was laughing, slurping his coffee through a sugar cube (a Norwegian tradition) and telling stories. The next, he was broken and battered. We were all so thankful he did not suffer; he would have hated to end up in a care facility, withering away.

All but one of his children made it home before he died and the last one arrived in time for the funeral. It was held on Friday, December 13, and the service was a wonderful tribute to a man who had lived his life serving others. What I enjoyed the most was the laughter; he had always been a joke-teller and entertained everyone with his tales. Some of his favourites were told at the funeral and the crowd loved them; each person remembering their own experiences of hearing Leroy's jokes. He had been a real father to me. It was a huge adjustment not to have him around. Death is so final. I have wished so many times to have him back again. I think of him every time I look in the cupboard and see the sugar cubes; every time I see a flock of geese. (When somebody would ask why one line is often longer when the geese were flying in a "v," he would always respond, "Because there are more geese in it.") Our family was so grateful for friends who supported us during difficult days and suffering the loss of Dad so close to Christmas. I have marvelled as I have watched Mom adjust to life without her partner of over fifty-five years. She has been an "over-comer." While devastated by the loss of a husband, she has accepted it willingly and graciously. Although she has grieved deeply, she does not mope. If she is having a particularly lonely day, she will go out for coffee with a friend or come to see us. She is a fine role model and I am grateful for the lessons she is teaching me about dealing with death.

One of the most frustrating aspects of the whole thing to me was living the intersection of personal and political life. In the House of Commons, we were debating the Kyoto Protocol. Our party had voiced strong disagreement with the deal and the direction the government was heading on climate change. I spoke to our whip, Dale Johnston, and explained what had happened to Dad. The big vote was scheduled for Monday. Dale was very understanding, but maintained how important it would be to get to the vote, if possible. Over the weekend, the vote was deferred until Tuesday. On the Monday evening, when Dad was near death, I said goodbye to him and Lew drove me to the airport so I could take the all-night flight to Ottawa. I felt so alone and so far from home and family. When I arrived at Toronto, I received Lew's message on my cell phone that Dad had died at approximately 1:00 A.M. while I was en route. I sat in the women's washroom in the Maple Leaf Lounge and wept, all alone. I carried on to Ottawa, voted that afternoon and returned home; I was gone less than twenty-four hours. One might ask why I bothered to go across the country for a vote that was a foregone conclusion. It is always a toss-up, trying to balance personal and political responsibilities. Even though I could do nothing to keep Dad alive, and stayed with him around the clock while his condition weakened, I still wanted to be there until the end. Yet, my professional duty called me to be at the other end of the country, voting on behalf of my constituents and standing with my party. Somehow, this seemed like a compromise solution. It was difficult, but in retrospect, I have no regrets about the way I chose to handle it.

There are times when it would not be an issue to miss a vote. However, Kyoto was a huge issue for our party and for me as an

Albertan. We had serious concerns with the government being a signatory to the Kyoto Protocol in 1997. David Anderson, the minister of the environment, has spent years trying to cajole Canadians and other countries into endorsing Kyoto. To date, the United States and Russia have not ratified it and it is doubtful they ever will. There are many scientific reports that do not support the idea that Kyoto will address the issues surrounding air pollutants and CO_2 emissions. In fact, the environment department's own meteorologist said there was no scientific connection between extreme weather and climate change. Our party supports a more practical plan based on technological innovation and a sensible approach to climate change that could be exported to other developing countries. Several of our provinces are already implementing such measures as encouraging energy-efficiency improvements, technological innovations and alternative energy sources that will reduce the intensity of CO_2 emissions. These practical plans need to be expanded throughout our country and to other nations. We recommend a Canadian Clean Air Act that would review current air-pollution standards to ensure they are up-to-date and workable. It would require the development of a national air-pollution database and provide assistance to provinces, territories and municipalities toward the development and adoption of new environmentally beneficial technologies. (Article by Bob Mills, MP, *The Hill Times*, p. 26, April 19–25, 2004.) Consequently, the importance of this issue took me to Ottawa and back in the middle of a family crisis. Nonetheless, I knew Dad would have approved; he loved nature and was opposed to the government's approach to Kyoto as well!

In January 2003, I took a trip out to Vancouver and Victoria to visit my family. Lew and I had talked about whether or not I would run again, but I wanted to talk it over with my mom and sisters as well. Not only had I faced many political challenges in the previous couple of years, but I also needed to take stock of my personal situation. August 7 would be our 10th wedding anniversary and we had never lived together full-time. I wasn't sure that I wanted to commit to another possible five-year run in Parliament. Also, Dad's very recent passing had brought me face-to-face with the reality of dealing with death from a distance. I found that difficult because I wanted to be closer to home to comfort, but also to be comforted in my own grief. It became tougher to get on a plane every week while wanting to be home more. I had never planned on being a career politician and suddenly it was fourteen years since my election. If I ran for another term, I wouldn't have a great deal of time to open another door to a new chapter in my life.

The Electoral Boundaries Commission had done a lot of work on riding redistribution after the last census. They had drawn up their preliminary riding boundaries and made substantive changes to the constituencies in Edmonton and the surrounding areas. Some of my colleagues and I had made presentations to the commission in the fall. Edmonton North's boundaries were to be changed somewhat, but many of the others were substantially redrawn. The theory of the commission was to mix urban and rural areas; consequently the outlying towns of St. Albert, Sherwood Park, Spruce Grove, Beaumont and Leduc would be joined with parts of Edmonton in pie-shaped ridings. This did not go over well with people who chose to live out of the city on acreages and in the smaller towns because it meant that parts of Edmonton North would be amalgamated into these rural areas, while Edmonton-Centre East would disappear. Their MP, Peter Goldring, mused that he might move back to Ontario and seek a nomination there. The more I thought about running again, the more it seemed this chapter of my life was done. After I hashed it out with my family and very close friends, I decided that it was time to close the door. You just plain know in your gut when the time has come for one thing to end and another to begin. I had a coffee meeting with my board of directors in Edmonton North on Saturday, February 22, 2003. I confided in them that it was time for me to move on. I appreciated their support and understanding and told them I planned to make an announcement on my upcoming anniversary on March 13. They kept it a complete secret; not one hint of a leak came out. The new Electoral Boundaries Commission maps came out on Monday, February 24, just after I got back to Ottawa. I opened the book to Edmonton and discovered that Edmonton East had been reinstated and Edmonton North was eliminated completely! I smiled and remembered the story of the billboard that had brought me to

Edmonton North in the first place. I'd had two wonderful terms serving these constituents and now it was gone, just like Beaver River.

A week later, I was appointed as our party's delegate to travel on an official visit with the Speaker of the House of Commons to Austria and Hungary. Lew was also able to go along with me and we all left on March 1. Our delegation was comprised of members from each party and some staff, for a total of eleven people. In Austria, we met with parliamentarians and many different individuals and committees. Austria had just held their elections on November 24, 2002. The People's Party won the election, but not a majority. Therefore, it formed a formal coalition with the Green Party. They had long-standing disagreements on various issues, such as the environment, education and the purchase of fighter jets, to name a few. However, they joined forces and formed a coalition government. It reminded me of the coalition that I had been part of back in Canada. The political will must be there to make it work, regardless of motive.

The city of Vienna is truly magnificent and we had an opportunity to experience some of its history and splendour. We visited the parliament buildings, the famous Hotel Sacher, the Museum of Fine Arts and the world-famous Vienna Opera House for a performance of *La Favorite*. Wow! We also enjoyed a reception at the residence of our ambassador, Ingrid Hall. I was impressed by the professionalism and expertise of our Canadian team that served in the embassy.

We were then driven to Budapest, Hungary for an official visit. We were chauffeured by a convoy of vehicles that travelled at seemingly supersonic speeds through the streets of Budapest, accompanied by police, who had flashing lights and waved off anyone who dared cut in to our entourage. It was a wild ride and we were amused by the importance our little delegation was accorded! We stayed at the guest house of the Ministry of the Interior, which had been used over the years by various dictators who had visited the city. We were overwhelmed by the beauty of Budapest, especially the parliament buildings, which were situated on the banks of the Danube River, unlike those in Vienna. We learned that every window in the parliament had been taken out several times over the years, to protect them during wars. It was sobering to stand on the grounds of parliament, the site of the Hungarian uprising in 1956, where many young people died trying to push for freedom and democracy. After so many years of socialism, Hungary had only had a democratic government for ten years. It was remarkable to witness the transition to democratic government over the last decade. Our delegation met with the president, the speaker, the Hungary-Canada Friendship Group and the Canadian Chamber of Commerce and were entertained at the official residence of our Canadian ambassador, Ron Halpin. His team impressed us just as much as the one in Austria. A trip to nearby towns was organized for us and we enjoyed witnessing the daily life of Hungarians in Esztergom, Visegrád and Szentendre. The history that we felt in those towns was tangible. It made Canada seem pretty young. We loved overlooking the Danube River, which had been such a huge part of European history, imagining people and cargo travelling along it centuries ago. A final highlight was a trip to the Budapest Opera House for a Royal Box viewing of the opera *Bluebeard's Castle* and ballet *The Miraculous Mandarin*.

We arrived back in Canada on March 11, grateful for the fabulous experiences of seeing a new and dynamic part of the world, but thankful to be home. My staff organized a press conference for 11:00 A.M. on March 13, the fourteenth anniversary of my election to the House of Commons. I announced that I did not intend to run for a fifth term in Parliament. As this signified the passage through a new door of my life, I will discuss it in the next chapter.

Throughout the spring, the PC leadership moved toward the finish line. There were some all-candidates' debates, but they were generally quite civil. One of the main issues was "unity with the Canadian Alliance." David Orchard pushed the others, especially the frontrunner, Peter MacKay. He did not appear interested in getting together with Stephen Harper and the Alliance. The leadership convention was held on May 31, 2003, and ended up providing one of the most bizarre twists of any convention in recent history. Grafftey and Chandler were dropped on the first ballot, Scott Brison on the second. On the third ballot, David Orchard was eliminated. The big question was: Who would he throw his support behind? The last two in the race were Peter

MacKay and Jim Prentice, the pro-unity candidate. As Orchard was so dead against any discussions with the Alliance, it seemed obvious that he would go with MacKay. What happened next shocked Tories and non-Tories alike. Word came out that MacKay was making a deal with Orchard to secure the leadership. In fact, a hasty meeting of the two produced a five-point document that they both signed. On the fourth ballot, Peter MacKay was victorious, winning 64.4 per cent of the votes to Jim Prentice's 35.6 per cent. News swirled around about "the deal." The pressure was relentless on Peter to make its contents known. Some days later, he produced the handwritten agreement that he and Orchard had both signed in the hotel room. The deal contained four main points:

> 1) No merger or joint candidates with the Canadian Alliance and the maintenance of the 301 rule (this was adopted at their last convention the previous summer and stated that their party would run a PC candidate in all 301 federal ridings);
> 2) A review of the Free Trade Agreement and North America Free Trade Agreement by a blue-ribbon commission, with the chair and members subject to joint agreement;
> 3) Cleaning up head office, including a change of national director with consultation and some of David Orchard's people working at head office; and
> 4) A commitment to put environmental protection front and centre, including sustainable agriculture, forestry, including reducing pollution through rail.
> (*National Post*, June 5, 2003)

When this agreement was made public, there were howls about MacKay making a deal with the devil and selling his soul just to obtain the leadership. It was a very rough period for him, perhaps an unnecessary one, since he likely would have won the race anyway. Stephen Harper said the level of influence that Orchard had in the party shocked him. He commented, "I am troubled by all of the contents of this. To hand an opponent sweeping control over policy, over future direction, over staffing, over major policy issues…I am just shocked by the sweeping terms of this."(*National Post*, June 5, 2003.) He also said that he was willing to sit down and discuss political cooperation at some point, but was concerned that the Tories had already ruled out too many options. On June 12 and 16, in Calgary and Toronto, Stephen outlined his plans for a "common cause" initiative to create a single slate of candidates. This idea was well received in Alliance circles, but also among Conservative members at the ground level. Many of the large financial backers had said for some time that the two parties had better figure out a way to cooperate or the funding would dry up. Belinda Stronach, CEO of Magna International, was a key figure in getting the two sides to the table. Attempts were made to bring Stephen and Peter together, but the fallout from the Orchard deal and media pressure made it tough. However, on June 26, Peter and Stephen met to discuss the "common cause" proposal. They did agree on three items: they would appoint representatives to have meetings, all options would be open for discussion and the group would provide recommendations to the leaders by Labour Day. We were glad to see the cooperation in the courtship ritual. This was a positive sign. Stephen then appointed as his representatives Ray Speaker (long-time provincial MLA and former Reform MP), Gerry St. Germain (former PC MP and Mulroney-appointed Senator who had joined our Alliance caucus some years earlier) and Scott Reid (Alliance MP from Lanark-Carleton who had served as Stephen's trusted advisor). They made this project their highest priority for the entire summer. Unfortunately, not much happened over the next two months. It seemed like a dance where neither partner was sure which move to make next. This two-step took place under the watchful and critical eye of the national media, who were anxious to report every nuance, conversation and apparent "deal-breaker." On August 21, the groups from both sides actually met and had some helpful discussions. It seemed as if both sides were going to contribute to the courtship. Things looked extremely hopeful. Peter's team was composed of Don Mazankowski (former PC MP and deputy prime minister), William Davis (former Ontario premier) and Loyola Hearn (a PC MP from Newfoundland). They agreed to meet again on August 30. In the interim, general comments in the media from both sides did not help and the August 30 meeting was torpedoed. Things looked as though they might fall apart permanently at that point. Nonetheless, Stephen's team prepared a proposal from the August 21 discussions regarding a single slate of candidates. From that, a fourteen-point proposal was drafted and sent to Peter on August 30, in place of the planned, but unexecuted, meeting. The points were:

1) The new party shall be known as the "Conservative Party of Canada" (CPC);

2) The CPC shall assume all the rights, assets and liabilities of the Canadian Alliance and the Progressive Conservative Party;

3) The PC and CA leaders are responsible for achieving support of their parties for the goals and legal establishment of the CPC by October 10, 2003;

4) The PC and CA will immediately each name eleven members to an interim governing body, with equal representation from each province;

5) The interim governing body will be responsible for ensuring filings with Elections Canada (by Nov. 10, 2003), drafting a constitution (by Dec. 31, 2003), establishing electoral district associations and overseeing candidate nominations;

6) The CPC will establish a trust fund capable of retiring the PC debt;

7) The CA and PC caucuses of both Houses will immediately establish the CPC parliamentary caucus;

8) The CPC parliamentary caucus will elect an interim leader and draft a statement of principles and policies;

9) The interim leader will serve as the leader of the Opposition and be responsible for election preparedness;

10) The CA and PC parties will each name two individuals to a leadership election organizing committee;

11) The leadership vote shall be conducted by mail-in ballot on the basis of one member, one vote. Membership cut-off shall be November 17, 2003. First ballot shall be completed by December 17, 2003. Any runoff ballot shall be completed by January 7, 2004;

12) The founding convention shall be held in Ottawa on February 19–21, 2004. It shall consist of ten delegates from each riding, plus members of the interim governing body, Conservative Party Trust, CPC parliamentary caucus, leadership election organizing committee, CA National Council and PC Management Committee;

13) The founding convention shall be responsible for the amendment and adoption of a constitution and statement of principles and policies;

14) Where possible, the selection of PC and CA candidates will be grandfathered to the CPC, and further CA and PC nomination meetings shall immediately cease. (Stephen Harper, memo to CA Caucus and Council, September 29, 2003.)

These proposals were amazingly detailed and very specific. There could be no doubt where Stephen Harper stood on the issue of merging with the PCs. The deal was on the table. Peter was notified that Stephen was prepared to take it to our membership for a vote. He asked for Peter's response. He did not receive one, but Peter agreed to kick-starting the talks again. The chats went back and forth and finally it was agreed to have the "emissaries" return to a face-to-face dialogue. After more discussions, it was agreed that the emissaries would meet again on September 22, that the Tory side would actually provide a counter-proposal, that the emissaries would meet until they reached an agreement in principle or a decision not to agree, and they would report the results to their leaders. The September 22 meeting lasted until September 23 and the report came back that a deal in principle was a possibility. A conference call was set up for September 26, but an agreement was not reached. It looked, again, like any deal was impossible. Our caucus had long discussions about the pros and cons of keeping the invitation on the table. Some were dead against waiting any longer. Harper said he would not wait indefinitely and mused that Thanksgiving would be about the longest he would or could wait. When you think about the mammoth task it would be to try to accomplish the fourteen points that Stephen laid out, it was a wonder that both sides didn't shut negotiations down completely. There was not much time left before both parties would simply have to start gearing up for the election on their own. The window of opportunity was closing. The press asked me if I thought this was nothing more than a backroom deal between the politicians. I replied, "Not at all. People across Canada, not just party members, have been crying out for a unified party that could pose an alternative to the governing Liberals. This is a case of the politicians trying to catch up to the public that is far out ahead of us." And truly it was. If we didn't get it right now, it was doubtful that we ever would.

However, after the stalemate of the September 30 meeting, things looked bleak indeed. As in many courtships, there is a period where everything looks like it might totally crumble. We seemed to be at that spot during this week. Stephen outlined what he thought were two large obstacles; one of these was the formula for the leadership vote. The CA believed in one member, one vote. The PCs favoured a system of assigning points to each riding, which would afford the same weight to a riding, regardless of the size of its membership. The other was the manner of setting policy at the founding convention. The Tories wanted it governed by the PC constitution and Stephen proposed the more populist approach that had been our hallmark: members debate and vote on policy and that becomes our final policy document, with a double majority safeguard; a majority of the members and a majority of the provinces. As late as Friday, October 10, no deal seemed even remotely in sight. On that day, Harper described MacKay as lacking "any spirit of compromise," and expressed his doubts that a deal could be done. (*Calgary Herald*, October 16, 2003.) Again, it looked like the possibility of unity was remote and getting more remote each day.

Those days were a roller coaster of emotion for both sides. We all had to work together in the House of Commons and took the odd swipe at each other. Both sides felt morally superior and tempers flared occasionally. On October 10, the House rose for the Thanksgiving recess, probably a good thing for all concerned. During the recess week, I was scheduled to speak to the Rotary Club in Edmonton. It would be a large group of professional people who wanted me to address the topic of "What will it take to unite the right and who will lead it?" I tried to write my speech, but every time I did, there was another stalemate between the two leaders. With each attempt to prepare for the speech, I felt more frustrated and exasperated. On the day before the Rotary Club meeting, I got to the point where I thought I might have to stand up in front of the crowd, shrug my shoulders and just say, "Beats me," then sit down again! Just before I went to bed on Wednesday night, October 15, I got a call from someone in caucus saying that Harper and MacKay were flying to Ottawa to strike a deal. "Yeah," I thought, "we've heard that one before." I went to bed, worried about what I could possibly say tomorrow at the lunch. Early the next morning, my phone rang. It was Wes from my Ottawa office, saying that they had come up with a deal and were having a press conference in half an hour. I watched it and realized that it really had happened. The body language of Peter and Stephen said it all. This was not a deal that had been forced on one side or the other. It was a joint effort of two men who were putting their egos aside and making an enormous contribution to their country. They were relaxed, relieved and rejuvenated. I jumped up off the couch and said, "YES! Now I can write my speech for the lunch today!" I went to my office, ran off copies of the agreement-in-principle and handed them out to the crowd, some of whom had been in meetings all morning and only heard the news when they came to the lunch. They got the deal "hot off the press." The agreement contained fourteen points, very similar to the original ones put forward by Stephen in the summer. These included the name of the party, principles governing the relationship between the CA and the PCs, founding principles, leadership election organizing committee, leadership selection, one-time process for leadership selection, membership, interim joint council, Conservative Trust Fund, transfer of assets and liabilities, completion of

ratification, critical path (timelines for implementation), first convention and standstill of nominations. It had been a mammoth task, but it
was now done. The founding principles included, amongst others: to
create a balance between fiscal accountability, progressive social policy
and individual rights and responsibilities; to build a national coalition
of people who share these beliefs and who reflect the regional, cultural
and socio-economic diversity of Canada; to develop this coalition,
embracing our differences and respecting our traditions, yet honouring
a concept of Canada as the greater sum of strong parts; and to operate
the Conservative Party of Canada in a manner accountable and responsive to its members. In addition, we were committed to a belief in
loyalty to a sovereign and united Canada governed in accordance with
the Constitution of Canada; the supremacy of democratic parliamentary institutions and the rule of law; a belief in the equality of all
Canadians; a belief in the freedom of the individual, including freedom
of speech, worship and assembly; a belief in the federal system of government as the best expression of the diversity of our country, and in
the desirability of strong provincial and territorial governments; a belief
that a responsible government must be fiscally prudent and should be
limited to those responsibilities that cannot be discharged reasonably
by the individual or others; a belief that the purpose of Canada as a
nation state and its government, guided by reflective and prudent leadership, is to create a climate wherein individual initiative is rewarded,
excellence is pursued, security and privacy of the individual is provided
and prosperity is guaranteed by a free competitive market economy; a
belief that the quality of the environment is a vital part of our heritage
to be protected by each generation for the next; and a belief that all
Canadians should have reasonable access to quality health care regardless of their ability to pay. These principles laid the groundwork of a
new conservative party that heretofore had often been at odds, but from
now on would be a single, united force on the national stage. The
courtship had been consummated. What a great day!

The next step was to obtain ratification from the membership of the
PCs and the CA. A date was set for the membership vote. Mail-in ballots were sent between October 27 and November 27 for the CA, using

our one-member, one-vote system. The PCs used a delegate selection meeting. The deadline for final ratification was December 12, 2003. The CA results came in with a resounding endorsement; the agreement was passed with 95.9 per cent approval! The PC vote was equally resounding; 90.4 per cent were in favour. By December 13, I was Deborah Grey, Conservative MP. Who'da thunk it?

CHAPTER 22

The Cycle Is Complete:
Exit Stage Right

THE WEDDING WAS OVER. Our new life had begun. We had wondered if it would ever happen; now here we were! The guests were happy, for the most part. The next part was for the couple to live together and make the necessary adjustments to married life. We lost a few people along the way who were neither interested in, nor able to, make the commitment to this union. André Bachand (Arthabaska), the only PC Member in Quebec, decided not to run again because the Alliance had remained low in the polls there and he felt being associated with it would not help his chances in his province. Also, Scott Brison (Kings-Hants) who had run for the leadership of the PCs, started making "anti-Conservative" remarks. The next thing we knew he was announcing that he was now a Liberal and when Paul Martin was sworn in as prime minister on December 12, 2003, he made Brison a parliamentary secretary. John Herron (Fundy-Royal) decided that he could not participate in the "unholy alliance" either and chose to sit out the remainder of the term as an independent. Also, Joe Clark (Calgary Centre) made loud noises that this was a terrible coalition (but wasn't it similar to the one we had been in with him?) and he would have nothing to do with it. We then realized that when Joe had talked about working together in the PC/DR coalition, he really wanted it to be on PC terms and was not interested in creating something new, like what we had now. On our side, we lost Keith Martin (Esquimalt-Juan-de-Fuca). I was not surprised by this move, because he had always been liberal in his thinking. Some thought it strange, though, since in the late fall he had stood up in caucus and pledged his undying support to our party and to Stephen Harper. Nonetheless, he sat as an independent for the rest of the term and ran in 2004 as a Liberal.

Our caucus began sitting together in January 2004. We were now a caucus of seventy-three with a Senate caucus of twenty-five. Many of my Alliance colleagues did not know the Senators, but the DR had worked with them in the coalition, so it was fun to be a liaison for both sides. As the Conservative leadership race was underway, we had an interim leader, Grant Hill (McLeod) as Leader of the Opposition, and Senator John Lynch-Staunton as the Leader of the Conservative Party. This went extremely well and we enjoyed getting to know each other. At the beginning, people were cautious, but there was an enormous desire to meld together and make the thing work. We knew that all eyes were on us and the media would be waiting for any opportunity to pounce. Fortunately, nothing happened to our caucus, but the Liberals started infighting. Paul Martin won the leadership race—or was it a coronation?—on November 15. Chrétien had announced that he was planning to retire in February 2004. There was enormous pressure put on him to step down earlier. He protested for some time, but eventually announced that he would formally leave on December 12, 2003. Martin took over that day and was sworn in with a new Cabinet. Immediately, there were complaints from the old guard and questions raised about the Chrétien-Martin forces. This went on for some time and never was resolved before the election call. Thank goodness the Conservatives got on well. Our leadership race provided some small fireworks, but nothing explosive or divisive.

Stephen entered the race as the front-runner. He had the organizational structure to begin with, much of it left over from his previous run, only two years earlier. He appealed to a broad base of conservative thinkers and really grew in the job. Many watched him mature in leadership and bridge-building skills with the Progressive Conservative element of the party. He appeared upbeat and very knowledgeable in the debates.

Belinda Stronach had been a long-time supporter of the united alternative movement. She, and other major financial backers, continued to put pressure on the two parties to get together or we would split the conservative vote for another decade, at least. I admired her tenacity and perseverance to move the ball forward. We had gotten to know each other and had been friends for some years, watching how this was all playing out. We talked to each other on the phone when she was thinking about throwing her hat into the leadership ring. I told her that I thought she would bring excitement and enthusiasm to the race. And she did! She gave up an extremely high-paying job as CEO of Magna International, an auto parts company. She was completely inexperienced in the political realm, but she grew and became more comfortable in the spotlight. It turned into a bit of "Belinda-mania" and our party drew a lot of media attention because of it. She committed to run for us in the next election, regardless of whether she won or lost the leadership.

Tony Clement was the third contestant in the race. He had also been a long-time supporter of the united alternative movement. Like Belinda, he was a PC from Ontario. It was essential to have someone from the PC side and especially from Ontario. I never was sure why two of them ran. It seems to me that this strategy was not the best, because they would split that vote. Nonetheless, he was in as well. Tony is a good, solid Conservative, with a long history of involvement with the PCs. He had served in the Mike Harris government in Ontario. He, and many others, had taken a pounding in the provincial election in November 2003, being replaced by Dalton McGuinty and the Liberals. This could have had something to do with the federal Conservative race, but I wonder if it was the double candidacy from Ontario that harmed them more.

The leadership race culminated on March 20, 2004. We used a weighting system so that ridings were each given points, which fairly equalized ridings, regardless of membership sizes. In Toronto, where the event was held, the candidates gave their speeches on Friday night. Peter MacKay and I were the co-chairs for the weekend event. It was fun to share the stage and poke fun at each other and ourselves. I said, "I love

that word Refoooorm!" And he retorted "And I love the word 'progressive!'" I shot back, "Oh, yes, the Progressives from the twenties. They
were our forerunners." We had a great time and we proved that conservatives really can have fun. Finally, the results of the first ballot were
announced: Stephen Harper, 17,296 (56.2 per cent); Belinda Stronach,
10,613 (34.5 per cent); Tony Clement, 2,887 (9.4 per cent). The membership had spoken loudly. They had chosen Harper by a sound margin
on the first ballot. It was thought that Harper would do well in the West,
but not particularly well in Ontario, where the race had two candidates
from there. He did very well there, as well as holding his own in Quebec
and Atlantic Canada. This proved that he had substantial crossover votes
from the PC side of the membership. It was encouraging to see that support, because people couldn't grumble on the regional breakdown.
There was no question; he had won, and won big.

We had a national caucus the following Monday, March 22. He
exhibited leadership to the entire group, many of whom were the Tory
MPs and Senators, who had never sat in the same room with him
because he had been on the leadership campaign trail when we started
sitting together in January. It was encouraging for me to see that this
thing really was coming together. It truly is an intercultural marriage we
are in. The Tory history is long, stretching all the way back to Sir John
A. MacDonald. They really feel that connection. Also, their national
infrastructure is deep-rooted. The Senate has contributed to that, but
also large donors who have given to the party for generations. In
Atlantic Canada, it is almost genetic whether you are a Liberal or a
Conservative. The Reform and Alliance tradition, on the other hand,
provides raw energy and a practical, populist approach to politics. We
do not feel as if we are born into a political family or ideology. That is
why many of us love and live by Nellie McClung's great line, "Never
retreat, never explain, never apologize; just get the thing done and let
them howl." We see a job that needs to get done and we just get at it. I
had always thought the combination of these two parties, if it could ever
happen, would be awesome. And I always had a feeling deep inside that
even if it did come together, I likely would not be a part of it. It was a
strange feeling, one I could not shake. I had always felt like the flag-

bearer, the forerunner, the trailblazer. I wondered for years if that were to be my whole role in the process. It may seem ironic that I had made my announcement not to run again long before the merger. But, then again, maybe not…

As a result of political and personal happenings, I had made my decision with family and friends some time before the merger happened. On March 13, 2003, a full seven months before Peter and Stephen penned the agreement-in-principle, I held a press conference to announce I would not seek a fifth term in Parliament. As I mentioned in the previous chapter, my riding association knew of my decision on February 22, but had kept it confidential until my announcement on March 13. The press assembled in my office in droves; there was barely enough room to hold them all. I enjoyed visiting with them when they came in to set up; I had known them all for so many years and done interviews with them about everything under the sun. This was a much happier occasion to host them than the last major press conference I held in my constituency office in July 2001. Things were much more stable for the party and I was much more settled personally. I began my remarks by saying,

> Fourteen years ago today, March 13, 1989, I made Canadian history by becoming the first Reform Party MP. I have seen tremendous growth, going from my one seat in 1989 to fifty-two seats in 1993 and to sixty seats in 1997, forming the Official Opposition. Our party merged with other conservative-minded people across the country and formed the Canadian Alliance in the spring of 2000. That fall, we won sixty-six seats and continued as the Official Opposition. Our present leader, Stephen Harper, served as my legislative assistant when I began in 1989. He has come full circle by serving as staff member, Member of Parliament and now party leader. He is doing an excellent job. Our party has paid off its debt, the caucus is united and we are holding the Liberals to account. I did not enter Parliament with the intention of becoming a "career politician." Therefore, after much thought, I have decided not

to seek a fifth term in Parliament. I am ready to pass the torch to a new generation of political reformers. They will continue the vision that Preston Manning began some fifteen years ago. I do not have any future career plans as yet. I look forward to finishing this term with Stephen Harper and my colleagues to hold the Liberals' feet to the fire. My husband, Lewis, and I are grateful for the support we have received over the years. I have enjoyed representing the people of Beaver River and Edmonton North in Parliament. Lew and I will always be thankful for the many friendships we have made across the country while in public life.

I then answered a barrage of questions about what my "real" agenda and reasons were. I had stated them all; there was nothing hidden or secret. I simply knew in my gut that it was time to move on.

Some months after my announcement, when the merger actually occurred, it started to fit together for me. I was asked over and over again, "Deb, this new party is so exciting. We need you to be a part of it. Won't you reconsider and change your mind?" I would scrunch up my face, close one eye, look upwards for three or four seconds, then say, "Okay, I've reconsidered. And no, I won't change my mind." You just know when you know....

For me, it is sad watching someone go past his or her "best-before" date. I have seen it in politics, preachers and professors. There is nothing worse than seeing a person past their prime, but hanging on like grim death to something that has slipped away on them. They seem unwilling or unable to admit it is time to move on to a new chapter in their lives. The saddest thing of all is that, if they refuse to accept a new door graciously, their input lessens and they often become totally ineffective. This seems like a terrible way to go out. I want to learn and grow during each chapter, yet be unafraid to let go and move on through the next door. Is it frightening? Yes. Is it secure? No. Is it comfortable? No. Is it necessary? Yes. If you don't grow and accept challenges, you atrophy in your mind, your soul, your spirit. If you refuse to renew, you rot. So many people want to cling on to what they have, thinking they cannot do anything else, afraid to move out of their comfort zone, afraid to let go of the trapeze they are on now. A trapeze is built in such a way that you cannot grab the next bar until you let go of the one you are on. There is no way to hold them both. So, as difficult as it is, you need to let go of the one you are clinging onto. I did that March 13, 2003, and have been in freefall ever since, not knowing what is coming next. But how exciting! I am choosing to renew rather than rot. Even though I knew I could likely get re-elected, (taking me to age fifty-five, when the pension would kick in), continue with a salary of $140,000 per year, putting money away toward that pension, it all seemed "too easy." If that is the only reason to stay, it is wrong. When you lose the fire in your belly for Parliament or anything else, it is wrong to keep at it, for your-self and others. Don't do it. I believe that would lead to a lot of regrets down the road. It could never be worth it, for any reason. We do not get a rehearsal for our career. There is one crack at it. A new challenge always seems preferable to regret, in my books.

Our two parties took that risk of letting go of our trapezes, also. We knew that remaining static, beating up on each other, would not help the Canadian public, or us. So, egos were put aside and an agreement was reached for the greater good. It was very difficult and some dreams had to die, but it was worth it. I think of Peter MacKay, young and ambitious, capable, personable; yet he realized it was necessary to lay down his leadership for this cause. He may yet obtain the leadership down the road, but there is no guarantee of that. However, he under-stood the importance of what needed to happen and let go of the trapeze of power and prestige. Thank you, Peter.

While Peter was relinquishing power, Paul Martin was clinging on to it, more and more tightly. He and his team had virtually chased Chrétien from power, wanting to obtain it as quickly as possible. The ironic part about that was the timing of the release of the Auditor General's report on February 12, 2004. An explosive report of money laundering and pay-offs to political pals, it dealt with what would come to be called the "sponsorship scandal." Sheila Fraser, the Auditor General, had conducted a lengthy investigation into the spending of $250,000,000 on "boosting Canada" in the wake of the Quebec referendum in 1995. It turned out that the federal government wanted to promote the idea of Canada, so they purchased billboards, plastered the logo of Canada all over buildings and projects, floated Canada remote-control blimps in hockey arenas and sponsored Canada parties and festivals. The money that was specified for various groups went through government-appointed advertising agencies. These agencies collected huge sums for simply passing on the government cheque to whatever group was receiving funding. The AG was outraged. She said she had never seen such a blatant misuse of government funds. By her team's calculations, fully $100,000,000 of the total spending of $250,000,000 went to these ad agencies, who simply handed the government money to the recipients. She said it was "shocking." It turned into a firestorm that Paul Martin did not recover from. He claimed to be "mad as h-ll" and said he was going to get to the bottom of the scandal. All the while, he maintained that he knew nothing about it. He was the finance minister, and although he might not have known where every single cheque went, surely he must have been aware of the program and how much it was costing. Surely the ledger didn't balance. The ad agencies were skimming a pile of cash off the top. Did nobody notice? Why did it take Sheila Fraser to come in and discover one of the biggest scandals in Canadian history? Did nobody notice how much of this money was being recycled back into the Liberal Party? Paul Martin blamed it on a few "rogue bureaucrats." A public inquiry was announced, but it would take until September 2004 to hear its first witness. The Public Accounts Committee of Parliament launched an investigation at the request of the prime minister. This is the only committee that is chaired by a member of the Official Opposition. My colleague John Williams (St. Albert) oversaw the committee and many of the witnesses appeared to give the standard line, "This was the government trying to save Canada from the separatists. There was no political interference." However, a few individuals testified that they knew what was going on behind the scenes; no written contracts, political masters giving orders to dispense cash, rules being bent or broken. The irony in all of this mess was that, while it had happened on Chrétien's watch, Paul Martin had chased him out before he was ready to go. If Chrétien had stayed on (as he had wanted to) until February 2004, he would have still been prime minister when the AG's report came down. Instead, Martin got pasted with it. His old nemesis, Chrétien, had dodged another bullet and it hit Paul Martin right between the eyes. Within two weeks of the report, Liberal support had dropped from 48 per cent to 39 per cent (Ipsos-Reid/CTV/*Globe and Mail*, January 15–February 12/04.) Soon after, Paul Martin's personal support had dropped from 60 per cent to 41 per cent (Environics Research Group March 29–April 18/04). In Quebec the numbers dropped drastically for the Liberals. They fell from 48 per cent to 37 per cent and the Bloc increased from 37 per cent to 45 per cent. (Environics Research Group March 29–April 18/04.) Chuck Guité, head of the Sponsorship Program, had boasted that he bought every billboard in Quebec for a total of $8,000,000. Whether federalist or separatist, Quebecers saw the federal government trying to manipulate them after the referendum. They were not amused and the polls reflected their dissatisfaction.

In the same period of time, the Conservatives went from 21 per cent to 28 per cent (Ipsos-Reid) and Stephen Harper's personal support went from 7 per cent to 19 per cent (Environics). Martin wanted to call an election in early April, but the polls spoke volumes. At best, he could win a minority government. April drifted into May and the writ had not been dropped. Constant polling was done to see if the Liberals' support could be shored up. It did not look promising for the man who had recently been crowned and seemingly could do no wrong. I think that Paul Martin believed he could drift in and the population would be thrilled to see him. He had had thirteen years to prepare for his ascension to the throne, and as of May 2004 he had introduced only one new bill to the House that was not left over from the Chrétien era; whistleblower legislation, theoretically to protect civil servants when they came forward to testify in the sponsorship scandal. What in the world was he doing all those years? He should have been preparing to actually govern, instead of touring the country on a perpetual campaign tour.

Because he was so low in the polls, Martin put off the election call. He had planned to drop the thirty-six-day writ on Sunday, April 4, for a May 10, 2004, election. However, the polls were not rebounding.

Consequently, he continued to tour the country, but that did not help. For many weeks, his numbers remained static at approximately 38 per cent. Things looked especially shaky in Quebec. The Bloc Québécois were poised to win 50 to 55 seats out of a total of 75. Apparently, Quebecers did not like the idea of having the government play the role of the "great white father," assuming that they knew what was best.

Martin was also on shaky ground in Ontario, where the Liberals had won almost every seat for the last three elections. It was predicted by the pundits that the Conservatives would win 20 to 25 seats and the NDP (under new leader Jack Layton) 8 to 10. Consequently, the Liberals could potentially be reduced by 20 seats in Quebec and at least 20 in Ontario. In early May, the Liberals had 168 seats, the Conservatives had 73, the BQ had 33, the NDP had 14, Independents had 9 and there were 3 vacancies; two in Ontario as Allan Rock had left after Paul Martin became prime minister and Mac Harb had been appointed to the Senate by Chrétien. Also, in Quebec, Chrétien's seat was vacant after his departure. In Manitoba, John Harvard resigned his seat to make way for Glen Murray, the mayor of Winnipeg, to run in his place. If the election went poorly for the Liberals, they could be reduced to 130 seats, well shy of a majority. With the new electoral boundaries, the 38th Parliament would consist of 308 seats, up from 301. Consequently, 155 seats were needed for a majority. Regardless of what might happen in the Atlantic Provinces or the West, Ontario and Quebec were the major battlegrounds.

During the spring, both major parties were posturing for position in the upcoming campaign. The Conservatives were pushing for answers and closure on the sponsorship scandal. We felt it was essential for Canadians to know exactly what went on in the scandal. The Liberals kept trying to end the committee's investigation and bring in a report, covering over all the wrongdoings of the guilty individuals. We kept fighting for all the details to be released, but it felt like a losing battle. In early May, the Liberals on the Public Accounts Committee tried to shut down the hearings, while there were still ninety witnesses to be heard from on the list that had been accepted by the committee. The prime minister said that the opposition was trying to filibuster and waste taxpayers' dollars. The point is that nobody had taken responsibility for the $100,000,000 that was paid to advertising agencies for simply transferring government cheques to recipients. Any report would be extremely inconclusive, as it would be based on bureaucrats that were following orders from their political masters to parrot the party line.

In preparation for the election, the Liberals proved their nervousness by running questionable polls in Ontario, where they were obviously weak. In April, they commissioned a poll to ask voters in Ontario, "Are you 'more or less likely to vote for the Conservative/ Alliance if you knew they had been taken over by evangelical Christians'?" Although the pollster wasn't made public, Liberal spokesman Steve McKinnon confirmed that their party had conducted the poll, asking about Conservative candidates who hold socially conservative views. (*Kingston Whig-Standard*, May 1, 2004.) This, in my estimation, is nothing more than religious intolerance. During the spring of 2004, there was a rash of vandalism in Jewish cemeteries in Montreal and Toronto. These acts are wrong, cowardly and hateful. Such intolerance is evil and we cannot come down hard enough on the perpetrators. Liberals criticized these acts, then turned around and levied their own on another group of people: evangelical Christians. How can this be acceptable in any way? Bruce Clemenger, president of the Evangelical Fellowship of Canada, wrote to Paul Martin demanding an official apology. In his letter he stated, "Only last week you were calling for religious tolerance in the wake of anti-Semitic violence. You properly denounced religious intolerance as un-Canadian. Tolerance for some, i.e. Jews, with exceptions for others, i.e. evangelical Christians, is a façade." (Letter from Bruce Clemenger to Paul Martin, April 23, 2004.) I have become weary of the double standard to which I have been subjected by the government of the day while I have been in Ottawa. If we are going to decry religious intolerance, then let's do it. But let us be consistent and not single out the evangelical Christians, many of whom support Liberal and NDP candidates anyway.

Not only were the Liberals demonizing the identifiable group of evangelical Christians (as if every evangelical were a Conservative), but poor old Joe Clark attempted to paint our whole party and Stephen

Harper as evil and untrustworthy. If it weren't so sad, it would have been laughable. On Sunday, April 25, 2004, Joe appeared on CTV's "Question Period" program. He dropped a bit of a bombshell by announcing, "Is Paul Martin with his baggage more dangerous for the country than Stephen Harper?"... "I would be extremely worried about Mr. Harper. I personally would prefer to go with the devil we know. I'm concerned about the imprint of Stephen Harper." (*Edmonton Journal*, April 26, 2004.) "I don't believe the Harper party can get away with the masquerade, the pretence that it is the Progressive Conservative party that is broad enough to attract support from a wide cross-section of Canadians." (*Edmonton Sun*, April 26, 2004.) These accusations were totally unfounded and, sadly, Joe appeared to be out of step once again. I have appreciated Joe over the years and think that he has done some good work for Canada. But it seems that he is always on the wrong side of the big strategic issues. It was said recently by someone that "Joe Clark has never missed an opportunity to miss an opportunity." That is so sad, but so true. I regret that he did not participate in the merger of the Alliance and PC parties. He had a lot to give and could have gone out on a real high. Instead, he chose to pout and leave on a bitter note, when it was totally unnecessary. Some said he lied about working toward the two parties coming together in the PC/DR coalition. I do not agree with that thesis. I believe that Joe, in good faith, thought the vehicle to advance the cause was the PC party and he could not imagine that any other configuration could accomplish the goal. But the old PC party was gone, the old Reform/Alliance party was gone and something totally new was about to be born. The excitement of that new birth was more than Joe could handle. I think he should have grieved it, accepted it and quietly released it. It would have been better than his attacks on Stephen and virtual endorsement of Paul Martin and the Liberals, whom he had fought against for thirty years in Parliament.

This proved that the run-up to the campaign was not going to be loving and kind. The Liberals released attack ads in the first week of May. In the two ads that were aired, the wording was stark, white letters on a black background that said: "If Stephen Harper becomes PM you'll have two health-care options. Be rich or don't get sick." This was so bizarre. Health care in Canada has been in such a mess for so long and the Liberals fancy themselves the saviours of the system. They forgot to mention that it is they who had been running that same system for most of its existence. Ironically, just after that ad was aired, Paul Martin himself went to a health-care clinic in Montreal that offered a series of private services if people wanted to pay beyond what they would receive with their public health-care card. The hypocrisy on health care was hard to believe.

Another ad targeted our party about the military. It was equally sinister and equally untrue. Same lettering, same kind of message: "If Stephen Harper was Prime Minister last year, Canadians would be in Iraq this year. Choose wisely. Choose Paul Martin and the Liberals." Of course, Stephen said nothing of the sort. Our military was active in Afghanistan. It was so badly cut back by the Liberal government for the last decade, we could hardly have sent soldiers to Iraq even if we had wanted to. What we had advocated was the importance of standing with our allies, Britain and the US, even with moral support. These attack ads proved my old theory that "only when you're nervous do you get nasty." They did not keep those ads running, which I thought was a good sign that the campaign might actually be fought on issues. I was wrong.

The sponsorship scandal continued to capture the news during the spring of 2004. On May 10 the news broke that Chuck Guité, the civil servant who ran the sponsorship program, and Jean Brault, the retired president of Groupaction, had both been arrested by the RCMP and taken to court in Montreal. They were charged with six counts of fraud and conspiracy, to the tune of $2,000,000. There was a debate in political circles about what this would mean. The Liberals thought it bode well for them because it looked like the culprits were caught and being brought to justice. Surely the scandal was over and all would be forgotten. On the other hand, many thought that this was just the tip of the iceberg and that Guité might be only the fall guy for his political masters, who likely would have been pulling the strings. It seemed ironic that these charges came only weeks after Jean Lapierre, the Liberals' star Quebec candidate, announced that it would be helpful if the police laid charges before the election was called. The truth was that these charges had nothing to do with the actual sponsorship scandal that arose from the February 2004 Auditor General's report. They were a result of Sheila Fraser's 2002 report that indicated serious problems with contracts arising out of the gun registry. Guité and Brault were charged with fraud relating to bogus contracts and duplications of reports to the department, etc. Somehow, the Liberals were trying to get Canadians to believe that these arrests would put the main sponsorship scandal to bed and make it seem that the true culprits had been caught. Consequently, the whole ordeal would be over and they could carry on with the election as planned. Nonetheless, the public did not seem to buy it. They remained deeply suspicious of the Liberals and their attempt to snow the electorate.

To make matters worse for the federal Liberals, mere days before the election call, the Ontario Liberal government brought down their first budget under the new premier, Dalton McGuinty. It was not a pretty sight for the Liberal government, provincial or federal. The budget brought in enormous health premiums for Ontario citizens, ranging from three hundred to nine hundred dollars per year. There were also large cuts to various services under the Ontario Health Insurance Plan, including physiotherapy, eye exams and chiropractic treatments. The reaction was incendiary. People were furious and their initial reaction did not dissipate. The Paul Martin Liberals tried to distance themselves from McGuinty and both the provincial and federal Liberals tried to lay the blame at the feet of the Mike Harris Conservatives. But the public did not buy this, either. Within days, the federal Liberals' support had declined by 4 per cent in the national poll commissioned by CTV/Ipsos-Reid/*Globe and Mail.* On May 22, the day before Martin announced the election, the standings were: Liberals—35 per cent; Conservatives—26 per cent, and NDP—18 per cent. (CTV/Ipsos-Reid/*Globe* poll, May 18–20.) The results from the same poll saw the Liberals decline in Ontario alone from 49 per cent to 42 per cent. This was not a great way to head into an election. On Saturday, May 22, the *Globe and Mail* headlines screamed, "Liberals Rattled by Decline in Ontario," as well as "Liberals Losing the Initiative on Health Care." A COMPAS poll conducted between May 15 and 19 showed the Liberals at 39 per cent, the Conservatives at 31 per cent and the NDP at 17 per cent. This, at best, could result in a minority government for the Liberals.

Nonetheless, the next day, Sunday, May 23, 2004, the prime minister and his wife, Sheila, walked from 24 Sussex across the road to Rideau Hall to visit the Governor General, Adrienne Clarkson. Our Canadian tradition is to "draw up the writ," a formal request to the GG for her signature and permission to dissolve Parliament in order to hold a general election. She signed the formal documents and the race was on for a June 28 election. It looked like a suicide mission for Paul Martin, but he maintained that he needed a mandate from the public to conduct health negotiations with the provinces later in the summer. He also boldly predicted that he would receive a majority government. This came as a surprise to pundits, pollsters and the public.

Martin relied on his tactics of telling Canadians they had a choice to make about what kind of Canada the voters wanted. In his press conference, he asked, "Do you want a Canada that builds on its historic strengths and values, such as medicare, generosity and an unflinching commitment to equality of opportunity? Or do you want a Canada that departs from much of its history—a Canada that rejects its valued tradition of collective responsibility?" In his press conference and response, Stephen Harper said, "You know, in this country, you can be Canadian without being a Liberal. The government seems to forget that." I thought it was an effective response to the superior-sounding prime minister who seemed to lay claim to being more Canadian than anyone else.

I spent much of the writ day at the CTV studio, as part of a political panel. After I left there, I stopped at several of our candidates' campaign offices. Some weeks before, Stephen Harper had asked if I would serve as one of the two Alberta co-chairs. I was pleased to accept and wanted to go around and cheer our candidates on. My first stop was at the office of Laurie Hawn, who was challenging Anne McLellan. It had been touted as one of the most-watched ridings in the country. Anne was dubbed "Landslide Annie" after she squeaked through in 1993 by twelve votes. Laurie was an excellent candidate; he was a fighter pilot who had served in the military for thirty years and had been in business for ten years. As of writ day, he had personally been at 21,000 doors in the riding of Edmonton-Centre. Surely this would be a wild run. We went on my motorcycle out door-knocking together. As he had been my pilot some years before when I went up in an F-18 at CFB Cold Lake, he billed this as "Deb Grey gets even!" Now I was at the controls! We didn't break the sound barrier, nor did we do any loops, but we sure got great media coverage! At the doorsteps, we noticed a visceral reaction to the sponsorship scandal, gun registry and Billion-Dollar Boondoggle. People were tired and angry about their hard-earned tax dollars going for such programs, when what they really wanted was good health care and efficient government. Our party offered them just that. Our chances with Laurie, a great candidate, looked good.

Also in Edmonton, we had a terrific candidate to challenge David Kilgour. David had been an MP since 1979 and switched from the PCs to the Liberals after the GST was introduced in 1990. He had been a popular representative, but there was overall frustration with his stand on the same-sex marriage issue the previous fall. He had missed the vote in Parliament, complaining of a sore back from an international flight. He was caught telling this story, then confessed that he had wanted to maintain his junior Cabinet position, so he would not break the solidarity commitment. Our candidate, a young, bright, articulate Sikh named Tim Uppal, had challenged Kilgour in the 2000 election as well. He had name recognition and developed a good team. In that constituency, like so many others, the sponsorship scandal seemed to be the last straw for the voters. They were furious with the government for assuming they could spend tax dollars at will. People wondered that if these amounts of money had been "uncovered" or "found out," how much else was out there that the public didn't know about? Also, this money should have gone to health care and essential programs for Canadians instead of just to Liberal-friendly ad firms.

In the first week of the campaign, Paul Martin made a huge fuss over announcing nine billion dollars for health care. This would have been welcome news, except that he had been announcing new money for health care for so long, people just didn't believe him. Even after this huge announcement, the polls reflected the public's cynicism. By the end of the first week, the Liberals' popularity was sliding. An Ipsos-Reid poll, conducted May 28–30, placed the Liberals at 34 per cent, the Conservatives at 30 per cent and the NDP at 16 per cent. Opinions of the leaders showed that Paul Martin "somewhat worsened" or "strongly worsened" by 47 per cent, whereas for Stephen Harper, "somewhat improved" or "strongly improved" by 32 per cent. In Ontario, the Liberal numbers had fallen from 49 per cent to a dead heat with the Conservatives at 36 per cent. Atlantic Canada was the only place where the Liberals managed a comfortable margin, at least for the time being, with 44 per cent compared to the Conservatives' 24 per cent. The Liberals had begun the campaign with 50 per cent just previous to the election call. The trends were showing that the air was coming out of the Liberal sails. Obviously, they would ramp up the rhetoric and try harder to demonize us.

Our campaign was not without its glitches. Early on, one of our candidates, Scott Reid, talked about official bilingualism in an interview. He voiced his opinion about the possibility of reevaluating the policy once we became government. The Liberals immediately pounced on this, thinking they could paint us as rednecks. Actually, Scott Reid, one of our bilingual MPs, is an expert on the issue and his views are supported by the public and many Liberals. However, it gave our opponents a chance to take us off-message. That firestorm lasted until another one of our MPs, health critic Rob Merrifield, mentioned in an interview that it could be helpful for women to have counselling regarding abortion. This also exploded into the national media and, again, our opponents tried to use it as "proof" that we had a hidden social agenda. It was overlooked that Paul Martin had said basically the same thing a short time earlier and that several Liberals also agreed with the principle. Nonetheless, the issue dogged Harper daily. He made it very clear, as he always had, that he did not intend to bring in legislation or a referendum on abortion. But, again, it drew us off-message. In spite of these incidents, we continued to rise slowly and steadily in the polls. On June 1, while Stephen was campaigning in Ontario, two Liberal cabinet ministers, John McCallum and Judy Sgro, confronted him and tried to heckle him. He dismissed them easily, and got great mileage out of their desperate-looking attacks. Aren't you supposed to hire rent-a-mob guys for those occasions?? Again, the public was left wondering what kind of a "Gong Show" the Liberal war room was running.

As the second week got underway, another Ipsos-Reid poll was released. It showed the Liberals at 32 per cent and the Conservatives at 31 per cent. Headlines across the country were not very encouraging for the Liberal party: "Knives Are Out as Poll Suggests Liberal Minority" (*Edmonton Journal*, Saturday, May 29); "Martin Admits Defeat May Be Possible" (*National Post*, Wednesday, June 2); "Liberals Could Lose: PM" (*Edmonton Journal*, Wednesday, June 2); "Sinking Feeling: Newest Poll Sees Support for Grits, Martin Way Down" (*Edmonton Sun*, Wednesday, June 2); "Liberals Cling to Lead...Voters Don't Trust Liberals, Pollster says" (*Globe and Mail*, June 5).

In early June, Paul Martin fleshed out his party platform on health care. It was a nine-billion-dollar package including shorter waiting lines, extending home care, training immigrant doctors and creating a drug insurance program. This sounded great; however, he had announced these things so many times before that the public simply did not believe him. After stripping twenty-five billion dollars out of the health-care system in his 1995 budget, his promises to restore it in the 1997 and 2000 elections went virtually unfulfilled (even though some funding was restored), so he had clearly lost credibility. We unveiled our health care plank as part of our platform launch on June 5, committing $18.2 billion over five years, upholding the Liberal government's 2003 Health Accord with the provinces, $2 to $3 billion a year on top of that for five years for home care, primary care and new medical equipment, and between six and eight million dollars annually to pay for the establishment of a national catastrophic drug plan. The Liberals cried foul and said it would be impossible to offer more money for health care and tax cuts at the same time. We maintained that this was nonsense; there would be many areas to save dollars. We would make sure there would not be another billion-dollar boondoggle, cancel the two-billion-dollar gun registry and scale back departmental discretionary spending, thus guaranteeing that another sponsorship scandal would never happen again. During the campaign, Martin tried to avoid the entire scandal. The problem was that he had promised the Canadian public he would get to the bottom of the mess before he called the election. I wonder if he thought that the voters would just take his word for it. Not very likely!

The sixtieth anniversary of D-Day on June 6 took Paul Martin away from the campaign to the beaches of Normandy. As the government had offered to pay the passage for some vets to attend but not others, Stephen Harper elected not to go, but offered his ticket to a veteran in his constituency. That was much appreciated, but I could not understand why the government failed to make a consistent offer to our veterans; either offer it to everybody or to nobody. It seemed especially sad, because this would likely be the last time these veterans could attend the commemoration, as they were all quite elderly. As I watched the ceremonies, I was struck again at the commitment of those young men, so many of whom lied about their age to go and fight for my freedom. Thank you all.

Immediately after returning from France, Martin flew to Georgia to attend the summit of the G-8 countries. Some people suggested this might be the best strategy for the Liberals to simply have Paul out of the country. During that same week of the campaign, former U.S. president Ronald Reagan died on June 5 and Martin announced that he would not be attending the state funeral. He faced some criticism for that decision. Also, within the Martin camp there were starting to be signs of serious internal dissension, which bubbled over into the public arena. Their national campaign manager, David Herle, said on an internal campaign conference call on June 9 that "we are in a spiral right now that we have to arrest." As a result, he and his team dreamed up more attack ads, about which he said on the same call, "They are devastating. People are drifting to the Conservatives in an aimless fashion... no one is paying attention... We are expecting the ads to be effective... We have to blunt [Harper's] momentum before it is too late." (*Globe and Mail,* June 10, 2004.) That same day, an Ipsos-Reid poll was released that showed us neck-and-neck; the Liberals at 32 per cent and us at 31 per cent nationally. (Ipsos-Reid, June 4–8, 2004.) Because of the timing of this poll, we could use it for a benchmark, as it came out at the same time as the attack ads. In the lead-up to the debates, headlines across the country could not have been much more discouraging for the Liberals: "A Blue Storm Threatens Liberals" (*Globe and Mail,* June 10); "Grits Continue to Bleed Across the Country" (*National Post,* June 12); "This Vote Could Do to the Grits What 1993 Did to the Tories" (*Ottawa Citizen,* June 13). This was not the kind of momentum a prime minister would want heading into the all-important debates.

The French debate was held on Monday, June 14, in Ottawa. This was the first time in many years that all of the leaders were fluently bilingual. A series of topics was covered and debates ensued on all of them, plus there was a time for open debate. There were no knockout punches scored, but Gilles Duceppe was unofficially credited with the win because of his merciless attacks on Paul Martin regarding the sponsorship scandal and Canada Steamship Lines. Paul Martin looked as good as he had throughout the campaign, held his own and got a few jabs in at his opponents.

The English debate was held the next night, also in Ottawa. The leaders had settled in to the groove and everyone (except Duceppe) was more comfortable in their mother tongue. Again, there were no knockout punches, but certainly lively debate. Martin made a strong case for the Canada that he would like to see and talked of Liberal values. Duceppe carried on his strategy from the previous night. Harper looked calm and reasonable, making a case for lower taxes, better funding for health care and more spending on the military. Jack Layton smiled the entire time, gestured awkwardly and seemed a little too keen about everything. He reminded me of Tigger, from *Winnie the Pooh,* bouncing around and trying so hard to be noticed. He constantly interrupted the others and at one point, Martin got testy and said, "Did your handlers tell you to talk the whole time?" After the debate, the pundits went to town with their analyses. Generally it was agreed that Harper had won the debate. Ipsos-Reid did an immediate poll and found that 37 per cent thought that Harper won the debate, compared to 24 per cent for Martin and 18 per cent for Layton.

The big show was now over and all the leaders hit the road. Paul

Martin seemed somewhat energized after the debate; perhaps he was just glad he had survived it. However, another poll was released by Pollara on June 17, placing the Conservatives at 36 per cent and the Liberals at 31 per cent. On June 18, a COMPAS poll indicated that our two parties were in a dead heat, with the Liberals at 35 per cent and the Conservatives at 34 per cent (COMPAS, June 17). With the regional breakdowns we were on track to get about 125 seats, the Liberals approximately 99, the Bloc around 55 and the NDP approximately 20. (Dr. Barry Kay, a political science professor at Sir Wilfred Laurier University, used polling data and extrapolated it to determine seat projections). Soon after the debates, buoyed by the polls, the Harper campaign team spoke of the possibility of forming a majority government. I believe this made us appear to be "counting our chickens..." Paul Martin decided this was the time to take the political risk of his life. He spent the rest of the campaign saying that he was in the fight of his life for Liberal "values." His team released their new attack ads and almost immediately voters began to question Stephen Harper and his Conservative "values."

Again, some of my Conservative colleagues provided fodder for the Liberals' fearmongering. The next weekend, our party mentioned that we could allow Air Canada to make its own business decision to move its head office from Montreal as well as follow other airlines' less restrictive regulations on official bilingualism. We were attacked as being un-Canadian. Many people thought this was simply wise business practice; others railed against it.

During the last week, a convicted murderer in Toronto confessed that viewing child pornography drove him to murder a young girl named Holly Jones. Our party issued a press release with a provocative headline, questioning whether Paul Martin, himself, supported child porn. This was clearly over the top. Whether or not Martin had introduced tough legislation on pornography is a valid debating point. However, even to insinuate that he personally supported child porn was extremely unwise.

In the last week, also, Alberta premier Ralph Klein announced that his government would be issuing proposals on health care two days after the election, that might challenge the *Canada Health Act*. Of course, Paul Martin leapt on those remarks and tried to demonize Harper and Klein. He was able to use the situation as a launching pad for his continued defence of "universal" health care and play the hero.

Also, questions continued to be asked about our "respect for the Canadian Charter if Rights." We do respect the Charter and the role of judges, but we also believe in the supremacy of Parliament and its responsibility as the place where laws are made. On the last weekend, a video of my colleague Randy White was aired, in which he discussed at length his views about the courts, the Charter and so on. The Liberals tried to use this as more evidence that we would ignore the courts.

During the last week, the polls flattened out and it seemed evident that the race would be too close to call. COMPAS had the Liberals at 34 per cent and the Conservatives at 33 per cent. Ipsos-Reid projected the Liberals at 32 per cent and the Conservatives at 31 per cent. They both predicted that the Liberals were climbing back slightly. Dr. Barry Kay of Sir Wilfred Laurier University projected 112 seats for the Liberals, 111 for the Conservatives, 60 for the BQ and 25 for the NDP.

Election day finally arrived, June 28, 2004. The last couple of days, I had felt a drift toward the Liberals. I sensed that Canadians were still angry with them, but that the attack ads were making them hesitant to support Harper. As Joe Clark had put it some weeks before the campaign actually began, Canadians might choose "the devil they know." The polls indicated that the results would be far closer than they actually turned out. The national results gave the Liberals a minority government of 135 seats, the Conservatives 99, the Bloc 54, the NDP 19 and 1 independent, my colleague Chuck Cadman, who had lost the Conservative nomination, but had a great deal of personal support in his riding of Surrey North. It was interesting to note that the Liberals could still not form a majority, even with the support of the NDP. In Atlantic Canada, the Liberals held their strength, capturing 22 of the 32 seats. The Conservatives received 7 and the NDP won 3. Scott Brison ran for the Liberals and won; John Herron ran for the Liberals and lost. In Quebec, the BQ benefited from the public's anger over the sponsorship scandal. They won 54 seats to the Liberals' 21. Jean Chrétien's riding of St. Maurice fell to the BQ after being Liberal for over forty years. In Ontario, the Liberals did far better than expected, winning 77 seats, compared to the Conservatives at 22 and the NDP at 7. Belinda Stronach won her seat; Tony Clement lost his. In Manitoba, the Conservatives obtained 7 seats, the Liberals 3 and the NDP 4. In Saskatchewan, the NDP were completely shut out, with the Conservatives winning 13 seats and the Liberals holding on to 1. In Alberta, we lost 2 seats, again, to the Liberals. Anne McLellan hung on to her seat by 711 votes and David Kilgour by 131. It was a real heart-break for our candidates who had worked so hard and come so close, again. In British Columbia, we lost a few seats, but won 21, while the Liberals got 8 and the NDP 6. Keith Martin ran as a Liberal and was re-elected. Canadians had spoken; they were not about to give Paul Martin another majority, but they were not ready to hand the reins of power over to Stephen Harper yet. Commentators were unanimous in their assessment that the Liberals had won again on the strength of the fear factor, by frightening voters, especially in Ontario.

Paul Martin will have a difficult time keeping this minority Parliament running smoothly. He must face the results of the public inquiry into the sponsorship scandal. He must also forge alliances with all parties. After vilifying Harper, he must now seek his advice and cooperation on virtually any legislation that he wants passed. Harper will be fair and forthright. Canadians will take note of this young, capable leader who unified the PCs and the Alliance, won the party leadership and ran an excellent national campaign, all within the space of eight months. The country will watch him and I think they will be impressed with what they see over the life of this fractured Parliament. Whenever the next election is held, no matter how long Martin is able to keep the government afloat, Stephen will still be under fifty years of age. He will continue to grow into a mature and confident leader; one that, I believe, will be the next prime minister of Canada.

And now, the political chapter is truly over for me. The election is done, the results are counted, a new government is in place, tentative though it is. My hill and constituency offices are both closed. My staff, Wes McLeod, Lana Fawcett Helman, Averil Grant, and Judy Pals, ensured that we finished well and are ready for a new chapter in their lives also. It feels strange not to be going to Ottawa to get sworn in with the new crop of MPs. I will not get to know them as I have every other Reform and Canadian Alliance caucus member throughout the entire history of our party. For me, this is the end of an era.

During the campaign, I was in Calgary to introduce Stephen at a huge rally. When he began his speech, he paid me a wonderful compliment. He said, "Ladies and gentlemen, Deb Grey is leaving politics, but not without leaving her mark on the Canadian scene. She has been a pioneer, a warrior and a legend." And to me, that is the best way to go out. As I contemplate the next chapter of my life, I am excited. Although opening a new door is often frightening, it is also an exciting challenge. If I have the attitude to walk through it with confidence and grace, then surely it will go well. If I refuse to renew, I will rot. Letting go of the trapeze allows me to fly, to dream, to hope. And fly I will. Why? Because I will Never Retreat, Never Explain, Never Apologize...

Acknowledgements

OW COULD I EVER HAVE MADE IT this far in my life without the unconditional support of my entire family, who have stood by me through every chapter? My mother is the best role model I could have asked for. She taught me strength, focus and a quiet determination.

My special friends Ev, Sandra, Maxine, Joanne and Marian (and so many others) have contributed to the rich fabric of my life. I am grateful to my political mentors Agnes Macphail and Nellie McClung for blazing the trail for me as an elected woman. Preston Manning has been a powerful force in my political growth; I was taught by one of the best. I have appreciated my personal friendship with him and his wife, Sandra. Thanks to the constituents of Beaver River and Edmonton North, who put an X beside my name so many times. It has been an honour to serve you in Canada's parliament. Thank you also to my entire staff for a job well done. I appreciate you all.

My husband, Lewis, is the wind beneath my wings. He has been the steady, behind-the-scenes support for my very public life. He has sacrificed a great deal and has been a full partner in my political career. After eleven years of marriage, we look forward to moving in together full-time! And, finally, I give thanks to my Lord, who has blessed me beyond belief. He has been faithful every step of the way, and Lew and I can hardly wait for the next adventure that He has lined up for us.

Index